DEMOCRACIES: CHALLENGES TO SOCIETAL HEALTH

RESEARCH IN POLITICAL SOCIOLOGY

Series Editor: Barbara Wejnert

Recent Volumes:

RESEARCH IN POLITICAL SOCIOLOGY   VOLUME 19

DEMOCRACIES: CHALLENGES TO SOCIETAL HEALTH

EDITED BY

BARBARA WEJNERT

University at Buffalo, NY, USA

United Kingdom – North America – Japan
India   Malaysia – China

Emerald Group Publishing Limited
Howard House, Wagon Lane, Bingley BD16 1WA, UK

First edition 2011

Copyright © 2011 Emerald Group Publishing Limited

Reprints and permission service
Contact: booksandseries@emeraldinsight.com

British Library Cataloguing in Publication Data
A catalogue record for this book is available from the British Library

ISBN: 978-1-78052-238-8
ISSN: 0895-9935 (Series)

Printed and bound by CPI Group (UK) Ltd, Croydon, CR0 4YY

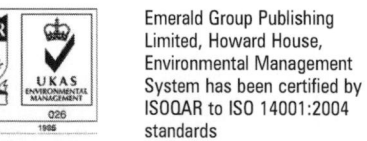

Emerald Group Publishing Limited, Howard House, Environmental Management System has been certified by ISOQAR to ISO 14001:2004 standards

Awarded in recognition of Emerald's production department's adherence to quality systems and processes when preparing scholarly journals for print

INVESTOR IN PEOPLE

CONTENTS

LIST OF CONTRIBUTORS

Seela Aladuwaka   Department of Humanities, Alabama State University, Montgomery, AL, USA

Ram Alagan   Department of Humanities, Alabama State University, Montgomery, AL, USA

Diana Austria   Department of Pediatrics, Stanford University, Stanford, CA, USA

Sitora Khakimova   State University of New York (SUNY) at Buffalo, Amherst, NY, USA

Melinda Landau   San Jose Unified School District, San Jose, CA, USA

Rasel Madaha   Department of Intercultural Studies, University at Buffalo, NY, USA and University of Dar Es Salaam (Mkwawa Campus), Iringa, Tanzania

Andrea Parrot   Department of Policy Analysis and Management, Cornell University, Ithaca, NY, USA

Nirupama Prakash   Department of Humanities & Social Sciences, Jaypee University of Information Technology (JUIT), Solan, Himachal Pradesh, India

Eunice Rodriguez   Department of Pediatrics, Stanford University, Stanford, CA, USA

Shiba S. Banskota   Women's Rehabilitation Centre (WOREC), NGO, Nepal

Elżbieta Sawa-Czajka   Centrum Edukacji Grupa ORLEN, Lublin, Poland

Barbara Wejnert   Department of Intercultural Studies, Global Gender Studies Program, State University of New York (SUNY) Buffalo, Amherst, NY, USA

PREFACE

My introduction to political sociology and particularly to the concept of democracy and its practical implication for societies started during my student years when I was a member of student chapter of the pro-democracy Solidarity Movement in Poland in 1980–1981. Participation in the Solidarity Movement taught me the unforgettable lesson about the power of individuals united by a common goal of building democratic society. I was able to witness how united citizens' concern about the future of their country could overpower totalitarian regimes (i.e., communist regimes), initiate their breakdown and, by voting and political participation, encourage policy makers and political figures to focus on betterment of societal living conditions. I also realize that democratization is a long process that starts with democratic political changes and democratic elections but it takes decades for their institutionalization and development, and it takes even longer to improve quality of people's lives in democratizing countries. Development of democracy requires experience, knowledge, and skills of domestic politicians and the existence of certain economic, political, and cultural structures conducive to democratic growth.

Since participation in student movement, the topic of democracy has captivated my personal attention as well as my research and academic focus. Initially I was convinced that adoption of democracy by a country is unquestionably related to many societal benefits, and society by using voting and election mechanisms is able to reverse evolving negative trends in economy, politics, or social policies. In my research I was able to observe that an introduction of democratic system concedes with opening of economic opportunities that broaden a country's access to a global market economy and a global trade system that generate higher quality of societal life. Democracy also exposes societies to different cultures, including globally dominant modern cultural systems. Both of these trends – global economy and modern culture – are beneficial for societies because they increase economic development, facilitate international contacts with other countries, and also facilitate diffusion of international economic opportunities and cultural practices. Thus it is difficult to disagree with Fukuyama arguing that democracy is the end of human history (Fukuyama, 1992) and needs to be promoted across the globe (Fukuyama & McFaul, 2007) and not as some scholars acclaim demoted (Snyder, 2000).

Over time, however, I have also noticed that democracy itself does not solve societal ills. Although potentially powerful people's impact on policy making in theory could direct societal development and hence it might be easier to solve societal problems in democratic countries due to active public participation in decision-making process, nonetheless democracies are no more free from social ills than nondemocracies. Though the benefits outweigh the costs of democratic changes the costs should not be forgotten. Especially when we consider the impact of democracy and development on *population health* the costs are significant though limitedly discussed.

The costs in societal health are especially visible among poverty-driven populations of democratic as well as nondemocratic countries. Poverty, in general, limits access to medical care and modern medical treatment. Poverty is also one of the most impactful segregators of society separating social strata in terms of their differentiated access to health-care facilities and modern medical treatments. Democracies by being more likely to be supported by international networks that help to open access to medical care, including internationally sponsored medical services, ease the struggle against poverty and unhealthy living conditions.

The World Health Organization (WHO) believes that by working closely with the private sector and NGOs to deliver information and services, governments can help derive the greatest benefits from national and international health resources. By increasing awareness of policy makers regarding the social and economic gains resulting from improvement in societal health, agencies such as WHO can help by informing country decision-makers about lessons learnt from worldwide experiences. The challenge is in finding the best means to integrate health issues effectively and fully with the development process to promote the role of society as an agent of change and to increase cross-societal access to information, technical and economic resources, skills, and opportunities.

International collaboration, openness of decision-makers to people voices, and consideration for democratic freedom of choice enhance provision of health care and potentiate health services. One such benefit, for instance, is the incorporation of tribal people into the mainstream medical treatment and hospital care. In many countries tribal people as well as impoverished, secluded rural communities do not seek modern medical help and allow diseases to take their course. Often it is difficult to persuade tribal people to seek modern medical help because of their firm, rigid, and well-developed system of traditional medicine, which, for instance, holds that disease is caused by hostile spirits, ghosts, or breach of some taboo. In this case, members of tribal communities seek remedies through magic–religious practices to propitiate the supernatural powers. As the result, tribal societies may attribute childhood mortality to fate, believing that death was caused by the curse of a family deity.

Democratic societies by pronounced equality and respect for human rights and by introduction of their societies to modern communication and modern lifestyle can outbalance neglect of modern medical services by tribal and rural societies and erudite their seclusion and perseverance in using magic–religious practices to treat illnesses. Thus, access to modern communication and societal exposure to modern lifestyle facilitate incorporation of positive elements of modern medicine and of mainstream societal culture into the culture of tribal or secluded rural communities. Considering democratic societies' openness to international collaboration it is hence essential to consider a broad network of health-care providers and practices to fully secure societal health and securely protect the population from spreading diseases.

Democracies pronouncing freedom and equality, and supporting individual development, find it easier to adopt policies that allow countries to combine traditional medical practices with modern medical care. In this sense, the use of traditional medicine (often called alternative medicine) such as herbal therapy, minerals treatments, tribal medicine, or climate therapy, does not replace but supplements modern medical treatments. Such an approach is particularly important for the enrichment of available medical practices. It also facilitates the preservation of indigenous cultural practices of tribal or rural people. Traditional medicine is more frequently used to treat illness than modern medical practices by traditional societies.

In many societies, for some treatments traditional cures constitute the mainstream techniques and are in practice for many centuries. Among traditional cures still utilized today is the use of the Salt Mine in Wieliczka, Poland, to cure asthma due to curative powers of salt ion laden microclimate in the salt chambers deep below the surface. Another commonly used alternative medical treatment is Baltic amber that is used as a natural curative by people of the Baltic countries over the centuries. Various amber products from amber chips to amber oil are the basic elements of many medical treatments. Similarly, in regions of India people use the indigenous medical science of India – Ayurveda which means 'science of life'. The term Ayus means 'span of life'; Veda means 'unimpeachable knowledge'. Hence Ayurveda is concerned mainly with prolongation of healthy life and prevention of diseases and only secondarily with curing disease. The knowledge was passed down from Brahma with the objective of alleviating human suffering and assuming long healthy life to all human beings.

Policy makers in democratic societies are not only more open to alternative medicine but also more likely to approve policies that support preventive medical treatments as part of modern and traditional medicine. Moreover, democratic societies are more likely to designate part of their budget to preventive medicine that uses both traditional and modern practices. Preventive medicine is essential for improvement of societal health to reduce misfortunes such as higher proportion of child deaths due to various infectious diseases, lack of proper care for elderly, malnutrition, premature births and birth accidents, coupled with unhygienic conditions.

In summary, democratization opens economic opportunities and generates higher quality of societal life. It also facilitates an impact of people on policy making which directly influences societal health and development of medical and health-care services, broadens access to health care, and supports approval of indigenous medical practices to supplement modern medical treatments. With this in mind, the *Intersection of Health and Democracy* issues become the leading topic among possible conceptual themes for this volume. Considering economic, and political interrelation with health it is then essential to approach societal health in a holistic way within the social, economic, and political context of people's lives.

Considering my professional and personal background, I joyfully welcomed an appointment as the editor of the journal *Research in Political Sociology* and treated it as the opportunity to create a collection of scholarly chapters devoted to issues concerning democracy, where voices of international as well as American scholars could be expressed. This is the second volume of this journal that I have edited. This volume presents a discussion about challenges and developments that are faced by health-care systems in democratic developed and developing countries. Among the leading chapters are articles on affordability and accessibility to medical care in well-developed, developing, and underdeveloped democracies. Represented countries are the United States, Poland, India, Sri Lanka, Tanzania, Indonesia, and Tajikistan. The discourse is presented from cross-cultural and comparative perspectives and includes discussions on countries' decisions regarding health-care system and the range of its societal coverage. It also illustrates an intersection of economic development and societal health, worldwide trends toward global economy and their impact on societal health, as well as the interconnection of societal ills with global development and with local cultures. This compellation of worldwide health trends concludes with a chapter that supports the research done in previous chapters and puts many of their basic tenets succinctly and summarily.

At this point, I would like to express my gratitude to the editor and managers of the journal at the Emerald Press, especially Stephanie Hull for her editorial assistance. My special gratitude extends to external reviewers for their endless effort in reviewing and commenting on submitted chapters, as well as editorial board members who shared important advice on the editorial process. Finally, I want to thank my family, husband Richard, and my sons Camille and Cyprian with wife Kate for their care, support, and patience, without which this volume would not have been possible.

REFERENCES

Fukuyama, F. (1992). *The end of history and the last man* (pp. 1–11). New York, NY: Penguin.
Fukuyama, F., & McFaul, M. F. (2007). Should democracy be promoted or demoted? *The Washington Quarterly, 31*, 23–45.
Snyder, J. (2000). *From voting to violence: Democracies and nationalist conflict*. New York, NY: W. W. Norton.

Barbara Wejnert
Editor

ISSUES IN HEALTH, DEMOCRACY, AND DEVELOPMENT

Barbara Wejnert

ABSTRACT

In democratic societies people can impact policy making and in theory can direct societal development. Hence, due to active public participation in the decision-making process, it might be easier to solve societal problems in democratic countries. Nonetheless, democracies are not free from social ills nor are nondemocracies. Though the benefits outweigh the costs of democratic changes, the costs should not be forgotten. Especially when we consider the impact of democracy and development on population health, *the costs are significant though limitedly discussed.*

The costs in societal health are especially visible among poverty-driven populations of democratic and nondemocratic countries. Poverty, in general, limits access to medical care and modern medical treatment. Poverty is also one of the most influential separators of society separating social strata in terms of their differentiated access to health-care facilities and modern medical treatments. Democracies by being more likely supported by international networks that help to open access to medical care, including international medical services, ease the struggle against poverty and unhealthy living conditions, but democracies are still unable to eliminate them.

Democracies: Challenges to Societal Health
Research in Political Sociology, Volume 19, 1–10
Copyright © 2011 by Emerald Group Publishing Limited
ISSN: 0895-9935/doi:10.1108/S0895-9935(2011)0000019004

The 19th volume of *Research in Political Sociology, year 2011* is devoted to health problems, challenges, and accomplishments in democratic societies across the world. It includes chapters analyzing health-care systems, health policies, obstacles to healthy societal behaviors, and health conditions that are experienced in the democratic and democratizing world. Defined broadly, democratic society includes developed Western democracies as well as less developed or underdeveloped countries that have a democratic system.

According to such a definition, the category "democracies" includes democratic countries that have well-established democratic systems and respect the broad network of peoples' rights, as well as democracies that are formally considered democratic states but de facto respect only a few rights or their governments are guided by limited democratic principles. Therefore, the collection of the 19th volume of *Research in Political Sociology* includes chapters addressing these issues in a broad spectrum of countries ranging from India, Sri Lanka, Tanzania, and Tajikistan to Poland, Indonesia, and the United States.

The worldwide diffusion of democracy has been more prominent in the last four decades (Wejnert, 2005), and it is often argued that the transition to liberal democracy brings substantial positive changes to peoples' lives. Democratic development leads to an increase in literacy, education, civil engagement, and human rights (Dahl, 1998; Garrett, 2004; Herspring, 2003; Shafer, 1994). Among the other positive changes is the growth of a middle class of educated professionals and intelligentsia, the principal carriers of democratic values, who foster civic engagement and the development of a civil society (Almond & Verba, 1989).

A worldwide integration of countries into a global market occurs simultaneously with democratization, and many positive societal changes are attributed to the emergence and development of this additional trend (Kellner, 2002). Industrialization, urbanization, and an increase in the overall well-being of citizens are symbolic manifestations of a cross-world transition into unified market economy. However, perceptions vary – for instance, according to neo-Marxists, due to the structure of the world's capitalistic economy, poorer countries (*semiperipheral* and *peripheral*) are disadvantaged in the global trade and hence are unable to catch up with the modernized, well-developed world (Wallerstein, 1998, 1999, 2001); in general, it is argued that the poorest and least developed states are benefiting from a global market and Foreign Direct Investment (FDI) that assists it. As a result of FDI, the manufacturing technology developed in richer nations is transferred to poor countries (Shafer, 1994). Hence, it is common among scholars to argue that the global growth is good for the poor

(Dollar & Kraay, 2000). Nonetheless, as chapters in this volume argue, global development, in spite of spreading democracy, does not secure the poor and does not necessarily improve societal health conditions (Rodriguez-Garcia & Goldman, 1994).

The Millennium Development Goals proclaimed by the United Nations provide a shared vision of a much improved world by 2015, where extreme poverty is cut in half, child and maternal mortality is greatly reduced, gender disparities in primary and secondary education are eliminated, women are more empowered, and health and environment indicators are improved. The last few years have seen a change in the concept of development, which now encompasses health, social, political, technological, economic, and human growth, and not merely economic growth. In the midst of all the spectacular progress on the development front, we are faced with many conflicts and challenges that need to be addressed (Annan, 2004).

Yet, only minimal efforts have been made to directly integrate health concerns as a priority into development processes. The interface between health, technology, and society in general can play a pivotal role in enhancing the quality of life of people. The relationship between health and development has undergone renewed scrutiny. There is a search for new models to deal with global threats, soaring medical costs, technological costs, gender disparity, poverty, and disease. Technological innovation offers a unique opportunity for partnership between health and development sectors to change the pattern of work and enhance health-promoting habits.

A study conducted by The World Bank on "Development in Practice, Improving Women's Health in India" (Wejnert & Prakash, 2009) has pointed out that investing in health is now being recognized as an essential component of social and economic growth. Investments in health can be recommended on several grounds, such as equity, human rights, existing gender disparity, and multiple benefits of women's improved health, such as the impact of the mother's health on her offspring and cost-effectiveness of health interventions (Lewin et al., 2001). It is essential to view health in a holistic way within the social, economic, and political context of peoples' lives. The health of a country's population ensures health and education of the next generation and economic well-being of households.

For instance, it has been argued that maternal deaths could be reduced by addressing health factors alone. Emergency care services including transport, regular visits and records by nurses, trained attendants, safe abortion services, and postnatal care can make a huge difference. On average half of the girls in Rajasthan (India) conceive by the time they are 17.6 years old. Almost half of Nepalese women are married and have children before they are 18 years old, while in Nepalese Hindu communities early marriages before menstruation (girls aged 13–14) are the most preferred. A girl conceiving before her 18th birthday has a 2.5-fold higher chance of dying than one over 18. Most of them are undernourished, anemic, and cannot sustain healthy pregnancies (*Times of India*, April 3, 2006). The gray areas also include literacy levels, family size, preference for sons, unsafe abortions, deliveries by untrained persons, and lack of proper emergency obstetrics care.

The health status of the world population is impacted by social, cultural, and economic variables. Thus, poverty directly determines access to health services and health care, as well as the likelihood of one's visiting doctors, health clinics, and hospitals. Most women still lack decision-making power at family and community level and do not have control over resources. They thus lack control over their reproductive rights, leading to a high maternal mortality rate.

There is an urgent need to understand various issues concerning health and consequently to alert policy, institutional, and peoples' initiatives at various levels worldwide to ensure sustainable, equitable, and just development for families from various socioeconomic backgrounds. This situation needs the urgent attention of academicians, medical professionals, women's studies centers, social scientists, NGOs, administrators, policy makers, national governments, United Nations, and international agencies.

It is in this context that the theme *Democracy, Development, and Health* chosen for this volume of *Research in Political Sociology* is highly relevant and apt. The challenge is in understanding processes and principles involved in societal health and its safety, and finding the best practices and innovative strategies, which have been successful in improving health and in reducing premature mortality.

The volume organizes the emerging health concerns in a conceptual framework that links together approaches to research on health, processes involved in health care, relevant policies, societal infrastructures, and effects of global economic and political processes on population's health. The framework is supported by case studies on specific medical problems, strategies, and policies concerning health that discuss health networks and situation in developed, developing, and underdeveloped countries in the world. Reports of researchers and health practitioners complete the theme of this volume.

For the purpose of this volume, the health issues were grouped into three thematic areas shown in Table 1. Of course, there are also other possible categorizations and other approaches to health that this volume was unable

Table 1. A List of Maternal Health Issues by Thematic Area.

Thematic Area	Maternal Health Issue
Concept of health in relation to global development	Influences on health: diffusing democracy and market economy; global communication system; local vs. global culture including tribal cultures; global development; technological innovations
Exemplification of health problems in case studies	Cross-world practicing of health-care provision: transitional societies; developing peripheries; postindustrial, modern countries; totalitarian and democratic regimes
Reports from research and practice	Scholars and practitioners remediation

to cover. Not all of the issues listed in Table 1 are also discussed in length in the volume. Rather, I have tried to cover the most important ones in each of the categories in Table 1 that are less frequently addressed or that need urgent attention.

Starting with a general analysis of processes of worldwide democratization and their effects on health, the volume offers many concrete suggestions and recommendations that could accelerate the process of health, understood as a holistic, affordable health for families based on an application of appropriate measures and technology. The chapter on worldwide democratization, development, and health-care systems addresses the need to revisit processes of global development and democratization. It answers an important issue of development and its effect on protecting peoples' health, arguing that global development does not secure equal access to health-care and medical services. It also indicates that implementation of equal access to health care could reverse the trends reported by the World Health Organization that more than 1 billion people in the world live in extreme poverty because advances in health, education, income-generating capability, and infrastructure did not reach them and their development has thus been handicapped (Rodriguez-Garcia & Goldman, 1994). Therefore, the efforts to directly integrate health concerns as a priority of the economic development process should be made. It also could reverse another trend reported by the United Nations Commission on the Status of Women that while women represent half of the global population, one-third of the labor force, they constitute majority of the 22 million people who die yearly from starvation, malnutrition, and lack of medical care (Morgan, 1984). To illustrate the problem, the chapter discusses health-care systems in democratized regions of Southeast Asia in comparison to Eastern Europe

Following the discourse on democratization, development, and health, the chapter on evolution of health-care system in Poland further illustrates the issue. Looking at the health-care system from historical perspectives, the pros and cons of health care in communist versus democratic Poland are addressed, concluded with a general argument that each of the system had some positive benefits for society in terms of provision of health services. Nonetheless, a seemingly better system in democratic Poland still requires improvements for societal health and life span to reach the level of a well-developed country.

The next chapter compares issues of health care in the most developed democracy, the United States, with a comparatively new democracy, Poland. Looking at the health data of pupils from California schools supported by conducted interview research, authors noticed that under the new Patient Protection and Affordable Care Act (ACA) the existing shortage of primary care physicians will drastically increase once the act is fully implemented. As a study conducted in California shows, the number of children from low-income families that have chronic illnesses like asthma, diabetes, and seizures is rapidly increasing; however, under the new act the access to primary care physicians is decreasing. To meet the health needs of children school nurses will need to substitute the medical primary care that physicians used to provide. Recent limits of school budgets however led to contraction of appointments for full time school nurses and indirectly limited health-care provision available to children from low-income families.

Following the general analysis of health-care provision in democratic countries, the next two chapters look into the impact of poverty in democratizing less developed countries of Tanzania and Tajikistan. The authors of both chapters connect poverty to rural–urban migration and its impact on population health. Although the chapters analyze two distinct countries one in Africa and one in Central Asia, the principles are very similar. The authors of both chapters argue that rural poverty causes internal migration of husbands to cities to look for employment opportunities in order to provide for their families. The dream of opportunities for employment in cities is further enlarged by commonly available media communication showing modern life across the globe and fueling the dream of convenient and affluent life in the city. The reality unfortunately is more problematic as majority of the men return empty-handed but often contracting infectious diseases including AIDS, or do not return, establishing a new family life in cities and abandoning their prior rural families. In either case, the outcome leads to degradation of family health and an increase in poverty due to contraction of illness or the number of children and family who cannot survive without the father, who is the breadwinner. As the chapters argue, accurate strategic communication at the national, as well as global, level could enable planners and policy makers to take the appropriate course of action in relation to rural population and sustainable development of economically less developed countries.

The next two chapters are devoted to the impact of societal culture on the spread of family violence. While one discusses the impact of cultural norms and values on a spread of domestic violence in Sri Lanka, the other analyzes the standard of living of rural women in districts of Rajasthan, in India. Both authors argue that women still face enormous obstacles in their search for redress of their rights when they suffer abuse in the name of custom or tradition. Especially, when the perpetrators of violence are men within the family, a greater pressure is exerted on women to maintain silence. For instance, as an author discussing family violence in India argues, female infanticide, anemia, poor nutrition, maternal mortality (558 per 100,000), child deaths from poor nutrition, and water-related diseases are the influencing factors broadening the scope of violence against women. Women and girl children are caught in a cycle of malnutrition. Sati and child marriage are age-old customs in Rajasthan. Incidences of sexual abuse and domestic violence are high. Not surprisingly, the state has one of the lowest rates for female literacy in India.

Two other chapters address the consequences of family violence on health. One focuses on forced child marriages, stressing that in many developing democracies that are traditional, the practice of child marriage and women's subordination lead to many societal health problems. One of them is the common practice of child marriage (marriage of girls aged 13–15) that coincides with the two and half times higher maternal mortality among young mothers under age of 18. Change of cultural practice could greatly reduce maternal mortality and at the same time improve the health of their offspring. As Shiba Satyal Banskota, states, in Nepal granting girls and women a right of decision making would not only improve women's societal position and well-being but also increase the well-being of society and the health of a nation. Both young marriage and subordination of women significantly hinder the development of Nepal and especially affect development and health of women, which remains the lowest among members of this society.

The Authors of the chapter "Natural Disaster, Gender, and Challenges: Lessons from Asian Tsunami" address a need for more adequate and appropriate information regarding the impact of disaster on health by focusing on the consequences of the tsunami and communication strategies.

At the most basic level, more adequate and appropriate information concerning maternal health is conducive to informed, responsible decision making concerning sexual and reproductive behavior; family planning and family life; and protected, healthy, and safe life of mothers and children. Appropriate information concerning general health and especially spread of disease at times of natural disasters could form a policy platform that would serve as an important point to initiate new policies and emergency provisions and which would be pertinent to societal health in a postdisaster setting.

Overall the thematic area includes reports of research on the interrelations between globalization and the status and problems of health in Europe, Asia, North America, and Africa. This series of analyses presents practices, policies, traditional customs, and state laws regarding maternal and reproductive health. Countries that are changing to global market economy and democracy; totalitarian and democratic regimes; developing peripheries and postindustrial, modern societies are the subject of analyses. In sum, the first and second sections show the impact of globalization on maternal health in the United States, Poland, Tajikistan, as well as in India, Sri Lanka, and Nepal.

Practical suggestions and remediation drawn from the conclusions offered by medical professionals and practitioners conclude the volume. Some chapters focus on a need to improve national and international networking to direct focus on interventions. There is a need to pool, supplement, and complement various resources. As indicated, involvement of medical students, non-government organizations, and community leaders should come together to reach the unreached and to make the poor and especially the rural poor understand their needs for safe environment and health. It is recognized that as far as health is concerned, people live dangerously all throughout their lives. Societal health can be achieved only if there is a shift in perception with an adequate understanding of the sociocultural and economic status of people and their ability to influence decision makers to incorporate issues of health in their policy agenda. Thus, a holistic approach should be taken to understand societal health and this includes medical, health-care, and social concerns. Without a holistic approach, better societal health cannot be achieved. This approach includes issues of:

- Gender equality in societies
- Less domestic violence
- Increased school enrollment
- Increased entrepreneurship

- Job availability specially for the poor
- Better access to health care
- Increased civil participation
- Better infrastructure of transportation and communication to reach disadvantaged populations and rural regions

Overall, this is a unique collection of chapters that focus on the processes and outcomes of the worldwide democratization and globalization of safe and healthy societies. It expresses the voice of interdisciplinary scholars and health practitioners from Eastern Europe, America, Asia, and Africa, as well as prominent policy figures including members of international organizations (e.g., UNICEF), government members, and directors of NGOs. The multidisciplinary approach to problems of societal health includes sociology, gender studies, economy, social policy, social geography, population management, and political science.

The collection of chapters in this volume of *Research in Political Sociology* posits that despite many trends that have been commonly perceived to enrich societal well-being, in addition to benefits, there are also costs associated with global development and democratization. Considering the interconnection of positive and negative outcomes of global democratization and development, numerous authors argue that in regard to health, the costs of global development are more substantial than expected. Thus far, development's costs to societal health have been largely overlooked, not only in terms of economic opportunities but also in terms of their impact on family health. These costs, however, limit the empowerment of the poor and endanger national health; therefore, they cannot be ignored.

There are many causes that underlie the unsatisfactory health status of societies in democracies of well-developed and lesser developed countries – too many and too equivocal for easy explanation. Comparatively, analyzing the effects of global development and democratic transition on health in democratizing well-developed countries as compared to developing countries across the world, I look into three major health-related problem areas. The first is deterioration of medical services and a progressive health policy and health-care system. The second is cultural change in societal roles of women, characterized by a devaluation of women's professional development, increased domestication, and decreased employment. The third relates to societal health and poverty and includes poverty-induced rural–urban migration, immigration, and societal safety in postdisaster environments. Much of this volume is devoted to the first and the latter. In view of the limited space and the authors' interest, the analyses in this volume are confined to major indicators of societal health and health-related topics, as well as health policies, with an understanding of a need to further broaden the scope of this interest and conduct further research on these important, but relatively ignored issues in the contemporary literature on worldwide democratization and development topics.

REFERENCES

Almond, G. A., & Verba, S. (1989). *The civic culture: Political attitudes and democracy in five nations*. Newbury Park, CA: Sage Publications.

Annan, K. (2004). Statement of the secretary general of the United Nations. Keynote address to the annual gala event of the International Women's Health Coalition, New York, January 15.

Dahl, R. (1998). *On democracy*. New Haven, CT: Yale University Press.

Dollar, D., & Kraay, A. (2000). *Growth is good for the poor*. Washington: World Bank.

Garrett, G. (2004). Globalization's missing middle. *Foreign Affairs* (November/December), 84–96.

Herspring, D. (Ed.) (2003). *Putin's Russia. Past imperfect, future uncertain*. New York, NY: Rowman & Littlefield.

Kellner, D. (2002). Theorizing globalization. *Sociological Theory, 20*, 285–305.

Lewin, J. A., Weisell, R., Chevassus, S., Martinez, C., Burlingame, B., & Coward, A. (2001). The work burden of women. *Science, 294*, 812–813.

Morgan, R. (1984). *Sisterhood is global*. New York, NY: Anchors Books.

Rodriguez Garcia, R., & Goldman, A. (1994). *The health development link*. Washington, DC: Pan American Health Organization (PAHO/WHO).

Shafer, D. M. (1994). *Winners and losers: How sectors shape the developmental prospects of states*. Ithaca, NY: Cornell University Press.

Times of India. (2006). News Series, April 3.

Wallerstein, I. (1998). *Utopistics: Or historical choice of the twenty-first century*. New York, NY: The New Press.

Wallerstein, I. (1999). *The end of the world as we know it*. Minneapolis, MN: University of Minnesota Press.

Wallerstein, I. (2001). Democracy, capitalism, and transformation. Paper presented at the Demokratie als Unvollendeter Prozess, Vienna, March 16.

Wejnert, B. (2005). Diffusion, development and democracy, 1800–1999. *American Sociological Review, 70* (February), 53–81.

Wejnert, B., & Prakash, N. (2009). Conceptual framework for integrating perspectives and approaches to problems of safe motherhood. In: Wejnert & Prakash (Eds.), *Safe motherhood in globalized world*. London: Taylor & Francis.

HUMAN RIGHTS AND HEALTH STATUS OF GIRLS AND YOUNG WOMEN IN AFGHANISTAN UNDER THE NEW DEMOCRACY: FORCED AND CHILD MARRIAGES

Andrea Parrot

ABSTRACT

Since many Afghans, especially in rural areas, favor traditional, customary, and tribal laws over national laws, they tend to disregard the constitution and national governmental structure under the new democracy that gives girls and women protection. These laws allow girls to attend school, and ban child marriage; therefore, the problems related to these practices should be decreasing. However, since many in the more rural areas of Afghanistan do not honor the regulations, laws, and rulings of the national government, serious problems still exist for girls and women. Those to be addressed in this chapter are high rates of illiteracy, child marriage, obstetrical fistulas, poor health, domestic violence, and self-immolation.

Democracies: Challenges to Societal Health
Research in Political Sociology, Volume 19, 11–25
ISSN: 0895-9935/doi:10.1108/S0895-9935(2011)0000019005

Since the 1980s, Afghanistan has endured Soviet occupation, civil war, Taliban rule (resulting in educational and employment restrictions for women), and war with the United States and its allies (Raj, Gomez, & Silverman, 2008). In 2001 a new democratic government was established that was supposed to have improved the status of women in the country, and has since signed on to international conventions and developed federal policies designed to improve health and human rights, particularly for women and girls. "In 2001, Afghanistan signed the Bonn Agreement, demonstrating a commitment to the establishment of a fully representative government sensitive to issues affecting women. In 2003, the country ratified the Convention on the Elimination of Discrimination against Women (CEDAW), and in 2004 it signed the Millennium Declaration to promote equality of the sexes and improve maternal and child health. Also in 2004, the Afghan constitution was signed into effect, granting women full citizenship, with legal rights and duties equal to those of men. In 2005, Afghanistan signed the Protocol for the Elimination of Forced and Child Marriage, and in 2006, it put forward the Afghanistan National Development Strategy, which includes as goals the elimination of discrimination against women and the promotion of women in leadership" (Raj et al., 2008).

DEMOCRACY IN AFGHANISTAN

As a fledgling democracy, Afghanistan's government does not resemble a centralized Western-style democracy. Afghanistan has been encouraged to adopt a Western model without consideration or incorporation of Afghan customs or culture. "States such as Turkey and Indonesia show that Islamic nations can construct their own forms of democracies, but it must be custom-tailored to make sure democracy can function in each local context" (Mohib, 2011).

A non-Western form of democracy has long been part of Afghan society, both through religion and culture. "Building on the existing democratic structures in the country, such as the *malik-ul-maluk* system, from the local to the national level, could produce the best form of representative parliament, one that comes from amongst the people, is affordable and sustainable for the country, and one that would ensure effective, grass-roots outreach for the government" (Mohib, 2011).

Few Afghans have confidence in their elected representatives, thus they are unlikely to exercise their right to vote, because they believe that corruption within the system prevents elected officials from exercising their representative function (Mohib, 2011). According to the Afghanistan Independent Election Commission (IEC), only about one-third of registered voters actually vote in their elections. Reports and independent studies documented various types of fraud and corruption that discounted the legitimacy of elections: low voter turnout, vote rigging, and ballot box stuffing – resulting in vote counting dragging on for months during the 2009 presidential elections (Mohib, 2011). The 2010 parliamentary elections exposed more flaws in the current system, when over 2,500 candidates ran for one-tenth that number of seats. Many of those who made it to the parliament are not truly representative of their constituencies, but instead are often warlords whose power has been bolstered through their strong political ties and bribery. Many in Afghanistan "take for granted the corruption and inevitable failure of elections to secure a representative central government" (Mohib, 2011). And although the constitution requires that at least one-quarter of the seats must be held by women, it is dangerous for many women to run for office, and those who are elected find it difficult to have their voices heard. Some women have received death threats and a number of candidates, and their campaign workers, have been murdered (Somerville, 2010).

In traditional Afghanistan governance decisions are made on both local and national levels by consultative councils of tribal elders and grand councils, respectively, throughout Afghanistan's history. An alternative, perhaps more sustainable, and effective approach to the current failed system must stem from traditional Afghan democracy, such as the *malik* system (Mohib, 2011) described below. Afghan societies have traditionally been governed on the local level. Customarily, communities rely on local nongovernment entities, such as tribal elders, composed of village leaders and religious leaders for legal matters, conflict resolution, and issues concerning social and economic needs. This is the basic Afghan localized system of governance – a tribal or village elder is selected, through consultation and mutual agreement within the community. The tribal elder then represents the village's needs and interests to external parties and deals with any internal matters. Very rarely do Afghan citizens living outside of urban centers feel inclined to contact local government officials or their respective members of parliament for issues or regarding services that *should* theoretically be provisioned by the central government under the current system (Mohib, 2011).

According to a 2010 national survey conducted by the Asia Foundation, when faced with social or economic problems, or in need of dispute resolution or services, the vast majority of respondents approach a nongovernment entity, either the village or religious leader (Mohib, 2011). The primary reason given for seeking out local governance entities was simply their faith that local leaders and nongovernmental entities would be honest and fair. In fact, the majority of respondents said they did not believe that the parliament was working in the interest of ordinary Afghan civilians, but rather, in individual political interests (Mohib, 2011).

This continued reliance on informal justice systems, mixed with knowledge of the history of Afghan governance, suggests that rural-dwelling Afghans (about 75% of the population) do not benefit or rely on parliament, or the country's electoral processes, as it exists in Afghanistan today (Mohib, 2011). This customary system of local governance is how Afghans have governed themselves for centuries, and how many continue to govern, regardless of the requirements and protections for women and girls in the new constitution.

STATUS OF WOMEN AND GIRLS IN AFGHANISTAN

Since many Afghans, especially in rural areas, favor traditional, customary, and tribal laws over national laws, they tend to disregard the constitution and national governmental structure under the new democracy that gives girls and women protection. Current national laws allow girls to attend school and ban child marriage; therefore, the problems that are related to these practices should be decreasing. However, since many in the more rural areas in Afghanistan do not honor the regulations, laws, and rulings of the national government, serious problems still exist for girls and women. Even if people did know the laws, they are often ignored because either there is no penalty associated with the law, or the law is simply not enforced. Those problems to be addressed in this chapter are high rates of illiteracy, child marriage, obstetrical fistulas, poor health, domestic violence, self-immolation, and death.

In 2007, the Supreme Court of Afghanistan approved a new marriage contract stipulating that the man needs to verify that his bride is 16 years of age; however, there is no law that penalizes those who arrange forced or underage marriages (2007 Country Report on Human Rights Practices, 2008). "There is no clear provision in the Criminal Procedure Law to penalize those who arrange forced or underage marriages. Article 99 of the Law on Marriage states that marriage of a minor may be conducted by a guardian. However, in March, the Supreme Court approved a new marriage contract stipulating that the man needs to verify his bride is 16 years of age, and that marriage certificates would not be issued for underage brides. In June 2006, the government set up a working group on early and forced marriages; however, this group appears to have informally dispersed. The

Afghanistan Independent Human Rights Commission estimates that up to 70 percent of reported cases of domestic violence have roots in child marriage" (2007 Country Report on Human Rights Practices, 2008). Another factor that contributes to this problem is that not all children who are born in Afghanistan, especially in rural areas or at home, have an official birth certificate. The parents can claim that their daughters are over 16, and there is no document to contradict this statement.

According to the United Nations Development Fund for Women, 70–80% of female Afghanis are forced into marriages, and 57% are married before 16 years of age; 84% of women are illiterate as compared with 69% of men, and women are half as likely as men to have completed primary school (United Nations Development Fund for Women [UNIFEM], 2007). Afghan women have a fertility rate of 7.5 births per mother (United Nations Development Programme [UNDP], 2007/2008) with a skilled birth attendant present at only 14% of births (UNIFEM, 2007; UNDP, 2007/2008). This results in Afghanistan's maternal mortality being the second highest in the world. Although there are no reliable statistics on the prevalence of sexual or physical violence against Afghan women, all available indicators suggest that it is a major problem, primarily perpetrated by husbands and in-laws (UNIFEM, 2007). In addition, self-immolation is becoming an increasingly serious problem among Afghan girls and women (Raj et al., 2008).

Structural violence (i.e., patriarchy, poverty, illiteracy) contributes to child marriage both by causing it and by preventing society and victims from confronting it effectively (Nikolic-Ristanovic, 2002). Therefore, it is not surprising that in spite of positive political changes and efforts made by civil society and women's movements, few substantial legal and institutional reforms have been effective in reducing the incidence and impact of child marriages. Expansion of neoliberal capitalism, deepening of the gap between poor and rich countries, and the dependent development of post-communist countries do not promise much chance for a strong welfare state (Sklair, 1991). The costs of economic change are very high, especially in poorer and war-torn countries (Parrot & Cummings, 2008).

CONDITIONS SUPPORTING FORCED AND CHILD MARRIAGES IN AFGHANISTAN

Education, religion, cultural values, family structure, socioeconomic status, traditional beliefs, myths, geography, economics, employment status, discrimination, patriarchy, government policies, criminal statutes, political unrest, and natural disasters all affect child marriage and in many cases, contribute to it (Parrot & Cummings, 2006). While the influences identified may operate as individual forces, they also often become integrated to support a cultural ideology that perpetuates child marriage and suppresses forces that may stand in opposition. There is little debate that male superiority and the cultural male dominance that stems from it are at the core of this practice that robs girls of their childhoods, health, education, independence, dreams, and in some cases, their lives (Parrot & Cummings, 2006, p. 23; United Nations Children's Fund [UNICEF] Trafficking Report, 2005a).

Social Conditions

As global stability fluctuates, changing family conditions appear to increase women's vulnerability. Political and social upheaval, changing environmental conditions, and exposure to changes in family roles may affect women's safety and standing in the home, aside from any culturally sanctioned practices that may coexist. The context in which women and girls are not valued as human beings is closely connected to changes within social, economic, and personal realms. These attitudes change as world circumstances change (Parrot & Cummings, 2006).

Regional Conflicts/Wars

Economic instability has been seen in Afghanistan as a result of many years of war and the loss of the males in the family in these conflicts. Consequently many women have found themselves unable to provide for their families. Because social, religious, and political policies (banning women from working outside of the home, and preventing girls from attending school) and warring factions create unsafe streets, there has been an increase in girls being kidnapped to be sold into sexual trafficking (McGirk, 2002). So because parents are afraid of this happening to their daughters, they may keep them home from school for their safety. In addition in Afghanistan, the age of arranged marriage for girls has become significantly younger, since many families have lost their livelihoods due to the many years of war and political conflict. Daughters are being offered as wives while they are still children to much older men in return for monetary compensation in the form of "bride price." These children often have no say in their futures and often face a lifetime of sexual servitude (Parrot & Cummings, 2008).

Political Instability

Education, religion, cultural values, and policies establish the lenses through which members of a community are treated. Communities that establish social norms where women are discriminated against and subjugated provide the backdrop to the commodification of women and girls where their primary value is to the family in the form of a bride price (Parrot & Cummings, 2006). In Afghanistan, younger and younger girls are "sold" when their fathers are given a "bride price" at the time of their daughters' marriage.

In Southeastern Afghanistan, UN officials reported cases of kidnappings, rape, and forced marriages of girls and women. Soldiers would storm into houses, pick the girls and women they desired, and take them to be forcedly married. If the girls' families tried to get their daughters back, they were forced to pay large sums of money (Human Rights Watch Report, 2003).

In Afghanistan, an estimated 80% of all marriages are forced; and because the conditions are so unbearable for the brides, it is not uncommon for those brides to commit suicide to escape the marriage (South Asia-Human Rights Index, 2008) The Afghan government corroborates this as well. Afghan women are often treated as objects through which tribal law accomplishes its goals of reconciliation and promoting stability. Girls are traded like currency (South Asia-Human Rights Index, 2008).

Child Marriages

Although marriage of girls under the age of 16 is illegal in Afghanistan under the new constitution, it still takes place because most people in the rural areas follow traditional customary laws, rather than constitutional law. Under most circumstances when children are married, they are considered property, usually of their parents or guardians, who make the decision for them. There are varied motivations for marrying children, and very few of them consider the child's welfare as paramount. Children are given or promised in marriage to guarantee virginity at the time of the contract, as a means to create family or political alliances, to pay off a debt, to earn money through bride price, to avoid pregnancy before marriage, to relieve an economic burden, to ensure obedience and subservience, and/or to maximize the number of children a woman can produce. Regardless of the motivation for forcing a child to marry, if they are unwilling participants, the marital conjugal obligations are required, and often forced throughout the female's life.

The families of child brides rarely permit the children to refuse the marriage. Community norms – social, economic, and religious – often make it nearly impossible for the girls to either avoid an early marriage or leave the marriage at a later date (Afghanistan Independent Human Rights Commission [AIHRC], 2006).

According to the United Nations (Report on the Violation of Basic Human Rights of Child Brides), child marriages are not uncommon in the rural areas of Afghanistan, but they are also reported in Egypt, Bangladesh, Ethiopia, Pakistan, India, and the Middle East. Many young girls are rarely allowed out of their homes unless it is to work in the fields or to get married. These uneducated girls are often married off at the young age of 11, although some are as young as 7. In Afghanistan, up to 80% of marriages are forced. The legal age to marry in Afghanistan for girls is 16; however, these laws are frequently ignored, especially in the more rural areas where child marriages are considered socially acceptable, and are quite common. As migration from countries where child marriage is common, child brides are being married in other countries where it is not the norm, such as England and the United States, where secret illegal weddings are being performed (AIHRC, 2006).

> ... Runaways; suicides; self-immolations; murders; sexual perversions; and psychological disorders are amongst the many negative consequences of child marriage (Women and Children Legal Research Foundation [WCLRF], 2008). These also include the increase of maternal and child mortality rates, and the low level of education for women which has a long term effect on the role these play in the country's political, social, and economic life (AIHRC, 2006).

According to a United Nations Children's Fund ("UNICEF") report, "girls who marry during their childhood do not develop properly, neither physically nor psychologically. They are frequently denied access to education and are subject to different types of diseases arising from abnormal births and isolation" (www.unicef.org/child protection information) (United Nations Children's Fund [UNICEF], 2005b).

Women and girls, even babies, are given away in marriage as compensation for crimes committed by the men in their families. This practice, called "swara" is intended to prevent bloodshed. Daughters and sisters are given away to resolve conflicts. Informal tribal councils often employ this approach as an accepted dispute resolution mechanism (Ebrahim, 2006).

This practice is an attempt to resolve disputes, so that killings do not go on for generations. Traditional wisdom holds that when girls are brought in from the enemy's family, any children born to her will belong to both families, which will put an end to feuds. However, this does not always happen. "I'll taunt and humiliate her for she's the price paid for my son's death," says a village elder. "He will accept her as part of the tribal council's decision and he will feed and clothe her, but she is not considered part of the family and cannot partake in any rituals or festivities" (Ebrahim, 2006).

The bride's sons are intended to replace the murdered family member. The aggrieved family accepts the girl and considers the obligation of revenge fulfilled, and their honor preserved. In Afghanistan, "Maryam's father murdered a man who taunted him for not acting like a true Pashtun. In settlement, little Maryam was sacrificed. Before she had outgrown her dolls, she was led away to her husband's home, deprived of any wedding celebrations. There she spends her life without honor, as payment for her father's crime. She is not invited to participate in any family celebrations. She walks a tightrope, and any mistake is blown completely out of proportion. She is a constant reminder to the family of the member that they have lost and she is treated accordingly" (About Afghanistan, Pashtun Swara, 2009).

In July 2007, Nazir Ahmad, a resident of Jalalabad reportedly settled his debt of $165, the value of nine sheep, by giving his 16-year-old daughter in marriage to the lender's son (South Asia-Human Rights Index, 2008). In February of 2007, 18-year-old Samiya (daughter of Gulzar and resident of the Teer village in Farkhar district of Takhar province) committed suicide in protest against her engagement by force to a 60-year-old man, who was already married to another woman (South Asia-Human Rights Index, 2008). Because Afghanistan is a primarily Muslim country, and because Islam allows men to take four wives, it is not uncommon for a child bride to be "sold" to a much older man who already has several wives. As a third or fourth wife, these child brides are often forced to have sex with their husbands and bear children when very young, but they are also sometimes treated very badly by the other wives. These girls are almost never able to divorce, are frequently victims of domestic violence, and are rarely welcomed home by their families of origins.

CONSEQUENCES OF FORCED AND CHILD MARRIAGE

Early marriage often causes many negative consequences for girls. Young brides are often denied educational opportunities, resulting in illiteracy. This can lead to a lifetime of poverty. Domestic violence is also not uncommon. If these girls are able to leave the marriage or they are widowed and they have to earn a living, they have trouble earning enough to support themselves and their children (Stritof & Stritof, 2011). Many child brides give birth when they are quite young, often resulting in severe health problems, such as fistulas (tear between the birth canal and the rectum or the urethra, resulting in constant leaking of fecal material or urine from the vagina), maternal mortality, or HIV/AIDS (Salopek, 2004). The best of these health consequences causes lifelong suffering and often social isolation, the worst prematurely terminates life.

Obstetrical Fistulas

Vesicovaginal fistula is an abnormal opening between the bladder and the vagina that results in continuous and unremitting urinary incontinence from the vagina (Wall, 2006). Some women also experience fistulae between the vagina and the rectum, resulting in constant leaking of feces from the vagina. These conditions cause women to suffer from terrible odor and relentless soiling of the ground on which they walk and the clothes they wear. These girls and young women are often rejected by their families and ostracized by their communities.

A woman's lifetime risk of dying as the result of a pregnancy-related cause is estimated to be 1 in 29,800 in Sweden, but as high as 1 in 6 in the most impoverished, least developed regions of Africa and Asia (such as Sierra Leone and Afghanistan) (Viswanathan et al., 2010). A woman's labor is obstructed when she cannot deliver her baby through her birth canal because her pelvis is too small to accommodate her fetus resulting in labors that last many days, usually ending in fetal and/or maternal death (Wall, 2006). The likelihood of obstructed and prolonged labor often resulting in a dead baby and seriously injured mother is increased in areas where early marriage and childbearing are common, because although growth in height stops or slows with the onset of menarche, the capacity of the bony pelvis normally continues to expand even after the girl has reached her full adult height (Moerman, 1982). These problems are exacerbated if girls have been undernourished throughout childhood and adolescence (Konje & Lapido, 2000), which is often the case in Afghanistan due to lack of resources following many decades of war. Although girls are capable of becoming pregnant at a relatively early age, their pelvises do not develop to their full capacity to accommodate childbearing until much later, and many will have their lives destroyed by obstetric injury even before they have entered true adulthood. The average age of a fistula patient is younger than 25 years, and many are as young as 13 or 14 years (Danso, Martey, Wall, & Elkins, 1996;

Gessessew & Mesfin, 2003; Kelly & Kwast, 1993; Muleta, 2004; Tahzib, 1983, 1985; Wall, Karshima, Kirschner, & Arrowsmith, 2004).

Probably the most important factors contributing to the high incidence and prevalence of obstetric vesicovaginal fistulas are socioeconomic (Harrison, 1997; Thaddeus & Maine, 1994; Wall, 1998). "Poverty is the breeding-ground where obstetric fistulas thrive. Early marriage, low social status for women, malnutrition, and inadequately developed social and economic infrastructures are all more common in poor areas. Most importantly, lack of access to emergency obstetric services is ubiquitous in the poor areas of the world"(Wall, 2006).

If child brides do not succumb to obstetrical fistulae or maternal mortality, they often find their circumstances so unbearable, that they try to leave the marriage through the only avenue left open to them, by committing suicide by setting themselves on fire.

Self-Immolation

"Self-immolation is the act of burning oneself as a means of suicide. Although reliable data on the scope of this practice is difficult to obtain in Afghanistan and elsewhere, there are indications that self-immolation is occurring at a notable and steady rate. In 2004, in response to an apparent increase in cases of self-immolation in the country, the Afghan government, the Afghanistan Independent Human Rights Commission (AIHRC), and the United Nations Assistance Mission in Afghanistan undertook separate reviews of identified cases to try to determine why the practice was occurring. Although formal analyses and reports were not generated from these reviews, researchers involved in them report that forced and child marriages, as well as violence perpetrated by husbands, in-laws, and husbands' other wives, were common precursors to acts of self-immolation. More recent data highlights the pervasiveness of the practice: the AIHRC and the Afghan Ministry of Women's Affairs report the identification of 106 cases of self-immolation in 2006; if these events are considered instances of violence against women, they account for 5 to 6% of all such violence reported that year" (Raj et al., 2008; UNIFEM, 2007).

In the study conducted by Raj and colleagues, the cases involved girls or women 12 years or older, with more than half of the patients being 16–19 years old. "In almost two thirds of the cases, the patients sustained burns over 70% or more of their bodies, and 80% of the cases resulted in death.

The majority of patients (80%) were married; 95% reported having little education and low or no literacy" (Raj et al., 2008).

The predominant causes or precipitating events of self-immolation identified by survivors or contacts were oppression of or violence against women. Forced marriage or engagement during childhood was identified in about one-third of the cases; practices involving forced marital exchange to settle a conflict between families or tribes in 18% of the cases; and abuse from in-laws in 16% of the cases (these categories were not mutually exclusive) (Raj et al., 2008). Although abuse by husbands was described as a common circumstance in the lives of Afghani women and girls, few identified this abuse as the primary cause of self-immolation. Often, self-immolation occurs after victims spoke out against or sought help in alleviating the violence to which they were subjected – but were ignored. As the sister of one victim explained, "My 18-year-old sister did not want to marry this man and asked my father several times not to give her to the farmer. But he ignored her pleas. One day I heard that my sister had taken petrol and committed self-immolation" (Raj et al., 2008).

Despite substantial efforts toward improving health and human rights in Afghanistan, persistent conditions permit violence against women, and Afghan women and girls continue to turn to the desperate remedy of self-immolation. Women and girls appear to see this horrifying act as a means of both escaping from intolerable conditions and speaking out against abuse, since their actual voices do not bring about changes that would allow them to lead safe and secure lives. More work is clearly needed to prevent and intervene in violence against women and to support existing policies aimed at improving the lives of Afghan women and girls (Raj et al., 2008).

CONCLUSION

The very highly publicized case in 2009 of Bibi Aisha, a child bride in Afghanistan, came to international attention when her nose and ears were cut off for attempting to flee from the abusive situation in her husband's home. This case highlights the plight of girls and women in Afghanistan, and the lack of human rights they experience despite the protections in place in the constitution of this new democracy. A photo of Bibi Aisha was published on *TIME* magazine's cover in August 2010. "Aisha had fled her arranged marriage to a Taliban fighter, but was captured and returned to the village where her husband, father-in-law and two brothers-in-law cut her nose and ears off after getting approval from the local Taliban mullah"

(Rubin, 2011). The only suspect arrested in the case, her father-in-law Mr. Sulaiman, was released in 2011. He was one of the people who held Aisha down while her husband cut her. "The mutilation took place in Chora, a remote area of Oruzgan Province. Left for dead, Aisha fled to the safety of a women's shelter in Kabul run by the advocacy group Women for Afghan Women, which publicized her plight a year later" (Rubin, 2011).

The suspect, Mr. Sulaiman, was released with the knowledge of the governor in south-central Oruzgan Province. According to police officials, Mr. Sulaiman had confessed to taking part in the attack in 2009, though he later insisted that he was innocent. The provincial attorney gave two different reasons for the release of Mr. Sulaiman: (1) that there was no one in Afghanistan to press the case against him because the victim was in the United States and (2) that he did not cut off the girl's nose himself. The other perpetrators have not been apprehended because the area is controlled by the Taliban and the police cannot enter it. Aisha's husband, Quadratullah, who is a Taliban commander, fled to Pakistan or goes back and forth, according to women's rights advocates who have tracked the case (Rubin, 2011).

While the rights of women and girls have been addressed in the new constitution of the fledgling democracy of Afghanistan, the laws and regulations protecting girls and women have not been embraced or enforced by many in Afghanistan since the passage of the constitution. There are so many different groups within Afghanistan that have very different customs and beliefs, and warlords that rule their sectors according to their own rules, that many Afghanis do not accept or honor the new constitution. This is due in part to the fact that local, traditional, customary laws are in conflict with the new rights afforded to girls and women under the constitution. The consequences of this lack of adherence to the constitutional guarantees for girls and women include illiteracy, forced child marriage, obstetrical fistulas, domestic violence, an increase in self-immolation, and death.

REFERENCES

About Afghanistan. (2009). *Pashtun Swara: A young Afghan girl is forced to marry*. Retrieved from http://www.about-afghanistan.com/pashtun-swara.html. Accessed on April 12, 2011.

Afghanistan Independent Human Rights Commission (AIHRC). (2006). *Evaluation report on general situation of women in Afghanistan*. Retrieved from http://www.unhcr.org/refworld/docid/47fdfad5d.html. Accessed on September 26, 2011.

Asian Centre for Human Rights. (2008). *South Asia-Human Rights Index 2008*. Retrieved from http://www.ecoi.net/188769::afghanistan/314492.312847.7951...mr.312930/forced-marriages-and-child-marriages.html. Accessed on May 30, 2011.

2007 Country Report on Human Rights Practices in Afghanistan. (2008, March 11). United
    States Department of State. Retrieved from http://www.state.gov/g/drl/rls/hrrpt/2007/
    100611.htm. Accessed on June 22, 2011

Danso, K. A., Martey, J. O., Wall, L. L., & Elkins, T. E. (1996). The epidemiology of
    genitourinary fistulae in Kumasi, Ghana, 1977–1992. *International Urogynecology
    Journal, 7*, 117–120.

Ebrahim, Z. T. (2006). *Pakistan: Girls as sacrificial lambs. Women's Feature Service.* Retrieved
    from   http://proquest.umi.com/pqdweb?did=1167646791&Fmt=7&clientId=8424&=
    309&VName=PQD&cfc=1. Accessed on September 19, 2006.

Gessessew, A., & Mesfin, M. (2003). Genitourinary and rectovaginal fistulae in Adigrat Zonal
    Hospital, Tigray, North Ethiopia. *Ethiopian Medical Journal, 41*, 123–130.

Harrison, K. A. (1997). Maternal mortality in Nigeria: The real issues. *African Journal of
    Reproductive Health, 1*, 7–13.

Human Rights Watch Report. (2003). *Killing You Is A Very Easy Thing For Us: Human Rights
    Abuses in Southeast Afghanistan, 15*(05). Available at http://www.cmi.no/pdf/?file=/
    afghanistan/doc/hrw-afghanistan0703.pdf.

Kelly, J., & Kwast, B. E. (1993). Epidemiological study of vesicovaginal fistulas in Ethiopia.
    International Urogynecology Journal, 4, 278–281.

Konje, J., & Lapido, O. A. (2000). Nutrition and obstructed labor. *American Journal of Clinical
    Nutrition, 72*, 291S–297S.

McGirk, T. (2002). Lifting the veil on Taliban sex slavery. *TIME* Magazine. Retrieved from
    http://www.time.com/time/magazine/article/0,9171,1101020218-201892,00.html. Accessed
    on February, 10, 2002.

Moerman, M. L. (1982). Growth of the birth canal in adolescent girls. *American Journal of
    Obstetrics and Gynecology, 143*, 528–532.

Mohib, II. (2011, June 27). A grassroots democracy for Afghanistan. *Foreign Policy.* Retrieved
    from   http://afpak.foreignpolicy.com/posts/2011/06/27/a_grassroots_democracy_for_
    afghanistan. Accessed on July 2, 2011.

Muleta, M. (2004). Socio-demographic profile and obstetric experience of fistula patients
    managed at the Addis Ababa Fistula Hospital. *Ethiopian Medical Journal, 42*, 9–16.

Nikolic-Ristanovic, V. (2002). *Social change, gender and violence: Post-communist and war-
    affected societies* (p. 130). Boston, MA: Kluwer.

Parrot, A., & Cummings, N. (2006). *Forsaken females: The global brutalization of women.* New
    York, NY: Rowman & Littlefield.

Parrot, A., & Cummings, N. (2008). *Sexual enslavement of girls and women worldwide.* London:
    Praeger.

Raj, A., Gomez, C., & Silverman, J. G. (2008). Driven to a fiery death – The tragedy of self-
    immolation in Afghanistan. *BBC News.* Retrieved from http://www.bbc.co.uk/news/
    world-south-asia-11334475. Accessed on June 10, 2011.

Rubin, A. (July 11, 2011). Suspect in mutilation of an Afghan woman is freed. *The New York
    Times.* Retrieved from http://www.nytimes.com/2011/07/12/world/asia/12afghanistan.
    html. Accessed on July 15, 2011.

Salopek, P. (2004). The bride was 7... In the heart of Ethiopia, childhood ends early. *The
    Chicago Tribune.* Retrieved from www.fistulacare.org/pages/resources/vrc/vrc-key
    words-geographic. Accessed on June 10, 2011.

Sklair, L. (1991). *Sociology of the global system* (p. 233). Hertfordshire: Simon & Schuster.

Somerville, Q. (2010). Risky climate for women candidates in Afghan elections. *BBC News*. Retrieved from www.bbc.co.uk/news/world-south-asia-11334475. Accessed on May 13, 2011.

Stritof, S., & Stritof, B. (2011). Child brides: The problem of early forced marriage. Retrieved from http://marriage.about.com/od/arrangedmarriages/a/childbride.htm. Accessed on May 1, 2011.

Tahzib, F. (1983). Epidemiological determinants of vesicovaginal fistulas. *British Journal of Obstetrics and Gynecology*, *90*, 387–391.

Tahzib, F. (1985). Vesicovaginal fistula in Nigerian children. *Lancet*, *2*, 1291–1293.

Thaddeus, S., & Maine, D. (1994). Too far to walk: Maternal mortality in context. *Social Science & Medicine*, *38*, 1091–1110.

United Nations Children's Fund (UNICEF). (2005a). *Guidelines for Protection of the Rights of Child Victims of Trafficking*. Available at http://www.unicef.org/ceecis/0610-Unicef_Victims_Guidelines_en.pdf

United Nations Children's Fund (UNICEF). (2005b). *Early marriage: A harmful traditional practice*. Retrieved from www.unicef.org/publications/files/Early_Marriage_12.lo.pdf. Accessed on June 10, 2011.

United Nations Development Fund for Women (UNIFEM). (2007). *Afghanistan: UNIFEM fact sheet 2007*. Retrieved from http://www.unama-afg.org/docs/_UN-Docs/_factsheets/07mayUNIFEM-fact-sheet.pdf. Accessed on April 29, 2008.

United Nations Development Programme (UNDP). (2007/2008). *Human development reports: Afghanistan, 2007/2008*. Retrieved from http://hdrstats.undp.org/countries/data_sheets/cty_ds_AFG.html. Accessed on March 18, 2008.

Wall, L. L. (1998). Dead mothers and injured wives: The social context of maternal morbidity and mortality among the Hausa of northern Nigeria. *Studies in Family Planning*, *29*, 341–359.

Wall, L. L. (2006). Obstetric vesicovaginal fistula as an international public-health problem. *Lancet*, *368*, 1201–1209. electronic version.

Wall, L. L., Karshima, J., Kirschner, C., & Arrowsmith, S. D. (2004). The obstetric vesicovaginal fistula: Characteristics of 899 patients from Jos, Nigeria. *American Journal of Obstetrics and Gynecology*, *190*, 1011–1019.

Viswanathan, K., Becker, S., Hansen, P. M., Kurnar, D., Kurnar, B., Niayesh, H., Peters, D. H., & Burnham, G. (2010). *Infant and under-five mortality in Afghanistan: current estimates and limitations*. World Health organization Bulletin. Retrieved from http://www.who.int/bulletin/volumes/88/8/09-068957/en/

Women and Children Legal Research Foundation (WCLRF). (2008). *Early marriage in Afghanistan*. Retrieved from www.wclrf.org/English/eng.../Early%20Marrige%20with%20cover.pdf. Accessed on April 5, 2011.

SCHOOL HEALTH: A WAY TO THE FUTURE?

Eunice Rodriguez, Diana Austria and
Melinda Landau

ABSTRACT

There is a need for rigorous research documenting the important role of school nurses in facilitating positive health outcomes among students. Poorly managed care can affect student absenteeism rates, which are associated with academic performance and school funding, and students in underresourced schools are at particularly higher risk of suffering chronic conditions (e.g., asthma, diabetes) that necessitate proper care and management. The San Jose Unified School District (SJUSD) Nurse Demonstration Project was developed as a five-year endeavor to expand school nursing and formally link school nurses to a school-based health clinic. The initiative provides for full-time school nurses at four elementary and middle schools in SJUSD, and a nurse practitioner at School Health Clinics of Santa Clara County. The objectives are to: (1) improve access to primary care and prevention services, specifically asthma and chronic condition management and (2) facilitate the establishment of a medical home for students. Evaluation of the project employs a mixed methods research design, including a logic model, an intervention and control study design (comparing outcome measures in the four demonstration schools with five "control" schools), parent, teacher, and school administrator

Democracies: Challenges to Societal Health
Research in Political Sociology, Volume 19, 27–41
ISSN: 0895-9935/doi:10.1108/S0895-9935(2011)0000019006

feedback, systematic nurse reports, and quantitative analysis of school health and administrative data, including health conditions and absentee-ism information. Key findings in Phase I of the project are discussed, including improvement in screening and referrals, follow-up care among students with asthma, and mean days absent due to illness. With increasing budget cuts to public schools, documenting the impact of full-time school nurses will remain crucial in leveraging support and resources for school health services. Findings of this project indicate that school nurses provide valuable services and could be a major player in providing and coordinating effective management and prevention of chronic disease among children.

INTRODUCTION AND BACKGROUND

The forecasted shortage of primary-care physicians a decade ago (Cooper, Getzen, McKee, & Laud, 2002) is now a reality that will continue to become more prominent once the Patient Protection and Affordable Care Act (ACA) is fully implemented. It is expected that 16 million people who are currently uninsured will be covered by Medicaid, which will add this important demand for services to those already provided to more than 76 million low-income patients who are already covered by Medicaid and the State Children's Health Insurance Program (SCHIP) (Rieslbach & Kellermann, 2011). As more children with chronic conditions, such as asthma, diabetes, and seizures, attend public schools, school nurses might not only play a vital role in maintaining their physical and academic well-being, but also help to fill some of the forecasted gaps in the care of children. In this chapter, we will first provide a brief review of school health research and the role of school nurses, and then describe the first phase and findings of a Nurse Demonstration Project initiated to add full-time nurses to several schools in California's San Jose Unified School District.

The National Association of School Nurses defines the goals of school nursing as to "advance the well-being, academic success and life-long achievement of students" (National Association of School Nurses, 2010) and identifies seven core roles school nurses fill to foster student health and educational success: providing direct care to students; providing leadership for the provision of health services; providing screening and referral for health conditions; promoting a healthy school environment; promoting health through education; serving in a leadership role for health policies and programs; and serving as a liaison between school personnel, family, health-care professionals, and the community.

There is a scarcity of rigorous research in this area. Yet, some studies have documented the important role of school nurses in facilitating positive outcomes among students (Guttu, Engelke, & Swanson, 2004), and others, such as Telljohann, Price, Dake, and Durgin (2004b) and Maughan (2003), have shown a positive impact on academic performance. Poorly managed care can affect student absentee rates, which are associated with academic performance and school funding. Students in underresourced schools are at particularly higher risk of suffering adverse health effects, given their greater likelihood to suffer chronic conditions (e.g., asthma, diabetes) that necessitate proper care and management.

Healthy People 2010 recommends that districts employ at least 1 nurse per 750 students to provide more psychosocial counseling services, better injury prevention services, and early detection of chronic illnesses, with the expectation that those services would not only affect well-being but would also increase academic performance. Yet, while half of the nation's schools lack a full-time registered nurse, the number of children with disabilities covered by the Individuals with Disabilities Education Act (1974) increased from 8.3% in 1976–1977 to 13.2% in 2008–2009 (NCES, 2010).

Chronic conditions among children have increased in the last decade. The rate of chronic health conditions among US children increased by over 50% from 1994 to 2006 – 12.8% to 26.6% – with the three most prevalent conditions being obesity, asthma, and behavioral/learning problems, such as attention-deficit hyperactivity disorder (ADHD) (Halfon & Newacheck, 2010; Van Cleave, Gortmaker, & Perrin, 2010). The prevalence of childhood asthma has doubled since the 1980s and now affects nearly 10% of US children and adolescents. Asthma is the third leading cause of hospitalization among children under 15 years of age, with the highest rates among low-income and minority populations, particularly African Americans. Pediatric asthma is the leading cause of school absenteeism and has been found to be associated with "reading problems, grade repetition, learning disabilities, and behavior problems" (Kohen, 2010; Levy, Heffner, Stewart, & Beeman, 2006; Moonie, Sterling, Figgs, & Castro, 2006).

School health studies have examined the impact of school nursing in settings with full-time (five days per week) versus part-time (two days per week) school nurses. Telljohann et al. (2004b) found that there was a "significant unmet need for access to health care services" among students in schools with part-time nursing. African American children of lower socioeconomic status who were identified with asthma and enrolled in elementary schools with a full-time school nurse missed 23% fewer days of school compared to those enrolled in schools where only part-time nurses were available. It was also found that students accessed available health services at their school almost two-and-a-half times more often in schools with full-time nurses than in those in which fewer nurses were available (Telljohann, Dake, & Price, 2004a).

Inadequate staffing threatens the school nurse's role as a medical home extender. Budget cuts have forced many public schools around the United States to decrease or eliminate nursing support. At the state level, only 21.5% of Californian postsecondary schools had a full-time nurse in 2008 (Brener et al., 2009). In addition, there is a high heterogeneity in their distribution throughout California schools. In 2006, the San Francisco area had the lowest percentage of schools with nurses with only 31% of its schools employing full-time nurses (Balaji et al., 2008).

The Santa Clara Country School District (where the San Jose Unified School District is located) serves as an educational home to not only many children of low socioeconomic status, but also to many children of immigrant populations. Immigrant children face additional challenges to obtaining health-care coverage. In 2000, about 50% of low-income noncitizen children and more than 25% of low-income citizen children with noncitizen parents were uninsured. In comparison, about one-sixth of low-income children from citizen families were uninsured (Ku & Lessard, 2003). While many of these students qualify for Medicaid or SCHIP, their access is hindered by the 1996 welfare reform law, language barriers, confusion regarding allowances, or fear that acceptance of such benefits will place them in future jeopardy. One of the most direct ways to address these shortcomings is via the school nurse. In providing guidance for parents and children in navigating the health-care system, the school nurse is able to satisfy his or her proposed duties and aid in securing a medical home for every child. However, as part-time school nurses are responsible for multiple schools, appropriate care and follow-up could prove insufficient. Even increased technology usage by school nurses, although presenting an opportunity to streamline health-related interactions between students and nurses and to evaluate their success (Vessey, 2002), is not a substitute for the required increase in nurse availability in the schools.

NURSE DEMONSTRATION PROJECT IN SAN JOSE UNIFIED SCHOOL DISTRICT: PHASE I

The Nurse Demonstration Project discussed here is an ongoing five-year endeavor to expand school nursing and formally link school nurses to a school health clinic located on a San Jose Unified campus. Sponsored by the Lucile Packard Children's Hospital and the Lucile Packard Foundation for Children's Health, the initiative provides full-time, credentialed school nurses at four underserved elementary and middle schools, and a nurse practitioner based at School Health Clinics (SHC) of Santa Clara County. The San Jose Unified School District (SJUSD) is a large and diverse district in Santa Clara County, serving 30,314 students across 40 schools during the 2007–2008 academic year. In 2007, 51.3% of SJUSD students were identified as Hispanic/Latino and 42.6% of students were enrolled in the free or reduced price lunch program. Fig. 1 describes phase I of the project presented in this chapter.

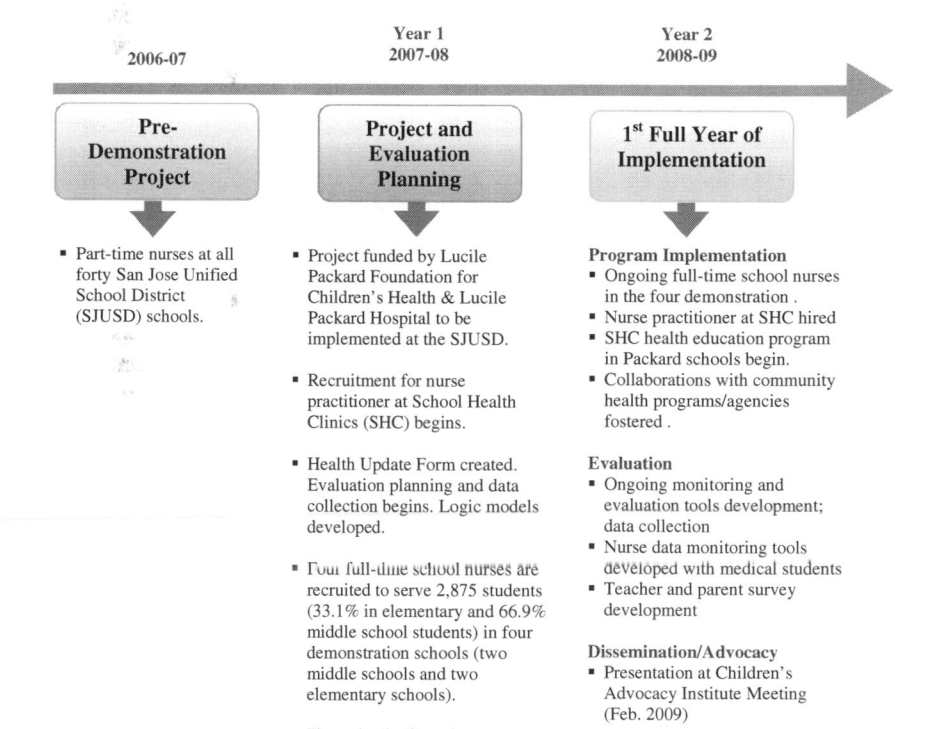

Fig. 1. Phase I Implementation in Demonstration Schools.

Project Objectives and Evaluation Focus

The main goals of the ongoing project are to (1) improve access to primary care and prevention services for students in kindergarten through 8th grade, with a special emphasis on chronic conditions and (2) facilitate establishment of a medical home for students who do not have one.

Phase I: Evaluation Activities

Evaluation of the project employs a mixed-methods design to assess the impact of the increased nursing time in (1) improving access to primary care and prevention services, specifically asthma and chronic conditions management, and in (2) facilitating the establishment of a medical home for students who do not have one. The American Academy of Pediatrics (AAP) characterizes a medical home as a "model of delivering primary care that is accessible, continuous, comprehensive, family-centered, coordinated, compassionate, and culturally effective" (Starfield & Shi, 2004; Turchi, Gatto, & Antonelli, 2007). AAP identifies six important components to a medical home, including provision of preventive care, assurance of ambulatory and inpatient care for acute illnesses, provision of care over an extended period of time, identification of the need for subspecialty consultation and referrals, interaction with school and community agencies, and data and health record maintenance (AAP, 1992).

   Key evaluation components include a logic model development and an intervention and control study design (comparing outcome measures in the four demonstration schools with five "control" schools) with parents', teachers', and school administrators' feedback, school nurses' systematic reports, and quantitative analysis of school heath and administrative data, including health conditions and absenteeism information. The logic models developed to guide the project evaluation are included in the appendix, and Table 1 describes the characteristics of the four demonstration schools and five comparison schools.

   Key outcome measures in Phase I of the project evaluation include school days missed by students due to illness; screening and follow-up of cases identified as needing further exploration after screening; use of emergency care as reported by parents; and satisfaction with the services provided by the nurses among parents, teachers, and administrators.

Table 1. Demographic Characteristics of Student Sample, 2008–2009.

	Demonstration Schools	Control Schools
Enrollment	2,877	3,204
Students enrolled in free and reduced lunch	81.9%	71.9%
Hispanic or Latino students	82%	73.2%
Students with chronic conditions	438 (15.2%)	504 (15.7%)
Students with asthma (% among students with chronic conditions)	195 (44.52%)	213 (42.26%)
Grade level		
Pre K–1st	11.9%	22.7%
2nd–5th	21.1%	40.0%
6th–8th	66.9%	37.3%

Results of Phase I: Demonstration Project

After a full year of project implementation we found evidence of a positive impact on schools where full-time nurses were placed in comparison to schools with part-time nurses. As indicated in Table 1, the demonstration schools comprise a diverse student population: 82% of whom identify as Latino or Hispanic with nearly 82% enrolled in the federal free and reduced lunch (FRL) program. The comparison schools are similar, with over 70% of students identifying as Latino or Hispanic and nearly 72% enrolled the FRL program. Students with chronic conditions comprise roughly 15–16% for both demonstration and comparison school populations.

The main findings of Phase I of the demonstration project regarding (1) improving access to primary-care and prevention services, specifically asthma and chronic condition management, and in (2) facilitating the establishment of a medical home, included (a) increased screening and follow-up, (b) a reduction on the number of school days missed due to illness among children with asthma and other chronic conditions, (c) a reduction in the number of recurrent emergency care visits, and (d) an increase in awareness and appreciation of school nursing by teachers and administrators.

Figs. 2 and 3 are examples of successful improvements in screening and follow-up due to the increased nursing time in the project demonstration schools. In 2009–2010, 97% of students who were screened and referred to a health-care provider for possible vision problems were examined by a vision

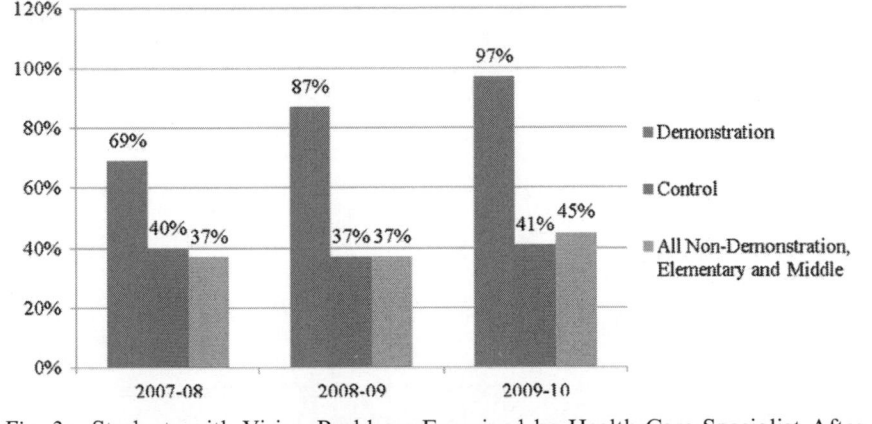

Fig. 2. Students with Vision Problems Examined by Health-Care Specialist After Nurse Referral. *Source*: SJUSD Nurse Monitoring Tools; Packard 2009–2010 (Year 3) Grant Report.

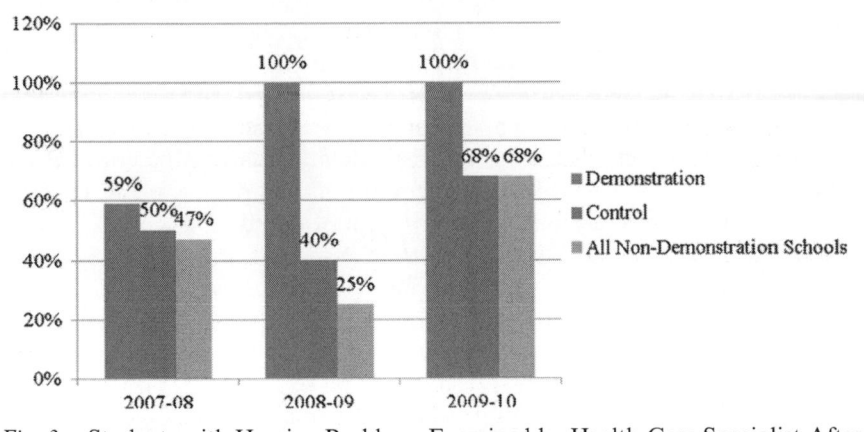

Fig. 3. Students with Hearing Problems Examined by Health-Care Specialist After Nurse Referral. *Source*: SJUSD Nurse Monitoring Tools; Packard 2009–2010 (Year 3) Grant Report.

specialist (which was 100% when excluding parental refusal after three follow-up attempts), an increase from 87% in 2008–2009 and 69% in 2007–2008 (Fig. 2). In contrast, referral rates for students in the control schools – as well as all elementary and middle schools not in the demonstration project – remain consistently around 40%. All nondemonstration elementary and middle schools (including the five control schools) comprise 29 schools serving a total of 18,640 students.

Similarly, 100% of students screened and then referred to a health-care provider for possible hearings problems were seen by a specialist in 2009–2010, a large increase from 59% in 2007–2008 (Fig. 3). Although referral rates for hearing problems increased slightly to 68% in 2009–2010 for control and nondemonstration schools, this rate remains far below the 100% referral rate in the demonstration schools. Including the five control schools, all nondemonstration schools comprise 36 schools serving a total of 27,133 students.

Table 2 illustrates changes in the number of school days missed due to illness among elementary and middle school students in the demonstration and comparison groups. Within the first full year of implementation of the project, the difference between demonstration and comparison schools in mean days absent due to illness increased from a 0.26 day's difference in 2006–2007 to nearly half a day's difference. Students in demonstration schools missed an average of 3.03 days due to illness in 2008–2009 (from 3.17 in 2006–2007), and this increased to a mean of 3.51 days missed due to illness among students in the control schools (from 3.43 in 2006–2007). This difference was more pronounced among elementary school students. If extrapolated to the entire school district (30,010 students in 2008–2009), this reduction of a half-day (0.48 days) difference between the mean days absent due to illness per student in the demonstration and control schools would translate to a difference of 14,405 school days for the academic year.

Table 2. Mean Days Absent Due to Illness, By Year and School Type.

		2006–2007: Before Project, with Part-Time Nurses	2008–2009: After First Full Year of Implementation
All students	Demonstration schools	3.17	3.03
	Control schools	3.43	3.51
Elementary school students	Demonstration schools	3.05	2.85
	Control schools	3.19	3.23
Middle school students	Demonstration schools	3.23	3.12
	Control schools	3.87	3.84

A telephone survey of parents yielded a low response rate, and only 183 surveys were completed in the demonstration and 178 in the comparison schools. Responses indicated that children in schools with full-time nurses were less likely to have repeated visits to the emergency room. While 26.3% of parents in the comparison schools reported taking their children to the emergency room two or more times during 2008–2009, only 16.7% in the demonstration school reported using those services twice or more.

In response to 2009–2010 e-mail surveys, teachers and administrators in the demonstration schools reported more awareness and appreciation of the work of school nurses. When asked about the type of impact the school nurse is making in the overall well-being of students with chronic conditions in their school, 75% teachers in demonstration schools reported a "very positive impact" compared to only 32.4% among teachers in control schools who reported the same. Additionally, 93.8% of teachers in the demonstration schools reported that a full-time school nurse was helping them teach more effectively, compared to 60% of teachers in comparison schools.

An additional outcome of the project has been the increased and strengthened collaboration between the district and community health agencies and partners. The full-time nurses have been able to successfully build and coordinate partnerships to provide dental screenings and follow-up care for students, facilitate parent, student, and staff health education sessions, as well as refer parents to appropriate resources for glasses, food, and clothing. One of the most important collaborations strengthened has been between the district and SHC of Santa Clara County, another partner with the demonstration project. With the support of a nurse practitioner with SHC and strengthened communication processes, referrals to SHC have increased and SHC health educators have been very successful in reaching students and staff in the classrooms to facilitate education sessions in the demonstration schools.

DISCUSSION

While the lack of randomized community trials pose a challenge to demonstrate the impact of school nurses, the increasing number of rigorous evaluations of school demonstration projects continues to build evidence on the beneficial effects of facilitating nursing care in the school, especially in those with a high proportion of underserved children.

The demonstrated successes and improvements in student screenings, referrals, follow-up, absenteeism, and even academic scores in the demonstration schools have provided leverage for other schools in the SJUSD to garner support for full-time nurses at their school sites. In 2010–2011, one additional school was able to secure funding to hire a full-time nurse, which increased to a total of three nondemonstration schools with a full-time school nurse in 2011–2012.

The demonstration project described here is ongoing. A cost-benefits analysis is under way. Focus groups with parents are being conducted to overcome some of the challenges presented by having a low response rate to phone surveys. Yet, at a time when there is both a shortage of primary-care providers as well as growing consensus about the need for interdisciplinary teams to provide effective management of chronic diseases (Fairman, Rowe, Hassmiller, & Shalala, 2011), a fast dissemination of results is important to give school health issues proper consideration. Our results indicate that school nurses provide valuable services, and could be a major player in providing and coordinating effective management and prevention of chronic disease among children.

ACKNOWLEDGMENTS

Preparation of this paper and the nurse demonstration project was supported through a grant funded by the Lucile Packard Foundation for Children's Health and the Lucile Packard Children's Hospital. The authors would like to thank Candace Roney, JoAnna Caywood, Sue Lapp, and Andrea Hong for their continued contribution to the project development and support of the evaluation efforts. They would also like to thank the school nurses who participated in the project, and undergraduate and medical students at Stanford University who have been involved in different aspects of the demonstration project and evaluation.

REFERENCES

American Academy of Pediatrics (AAP). Ad hoc task force on definition of the medical home. The medical home. *Pediatrics, 90,* 774.

Balaji, A. B., Brener, N. D., McManus, T., Hawkins, J., Kann, L., & Speicher, N. (2008). *School health profiles: Characteristics of health programs among secondary schools 2006.* Atlanta, GA: Centers for Disease Control and Prevention.

Brener, N. D., McManus, T., Foti, K., Shanklin, S., Hawkins, J., Kann, L., & Speicher, N (2009). *School health profiles 2008: Characteristics of health programs among secondary schools.* Atlanta, GA: Centers for Disease Control and Prevention.

Cooper, R. A., Getzen, T. E., McKee, H. J., & Laud, P. (2002). Economic and demographic trends signal an impending physician shortage. *Health Affairs, 21*, 140–154.

Fairman, J., Rowe, J., Hassmiller, S., & Shalala, D. (2011). Broadening the scope of nursing practice. *New England Journal of Medicine, 364*, 193–196.

Guttu, M., Engelke, M., & Swanson, M. (2004). Does the school nurse-to-student ratio make a difference? *Journal of School Health, 74*, 6–9.

Halfon, N., & Newacheck, P. W. (2010). Evolving notions of childhood chronic illness. *JAMA, 303*, 665–666.

Kohen, D. (2010). Asthma and school functioning. *Statistics Canada, 21*, 35–45.

Ku, L., & Lessard, G. (2003). Gaps in coverage for children in immigrant families: The future of children. *Health Insurance for Children, 13*, 101–115.

Levy, M., Heffner, B., Stewart, T., & Beeman, G. (2006). The efficacy of asthma case management in an urban school district in reducing school absences and hospitalizations for asthma. *Journal of School Health, 76*, 320–324.

Maughan, E. (2003). The impact of school nursing on school performance: A research synthesis. *Journal of School Nursing, 19*, 163–171.

Moonie, S., Sterling, D., Figgs, L., & Castro, M. (2006). Asthma status and severity affects missed school days. *Journal of School Health, 76*, 18–24.

National Association of School Nurses (NASN). (2010). *The definition of school nursing.* Retrieved from http://www.nasn.org/RoleCareer. Accessed on July 19, 2011.

National Center for Education Statistics (NCES), U.S. Department of Education. (2010). *Chapter 2: Digest of education statistics.* Retrieved from http://nces.ed.gov/programs/digest/d10/ch_2.asp. Accessed on July 18, 2011.

Rieselbach, R., & Kellermann, A. (2011). A model health care delivery system for Medicaid. *The New England Journal of Medicine, 364*, 2476–2478.

Starfield, B., & Shi, L. (2004). The medical home, access to care, and insurance: A review of the evidence. *Pediatrics, 113*, 1493–1498.

Telljohann, S., Dake, J., & Price, J. (2004a). Effect of full-time versus parttime school nurses on attendance of elementary students with asthma. *Journal of School Nursing, 20*, 331–334.

Telljohann, S. K., Price, J. H., Dake, J. A., & Durgin, J. (2004b). Access to school health services: Differences between full-time and part-time school nurses. *Journal of School Nursing, 20*, 176–181.

Turchi, R. M., Gatto, M., & Antonelli, R. (2007). Children and youth with special healthcare needs: There's no place like a (medical) home. *Current Opinion in Pediatrics, 19*, 503–508.

Van Cleave, J., Gortmaker, S. L., & Perrin, J. M. (2010). Dynamics of obesity and chronic health conditions among children and youth. *JAMA, 303*, 623–630.

Vessey, J. (2002). An evaluation of commercial school health software for use in multisite research studies. *Journal of School Nursing, 18*, 95–100.

APPENDIX: PROJECT LOGIC MODEL

Goal 1: Managing Chronic Conditions (Focused on Asthma).

Inputs	Activities	Outputs	Short-Term Outcomes	Midterm Outcomes	Long-Term Outcomes

• School nurses
• School health clinic
• Nurse practitioner
• Community resources
• Health education materials
• Teachers
• Student records
• Parent volunteers
	• Teacher education
	  ○ Developing standard presentations about chronic diseases for use by district
	  ○ Increased ability to provide 1:1 teacher training as required by student health needs
	• Case management
	  ○ Increased ability to identify students with chronic health problems which are ineffectively managed
	  ○ Increased ability to refer and follow-up with health-care providers and parents
		• Number of teachers educated about chronic diseases
		• Number of contacts with parents
		• Number of referrals made to clinic
		• Number of exchange of information forms in place with clinic
		• Number of rescue treatments given
		• Number of students
			• Teachers report increased knowledge of how to handle their students' medical issues
			• School nurses, nurse practitioners, and other health-care providers are able to discuss and coordinate care of students
			• Families are more aware of resources to help manage chronic diseases
			• Parents demonstrate increased knowledge of ways to receive urgent care besides visiting the emergency room
				• Decrease in number of urgent care and/or ER visits for asthma problems
				• Decrease in number of school days missed
				• Decrease in number of "rescue" treatments given
				• Increased number of students receiving follow-up care after diagnosis
				• Better compliance with treatment of chronic diseases
				• More students with asthma will receive treatment meeting the current asthma management standards
				  ○ Have an asthma care plan in place
					• Students with chronic medical conditions will have better secondary preventive care.[a] The focus will be on asthma, which affects a high proportion of students in the district.

- Student education
  - Observation of inhaler treatments to increase compliance and effectiveness of use

- More effective coordination of care between clinic and school
  - Improved nurse practitioner tracking tools
  - Increased ability to refer and follow-up referral to health-care providers

being sent home from school or missing school

- Number of students with asthma vaccinated
  - Receive a flu vaccine

Goal 2: Establishing a Medical Home.*

Inputs	Activities	Outputs	Short-Term Outcomes	Midterm Outcomes	Long-Term Outcomes
• School nurses • School health clinic • Nurse practitioner • Community resources • Health education materials • Teachers • Student records • Parent volunteers	• Identifying children without insurance • Helping families without insurance • Nurse coverage locate federal and state insurance resources • Referral to school clinic • Encouraging follow-up care at clinic • Referring parents to community resources	• Number of referrals to clinic • Number of children without insurance identified • Number of students establishing a relationship with primary-care provider • Number of follow-up visits to clinic • Number of referrals to community resources	• School officials gain knowledge of students lacking insurance • School officials gain knowledge of health-care barriers • Parents gain knowledge of community resources • More parents identify school as a possible resource for health knowledge	• Increase in number of students with insurance • Increase in number of children who have a regular doctor (continuity of care) • Increase in immunization	• More students in the district will establish a medical home

*If Goals 1 and 2 are accomplished, this could potentially lead to a decrease in absenteeism and better academic outcomes.

HEALTH, DEVELOPMENT, AND DEMOCRACY: HEALTH SYSTEMS IN SOUTHEAST ASIA AND IN EASTERN EUROPE

Nirupama Prakash and Barbara Wejnert

ABSTRACT

So far only minimal efforts have been made to directly integrate health concerns with priorities of the processes of global economic development. Nonetheless, there is search for new models to provide sufficient medical care and to encumber global threats, soaring medical costs, technological costs, poverty, and disease. Using example of health conditions and health policies implemented in countries of Southeast Asia in comparison to Eastern Europe, the chapter emphasizes success achieved and in the process of achievement in provision of health care to societies in these countries.

INTRODUCTION

Development is defined as the process of improving the quality of life through changes that result in higher productivity and standards of living, greater political participation, and access to basic goods and services. It

Democracies: Challenges to Societal Health
Research in Political Sociology, Volume 19, 43–56
Copyright © 2011 by Emerald Group Publishing Limited
ISSN: 0895-9935/doi:10.1108/S0895-9935(2011)0000019007

involves progressive change in socioeconomic and political status. Therefore, development encompasses social, political, economic, and human
development, not merely economic growth. This all encompassing concept
of development should be used to guide the formulation of policies needed
for the resolution of global social threats such as AIDS, poverty, and
environmental degradation, which affect the populations in all countries of
the world, regardless of their position in the world economic system.

So far only minimal efforts have been made to directly integrate health
concerns as a priority of the economic development process. The relationship
between health and development has now undergone new scrutiny. There is
search for new models to deal with global threats, soaring medical costs,
technological costs, poverty, and disease. More than 1 billion people in the
world live in extreme poverty because advances in health, education, income-
generating capability, and infrastructure did not reach them, and their human
development, thus, has been handicapped. Empowering these individuals to
become productive members of their societies involves implementing development strategies and public policies that would make available basic health,
shelter, nutrition, information, and skills for effective income generation.

While a global approach is certainly needed, world conditions of extreme
poverty, inequality, and pressure on the environment demonstrate an urgent
need to move from macro concepts and global policies to empirical concepts
and convert them into coordinated local policies and actions.

With worldwide development, the concept of health has evolved and
expanded. In early 1900s, health was defined biologically, restricting health
to absence of death, chronic diseases, and physical disabilities. Decades
later, health underwent de-biologization. The social variables of environmental hygiene, health, safety at work place, etc., are also included.
Presently health, by its definition, is an integral part of development. The
constitution of the World Health Organization (WHO) defines health as a
state of complete physical, mental, and social well-being and not merely the
absence of disease and infirmity.

Those who prepared the WHO constitution almost 50 years ago had the
remarkable foresight to see health within the context of human rights, peace,
and security. For example, the WHO constitution affirms

- The enjoyment of the highest attainable standard of health is one of the
  fundamental human rights of every human being without distinction of
  race, religion, political belief, and economic or social condition.
- Health of all peoples is fundamental to the attainment of peace and security
  and is dependent upon the fullest cooperation of individuals and states.

• The Health for All (HFA) movement launched at the 30th World Health Assembly in 1977 was based on recognition of the link between health and development. HFA acclaimed the universal attainment by the year 2000 of a level of health that permits people to lead socially and economically productive lives as a primary goal for all societies.

The need to protect these rights and ensure adherence to the responsibilities they mention is more relevant today than ever before. This recognition is reflected in the concepts of "health security" and "health accountability." Health security is founded on equity. It is founded on the principle that all human beings may live free from the risk of preventable illness and injury and will have equal access to quality health care that is both affordable and relevant. Health security means more than a system of schemes to guarantee access to health care. It includes the right to food in sufficient quantity and quality, information needed for self-reliance, and a working and living environment where known health risks are controlled.

It also means empowering people to make the right choices in health, and building their capacity to keep themselves and their families healthy. This calls for various forms of social and economic support, and better knowledge and awareness. It also calls for intersectional collaboration of various social systems as an essential element in health development. Health accountability begins with the obligations of the states and the responsibilities of health professionals to provide health services to all. It also includes the state's acceptance of responsibility for the impact on health development and other policies.

In more recent years, a more holistic, multisectional approach to determinants of health has emerged, which attempts to integrate medicine with economic and political processes, and sociocultural factors. Here, a variety of social, economic, political, and cultural issues are seen as additional determinants of a society's health. World development efforts in the 1950s and 1960s emphasized economic development strategies of industrialization over social investment in areas such as health and education. Most experts assumed that the prosperity derived through economic growth would "trickle down" to reach sectors such as health that were not directly involved in the activities being promoted.

While economic growth can stimulate growth in the health sector of the economy, it is not necessarily true that this growth lead to the achievement of health goals. Indeed, economic growth, new health technology, increased education, and government intervention succeeded in bringing about significant declines in death rates and childhood diseases. But periodic reviews of the world conditions by national governments and international agencies have revealed the continued existence of large population groups of poor, sick, and illiterate people marginalized from national economies in both developed and developing countries.

By 1970s, some perceived the emergence of negative effects of certain developmental efforts on health. This led to debates over urbanization, use of pesticides, infant bottle feeding, etc. New strategies were developed. UNICEF and WHO embraced a community-based approach to health. This includes topics on health auxiliaries, appropriate technology, community education, and disease control. This accompanied efforts by many developing nations to develop their own expertise in health education, management, and delivery of health services.

The concepts of health and development have evolved to a point where they are intertwined. The principal objectives of public policy for health are relief from suffering, improvement in health status, control and responsibility for health at the individual and household level; dealing with occupational and environmental health concerns; and managing potential disease threats within and among countries. These objectives should be broadened to include consideration of health concerns as they affect and are affected by processes of socioeconomic development.

HEALTH AND DEVELOPMENT
IN A CHANGING WORLD

The world is becoming so interdependent that in relation to health, it is now becoming difficult to talk of a region or a country in isolation. In the past few years, there has been an unforeseen but far-reaching global trend toward the democratization of political systems. This has been accompanied by much greater participation of people determining their own future.

WHO has endorsed these two concepts and the policies and programs have been given overall orientation to ensure that all people, irrespective of their course of life and the circumstances surrounding their lives, enjoy health security, and that governments and health professionals display their obligations toward health accountability in providing health services to all. On the other hand, while the end of the "Cold War" relieved the tension between the East and the West, regional, intercountry, and intracountry conflicts and warfare have persisted. Hopes have been high for reduced spending on arms and increased spending on health development. According to many policy makers, financial resources should be diverted toward accelerating human development.

The demographic shift in the world population in terms of increase of population, including increase in geriatric population, especially in developing countries, has very significant implications for planning, financing, and delivery of health services in the coming decades. It is expected that by the year 2025, about 60% of the world's population will live in urban areas. The megacities (large urban populations of 10 million or more) have huge numbers of very poor people concentrated in slums, where poor housing and squalid living conditions exist. All these contribute to ill-health and an unsatisfactory quality of life. Poverty is the main cause of short life expectancy, malnutrition, and disability. It is the basic reason why babies are not vaccinated and clean water and sanitation are not provided in communities; why mothers die at childbirth, and why lifesaving drugs are not available in many countries. Poverty is the single largest contributor to mental illness, suicide, and family and social disintegration.

Improvements in the world economy have helped to supply diverse goods and services, and this has led to widespread improvements in the standard of living for most of the world's population. Nevertheless, the gap between the developed and the developing countries has increased. So also has that between the developing and the least developed areas. In the backdrop of such a global scenario, we need to examine the main determinants of health in the Southeast Asia Region (SEAR), especially in democracies of this region, and compare them to determinants of health in developing and democratizing countries of Eastern Europe.

The Global Market, Public/Private Mix Health Care, and the Role of Governments

Most countries in the SEAR and of Eastern Europe have been in the process of restructuring their economies to adjust to the global market. Privatization of state activities and public enterprises has been a major outcome of this process. This same process has also affected a wide range of public services, especially welfare-oriented programs including health services and special target programs for the disadvantaged and the poor.

The changing pattern of health care, from a predominantly public sector to one where the private sector is becoming increasingly important, poses newer challenges to managers of health services. These ongoing changes in the countries of SEAR and Eastern Europe call for a closer look at the role of the private sector in the overall national health development strategies. Therefore, the issue of what makes for an appropriate mix of public and private sector in the provision and financing of health care has to receive the attention of health-care managers and planners. Both in Southeast Asia and in Eastern Europe, the growth of the private sector does not diminish the importance of the state and the public sector as determining agents of the National Health Policy. It alters the conventional role of the state, and endows it with an even more critical and essential role.

In the coming decade, it will be necessary for health policy makers, planners, and managers to look objectively at the needs of the public above those of the providers and interest groups, to look at the needs of preventive and curative services, and to formulate a judicious mix of such services. They will need to determine the complimentary role of the private and public sectors in the given country, and harmonize their respective advantages using a realistic mixture of incentives, controls, and other policy instruments.

In this situation the government has three major roles to play. First, the government has a role as a policy maker and regulator. Government will have to ensure that measures are taken to maintain an acceptable level of equity and that increasing reliance on the private delivery of health care does not disadvantage the poor, the elderly, and the most disabled members of society.

The second role for the government is to serve as a source of accurate, timely information. By providing key pieces of information to those concerned in the health-care system, governments may improve the efficiency and equity of health sector operators.

And third, the government has an important advocacy role through the evaluation of financing and provision policy changes. It can review the experiences of other countries, carry out studies or situational analysis and needs assessments, and assess manpower and technology alternatives before enlarging the scale of innovations.

Advances in technology will continue to be the main level of socio-economic transformation all over the world. However, technological innovations have not benefited all people equally. Many people do not benefit fully from available health technologies because of lack of accessibility and cost implications. Technological innovation offers the opportunity for partnerships between health and development sectors to change the patterns of work and enhance health-promoting capacity. For example, where simple technologies such as iodizing salt have been widely applied, the incidence of goiter has been reduced at a very low cost. More sophisticated technology also has its uses, but it should be used in a judicious manner.

Priority Issues in Health Development

There are some critical issues, which have a direct bearing on health as a whole. These issues are poverty and its consequences, the emergence of market economies, and the search for newer ways of health-care financing and issues related to health of women. Poverty worsens the spread of disease, but, equally important, the impact of ill-health has the capacity to intensify poverty or push groups and societies below the poverty line. Among the many examples of this are malnutrition, cholera, and tuberculosis. Cholera, which is directly associated with the lack of adequate housing, clean water, and sanitation, has increased over the last decade. Social disintegration related to poverty and unemployment is shown by indicators such as the harmful use of alcohol, drugs, and violence. In turn, sick people limitedly contribute to the workforce that enhances progress in economic development.

Hence, the future perception of health requires the interactive approach in terms of health being a cause and a consequence of countries' level of development. Future research also requires a comprehensive view of health that includes maternal and child health as equally important as infectious and communicative diseases.

THE CASE OF HEALTH SYSTEM IN SOUTHEAST ASIA

Demography

The SEAR comprises 10 countries with a combined population of 1.5 billion people living in 6% of the total land area. The populations of Bangladesh, Bhutan, India, Maldives, Myanmar, and Nepal will increase by at least 30% between the years 2000 and 2010. In Korea, Indonesia, Sri Lanka, and Thailand, the population increase will be around 18%.

Southeast Asia has a higher child (0–14 years) population than the world as a whole, but lower proportions of adults aged 15–64 and of elders aged 65 years or more. Two countries of Southeast Asia region (Myanmar and Nepal) spend less than 1% of their GNP on health: five countries (Bangladesh, Bhutan, India, Indonesia, and Sri Lanka) spend more than 1% but less than 5%; and Maldives and Thailand spend more than 5% of their GNP on health. In Bangladesh, Bhutan, Maldives, Nepal, and Sri Lanka, the percentage of national health expenditure spent on local health services is higher than 50.

Health Systems

The physical infrastructure and/or functioning of health systems seems to be inadequate in Bangladesh, Bhutan, and Nepal. The situation is better but also needs improvement in India, Maldives, and Myanmar. In other countries (Korea, Indonesia, Sri Lanka, and Thailand), the physical infrastructure is reasonably good and a basic network is in place.

In Korea, Sri Lanka, and Thailand, between 80% and 100% of the population has access to local health services or to all elements of primary health centers. In the remaining countries of the region, the coverage is lower. The quality and quantity of human resources for health need improvement in most SEAR countries. There are shortages in most categories of health personnel in Bhutan, Indonesia, Maldives, Nepal, and Sri Lanka. Other countries (Bangladesh, Korea, India, Myanmar, and Thailand) have sufficient or excessive number of doctors but shortages in other categories of personnel.

In all countries a shortage of professional nursing and midwives personnel is recognized. In almost all countries there is need to improve the distribution of health personnel, which at present is usually uneven, with excess in urban areas and shortages in rural, especially hilly areas. Overall the health situation in the SEAR is characterized by the slow decline of crude death rates as well as by the gradual increase in life expectancy.

The infant mortality rate (IMR), an important comprehensive indicator of standard of living, which also reflects the level of education and the effectiveness of the health-care system, has declined during the last decade in virtually all countries of the region, but still remains high (60–102 per 1,000 live births) in some. The maternal mortality rate (MMR) has shown a slow overall decline during the last decade.

Success Achieved and in the Process of Achievement

The main change in morbidity and mortality patterns in the countries of the region during the last 10 years has resulted from a decline of polio, measles, and neonatal tetanus, and declining incidence and prevalence of leprosy in the region. There has also been a decline in the number of registered cases of guinea worm diseases in India since 1984, and decline of leishmaniasis in some countries during the past years.

The less optimistic side of the regional health situation is determined by the high incidence and prevalence of acute respiratory infections, diarrheal diseases, malnutrition and nutritional deficiency disorders, vector-borne diseases (especially malaria), and tuberculosis. The persistence of malaria and tuberculosis; the resurgence of plague; the emergence of chronic noncommunicable diseases such as cardiovascular diseases, cancer, and diabetes; the emergence of other infectious diseases such as dengue fever, encephalitis, and cholera; and the pandemics of AIDS and HIV infection are the challenges for the future (Rodriguez Garcia & Goldman, 1994).

Future Agenda

The process of epidemiological transition needs to be carefully studied to decide upon health interventions. As an example, if one were to study the causes of mortality rate under the age of five in a typical developing country, it would be clearly seen that infectious diseases are the predominant causes. The causes of adult mortality also show a similar pattern, excluding measles and neonatal tetanus. Under these circumstances, if health authorities vigorously combat infectious diseases such as diarrhea, malaria, and vaccine-preventable diseases, reduction in infant and overall mortality can be achieved.

Forecasts for the next 10 years envisage morbidity and mortality burden still dominated primarily by infectious diseases with the beginning of shift toward noncommunicable chronic diseases for Bangladesh, Bhutan, most of the states of India, Maldives, Myanmar, and Nepal. Noncommunicable diseases and accidents will affect to a greater extent in the more advanced countries of the region, which have achieved higher level of life expectancy. The HIV/AIDS epidemic will be present throughout the region, being close to its peak in India, Myanmar, and Thailand, and rapidly spreading in some other countries.

THE CASE OF HEALTH SYSTEM IN EASTERN EUROPE

Demography

The region of Eastern Europe comprises Albania, Bosnia and Herzegovina, Bulgaria, Croatia, Czech Republic, Hungary, Macedonia, Montenegro, Poland, Romania, Serbia, Slovakia, and Slovenia. All of these countries were previously communist states with similar economic and political system and similarly organized health-care system. All of these countries transformed from communism to some type of democracy and from control by state economy to a market economic system. The political transition interacted with economic transition leading to initial decrease followed by slow increase of living conditions. The increase of living conditions coincided with the diffusion of the Western Europe model of living and opened new life opportunities for a younger, educated generation. Initial economic hardship, combined with new lifestyle resulted in new demographic trends of population *aging* and *population decline*, and intensified *migration*. These three factors contributed to a rapid decline in population that is expected to be more visible throughout the twenty-first century. As is predicted, by 2100, Eastern European population will decline by half (Lutz, Sanderson, Scherbov, & Samir, 2008).

Unlike in the communist period, presently the Eastern European region is the only region in the world experiencing a contraction in population, which stems from both a natural decrease in the population (i.e., crude death rates exceeding crude birth rates) and emigration. The highest crude death rates in the world are found in this region; so too the lowest fertility rates (Heinegg, Melzig, Pickett, & Sprout, 2005). Over the years 1991–2002, the region faced, on average, contraction of −0.1% of population and since 1994, the natural change in population in the region has been negative. The worst situation is expected in Ukraine and Bulgaria, where the population is expected to fall sharply by 20–22% by 2025. In the Baltic countries of Estonia and Latvia, demographic prospects are not very promising either, but their economies are stronger than in Bulgaria. Even relatively rich countries such as Hungary and the Czech Republic should be worried since old populations tend to mean slower growth of economy. There are fewer workers. Older people are (on average) less productive and countrywide health-care and pension bills rise.

Bad demographics are believed to be a communist-era fluke. Under the communist system, women were highly educated but living conditions were poor. The system also required that women were workers and mothers (Wejnert & Spencer, 1996). In postcommunist democracies, women exposed to new Western standards of living cut the number of children they bear and decided to postpone procreation age (Wejnert, 2002). For example, in Poland, the common age for bearing a first child increased from 22 in 1989 to 26 by 2001 (*The Economist*, 2011).

The second factor influencing the countries' population is emigration, with the top emigrating country being Albania that experienced decrease of its population by almost 25% in the last decade. Although the population in the region has been and is increasing and the educational attainment of the working-age population coincides with a positive economic growth, the region of Eastern Europe varies economically. The GDP for an average country in the region is $7,857 per capita, with three countries – Czech Republic, former East Germany, and Poland – having the highest per capita GDP and the highest growth rate of GDP.

Development and Economics

The variations in GDP growth within Eastern Europe reveal much about the economic profiles of these countries. The region breaks down roughly into three groups: (1) Poland, the region's largest and most robust economy and the only European country that achieved positive GDP growth in 2009, (2) four countries projected to attain modest GDP growth in 2010 (Czech Republic, Slovenia, Slovak Republic, and Romania), and (3) five countries whose economies are expected to contract in 2010 (Hungary, Bulgaria, Estonia, Lithuania, and Latvia). The International Monetary Fund (IMF) predicts that contraction of economy of many countries within this region will persist with the greatest contraction already observed in Hungary, Bulgaria, Estonia, Lithuania, and Latvia. In 2009, regional economic output fell by 5% and was lower than an average European, the United States, and Latin American reduction.

With the introduction of democratic transition and economic integration within European Union, after initial hardship, the living conditions improved and with them the life expectancy started to steadily increase. On average the life span for women is much higher than that for men; for example, in Poland, female life expectancy is 80.25 years versus male 72.1 years. However, once under way, the post-1989 increase in life expectancy in these countries has continued at a steady rate that is very similar to Western Europe.

Public and Private Health Systems

The health-care system in Eastern Europe is a mix of private and public insurance plans. *Public health insurance* is required in all Eastern European countries, and the services covered by it are in public hospitals and clinics and are free of charge. The main benefactors of these insurance plans are poor people who are able to receive medical help but cannot afford services provided by private doctors. The government pays general practitioners or "family doctors" on a contractual basis per socially insured patient treated.

The overall standard of provision in the public sector is quite poor, and hospitals and clinics are overcrowded and inadequately equipped due to governmental underfunding. Many patients offer doctors out-of-packet "rewards" to secure better service in public medical facilities. Such "rewards" are especially popular for services provided by selected medical doctors who are specialists in chronic illness, perform a major surgery, or assist in the childbirth. General practitioners and doctors who are specialists use rent-free clinics and equipment, as well as laboratories of clinics, when offering services with "rewards." At the same time, they often borrow capital from banks to open their own private practice.

This situation affects people's health, as for example, former Yugoslavia is overwhelmed by respiratory and digestive tract diseases, and the occurrence of tuberculosis in Romania is higher than in sub-Saharan Africa. Local health-care authorities started to complain about the state of government-provided health services. For instance, Professor Pavel Pafko, head of the Third Surgery Department in Charles University Faculty Hospital, Prague, said, "In the public's mind the idea of 'free health care' survived ... as does the idea that all of us are equal as long as we are healthy" (Pafko, 2000).

Private medical insurance, which covers private clinics and visits to private doctors, is generally good but expensive (EurActiv, 2010). There is also insecurity of coverage in case the insurance suffers a bad run on claims, which is not uncommon, considering the relative short time of the existence of these insurances. Private insurance has also other limitations. The number of private clinics is small and located primary in the largest cities. Treatment options are much more limited than in public hospitals. But most importantly, coverage of private insurance is limited. It covers dental care, long-term hospital stay, and serious illness in contrast to public insurance that covers all type of medical treatments and visits (Kulish, 2008).

Nonetheless, short supply of highly qualified doctors in governmental hospitals (medical doctors compare salaries and quality of life with medical specialist in Western Europe and frequently choose to move to the Western countries in search for a better life), led to steady increase of public interest in private insurance. As a result, throughout the region, the private medical insurance doubled in growth since the mid-1990s.

Success Achieved and in the Process of Achievement

In most countries patients are dissatisfied with both private and public plans. However, Romania is an exception where based on the health law passed in 1997 it was made mandatory for each patient to pay one-third of their health bills to providers and hospitals to assist the government in subsidization of health-care resources. The individual payment is, however, assessed based on a projected global budget. This country is also experimenting with methods involving fee-for-service reimbursement. In consequence, Romanians are the only people who are satisfied with their medical health care in the region of Eastern Europe.

Future Agenda

The problem with health care in Eastern Europe is that practice and theory remain far behind Western European counterparts. Two main factors influence such a situation. First, continuously unhealthy lifestyle results from populations' nutritional habits, tobacco and alcohol consumption, post-communist spread of drugs, and addictions. The impact of an unhealthy lifestyle is additionally enhanced by unhealthy, poor living conditions and environmental pollution. Second, there are insufficient governmental resources to cover the medical needs of the regions' citizens. Third, the population is aging and its growth rate is negative. Under these circumstances, it is most likely that population health in democratizing Easters European countries will be still decreasing as many people cannot afford adequate and sufficient health care, whereas free-of-charge care is inadequate. And fourth, the economic growth of Eastern Europe lags far behind the developed countries (the exception is Poland that recently was classified as one of the developed countries in the world). According to the Human Development Index (HDI) in 2010, Poland was ranked as the 41st country in the world with its HDI of 0.795 and increased by 0.0004 in comparison to 2009.

CONCLUSION

The developing and democratizing region of Southeast Asia and Eastern Europe are still facing many unsolved problems regarding the health of the populations. It may appear that one of the solutions could be mixed public–private health insurance coverage that could be afforded by all citizens and would cover costs of doctors and clinics of patients' choice. Indeed, such a scenario is proposed as a solution in the case of Southeast Asia.

At the same time, in the region of Eastern Europe the two types of insurance already exist, but they still do not solve numerous problems of sufficient and affordable societal health care. It is due in part to relatively new and experimental coverage by private insurance providers, as well as insufficient funds in state budgets devoted to the coverage of cost of public medical care supported by public insurance. It is also partly due to limited focus of governments on societal health issues that spans beyond the provision of better infant, child, and maternal care, the popular indicators of infant and maternal mortality rate. This indicator is often used to measure the overall level of a country's development.

In the current climate, a new solution could be some form of international health insurance that is competitive to private insurance but offers coverage of better and broader services in all types of medical facilities. We believe that additional choice is essential in Eastern Europe, as well as Southeast Asia, particularly for poorer families and older patients, and especially in the combat of noncommunicable diseases such as cardiovascular diseases, cancer, and diabetes. Large international insurance could perhaps better prevent the emergence and spread of other infectious diseases such as dengue fever, encephalitis, cholera, and the pandemics of AIDS and HIV infection. Regardless of visible improvement in provision of medical care, both regions are facing challenges in population health in the future.

REFERENCES

EurActiv. (2010). Health care systems in Central and Eastern Europe. *Newsletter*, January 29, pp. 1–3.

Heinegg, A., Melzig, R., Pickett, J., & Sprout, R. (2005, June). Demography and health in Eastern Europe and Euroasia. Program Office Bureau for Europe & Eurasia. U.S. Agency for International Development. Working Paper Series on the Transition Countries.

Kulish, N. (2008). Health care fees trouble Eastern Europe. *The New York Times*, May 26, p. 2.

Lutz, W., Sanderson, W., Scherbov, S., & Samir, K. C. (2008). Demographic and human capital trends in Eastern Europe and Sub-Saharan Africa. Migration Policy Institute. Transatlantic Council on Migration, New York, November.

Pafko, P. (2000). Trying our patients. *Central Europe Review*, March, 1.

Rodriguez Garcia, R., & Goldman, A. (1994). *The health-development link*. Washington, DC: PAHO/WHO.

The Economist. (2011). Demography in Eastern Europe. Red fades to grey. July 7–August 3, p. 1.

Wejnert, B. (2002). Effects of global democracy on women's reproductive health: 1970–2005, cross-world analysis. In: B. Wejnert (Ed.), *Safe motherhood in globalized world* (pp. 14–37). London, UK: Routledge Press.

Wejnert, B., & Spencer, M. (Eds.). (1996). *Women in post-communism* (pp. 3–19). Greenwich, CT: JAI Press.

TRANSFORMATION OF HEALTH SERVICES IN POLAND SINCE 1989 DEMOCRATIZATION

Elżbieta Sawa-Czajka

ABSTRACT

After 1945 all countries of the communist Eastern Europe implemented a uniform model of health-care system and health policies called socialist Health Services that provided universal, free of charge health care to all citizens. The initial model underwent many reforms with the largest change taking place during the country's democratization and transition to a market economy system after 1989. The processes of the democratization of the political life and economic changes included privatization of the health-care and medical services. In addition to state hospitals, medical care was provided by private doctors and these services were fully paid for by patients. The private medical care was greatly available but was not controlled by the state until a few years later when the state developed networks of state-regulated services, including public and independent health-care centers. Among other changes of the recent decades was establishment of accreditation system in Polish medical institutions implemented in Poland after 1997. As of 2011 there are 98 accredited Polish hospitals. The prevailing mix-health-care system (private and public) is divided by differences in quality of services, with

Democracies: Challenges to Societal Health
Research in Political Sociology, Volume 19, 57–69
Copyright © 2011 by Emerald Group Publishing Limited
All rights of reproduction in any form reserved
ISSN: 0895-9935/doi:10.1108/S0895-9935(2011)0000019008

*much higher quality medical services being offered by private clinics than
by state-sponsored hospitals.*

After 1945 all countries of the communist Eastern Europe implemented a
uniform model of health-care system and health policies called socialist
Health Service. The model was based on principles designed in the 1930s by
Nicolai Siemiaszko, the former Health Commissioner in the Union of Soviet
Socialist Republics.[1] According to the uniform model, in each country
(a) every citizen was guaranteed a universal access to health-care and
medical services, (b) Health Services were to be financed by the state budget,
(c) doctors and medical staff were federal employees on state salaries, (d) all
medical services, treatment, and medical care were free of charge, and (e) the
only exception was a small co-pay for some medications.

Health services were uniform across all countries and across all social
groups within countries and were controlled centrally by the government of
each country; the entire population had equal access to health care and
benefits, the system goal provision of medical help and protection of health,
as well as health prevention (Wlodarczyk, 1996).

Such development of the health-care system in the post–World War II
Poland followed the stages given below:

Stage I – years 1945–1954. Widening the benefits of social security and
health care to fastly growing postwar population. In 1952, the Constitution
of the Polish People's Republic recognized the right to health protection as
an *essential civil right*.

Stage II – years 1955–1970. In this period the development of the Health
Service and improvement of its organizational forms became less important
as the Polish government mainly concentrated on the training of medical
staffs and development of broader medical cadres as well as establishment of
new research and educational institutes. New medical specializations, such
as occupational medicine as a strong, extended division of the industrial
health-care branch of health services, were established and implemented at
this time.

Stage III – from 1971 till 1980s. This period was associated with the new
socioeconomic development strategy of a country. The new development
program of health care was accepted and it focused on the intensification of
prior strategies and goals including extension and development of medical
staffs, as well as the basic infrastructures of medical care. Many
organizational changes focused on the integration of outpatient care with

hospital care and the appointment of teams of *health-care providers*; the Nationalist Fund of the Health Care budgeting payment for state-supported health care was created, and above all a health care free of charge was expanded practically to the population of the entire country irrespective of character and sector of employment (Wlodarczyk, 1996).

Stage IV – started in the beginnings of the 1980s, clearly aiming at protective health care and strengthening the health of the entire nation. This new policy established a new principle in its approach to health claiming that not only the government but also the individual person and individual family were to bear the burden of responsibility for the societal health. Health services were expected to be provided at the nursery school, school, workplace, and at community level (Dobska & Dobski, 2003, pp. 13–15).[2]

Such organization of the health-care system, with some alterations, continued until the end of the existing communist regime and the end of the communist state in the Polish People's Republic in 1989. The beginning of the political transformation in Poland was particularly difficult because it assumed the reconstruction of all social spheres and reconstruction of many social institutions (Sawa-Czajka, 2010). The processes of the democratization of the political life and economic changes introduced by the market economy system had many pros and cons. Among the negative outcomes were unemployment, paid educational services, including university-level education, and paid health services. Especially the health-care and medical services underwent significant changes and reforms. First, private doctors provided a new type of medical service that was fully paid for by patients. This form of health care was quickly instituted and included services for surgeries provided by private surgeons. These surgeries were free from any scrutinized state control but were broadly available. At the same time the network of state-regulated services, including public and independent health-care centers, started to develop. Not only did this engender a competition between private and public sectors of medical services it also initiated a tradition of cooperation between the private and public units, complementing each other's benefits. Health services started functioning as a vital arm of the economy with the participation of state-run institutions, and state and private institutions were answerable for citizens' health safety.

First efforts of health reforms took place in 1991. The reform of the health-care system started when it was possible for a health-care center to be self-reliant with the "Act on Health Care Centers"[3] constituting the base for building the market of health services (Dobska & Rogoziński, 2008).[4] Although it was repeatedly amended and changed, it was the first act reforming the Health Service and enabling the implementation of market mechanisms in the Polish health system (Ksykiewicz-Dorota, 2004).[5] As per this regulation the defined health-care center, which was the basic structure of medical care, comprised a "team of persons and property means singled out organizationally, created and held with a view to grant health benefits, prevent coming into existence of illness and injuries, promote the health education, and as far as possible educate persons doing medical jobs."[6] The decisions contained in Article 2 enabled the management of the institution to decide on the internal organizational structure and adapt it to the needs and profile (Dobska & Dobski, 2003).[7]

New legislation assuring fresh opportunities in the health-care sector provides:

– regulations that govern the patient's categorization and award of benefits, whether it is free medical care or with partial payment or full payment (however a detailed list of benefits in individual groups is yet to be made),
– enabling the flow of benefits to the public sector,
– introducing the new organizational form in the form of independent public health-care center (Dobska & Dobski, 2003).[8]

The act defined forms of activity of health-care centers segregating them based on:

1. public units having the incomplete legal personality created and supported from public means by chief and central administration authorities, province governors, communes, and state enterprises (e.g., Polish State Railways);
2. independent public units created and held through the same, as above legal subjects, but having the full legal personality and self-reliance of acting on one's own account, with benefits and income which cover its activity expenses;
3. nonpublic units created and held through churches and religious connections, insurance institutions, workplaces, associations, foundations, and other legal persons or foreign entities. These plants were popularly called "private," and could grant health benefits using budget means or on commercial principles (Dobska & Dobski, 2003).[9]

The essential document increasing the autonomy of health-care centers was a regulation issued by the Department of Health and the Social Welfare in 1993, in the matter of principles of reaching contracts.[10] A provision of transferring public funds allocated to health care was included in it – in specific conditions – covering the public sector and private sector providers of health services. Changes in legislation pertaining to financing of health care necessitated the first service medical contracts with provincial authorities (province governor), which were signed in 1996. An Act enabling nurses and midwives to practice their profession also came into effect in 1996.Nurses were eligible to sign civil-legal agreements (contracts) and claim nursing benefits.

In 1997 Poland entered the Bioethical Convention of the European Council, which was an important step with regard to changes associated with the political transformation, and it guaranteed all citizens equal access to quality medical care.[11] Also, the Constitution of the Republic of Poland passed on April 2, 1997, in Article 68 guarantees the Polish people the right to health protection. "For citizens, irrespective of the material situation, official authorities provide with the equal access to health benefits, financed from public means. Official authorities are obliged to provide the special health care for children, expectant mothers, persons with disabilities and old age people. Official authorities are obliged to fight epidemic disease and prevent negative health consequences from the effects of environmental decay."[12]

Until the end of 1998 the entire health-care system in Poland was controlled by public health-care centers run and financed by the state government. In 1998, M. Dobska and K. Rogoziński brought in reforms in health care in Poland "in the form of budget units or budgetary units financed from the government by the Department of Health and the Social Welfare or the province governor. Some communities as part of the realization of decisions of the so-called act on large cities[13] financed the health care from own budgets. Apart from that the certain part of institutions of the health care was financed by other ministries (so-called departmental Health Service). Apart from that on the internal medical market private individuals acted which for granted benefits collected charges in the commercial system. In case of public institutions one subject (province governor, commune) served as both the organizer of medical services, and the financing body. Such a system didn't induce the health-care units either for caring about the rationality of expenses, or for the essential restructuring, however it supported for pathological behaviors, that is among others for practice of private extra charges of patients for benefits get at public units" (Dobska & Rogoziński, 2008).[14]

Implementing methods of estimation of medical procedures and their qualities was an element of the reform of the system. Health benefits were considered part of the service industry; the patient was the buyer (customer) like in every market economy, in which the market is focused on profit. The higher the quality of services the higher the profit. Accreditation of procedures and qualities of work of medical institutions based on specific standards is one of most well-known and tested methods of quality assurance. The accreditation system in Polish medical institutions was implemented in Poland after 1997. As of 2011 there are 98 accredited Polish hospitals.[15]

Apart from accreditation, the possibility of implementing quality systems in health care was governed by a certification of medical units according to the ISO 9001: 2000 norm. "ISO 9001: 2000-it is the most popular quality management system. Correctly worked up and introduced the system is the perfect tool for effective managing of the medical institution. Many times doctors not having too great management experience for managing human teams are owners or managers of such institutions. The transformation of the system and the reform of the health-care system extorted the need to contend with problems, which earlier they didn't have any contacts with. Many of them had to meet requirements put by health-insurance funds and later institutions financing the Health Service becoming the employer and the manager simultaneously. With the ISO 9001: 2000 the best advantage is the fact that management and quality control system is individually adapted to needs of the specific institution and drawn up by consultants based on accurate analysis of the baseline situation. It is undoubted advantage over all courses and trainings in the field of the management, handing very theory over often, many times not very useful in the everyday practice. Even the most interesting lectures aren't able to replace the thorough and objective problem analysis, being held where it is done i.e. in a doctor's surgery, in registration office, in waiting room, during the conversation with the patient or the staff. ISO 9001: 2000 norms create a chance for drawing up the new way of managing the medical institution set to the effectiveness, patients' satisfaction and constant refinement of provided services. To this purpose trainings of all employees of the institution are being conducted: of senior staff, of doctors, of nurses, of receptionists, of technicians. Conception of norms of ISO 9001: 2000 is widely applied in countries of the European Union. Many medical institutions try to obtain the ISO certificate seeing the guarantee of the development and competitiveness on the medical market. ISO norms clear up a lot of matters with which the managers managing the hospital, the clinic, the individual practice must usually cope with. ISO is used for all medical industries. It lets to have a quick insight into what in the given moment is happening in the institution, to rationalize costs, to analyze activity in past periods, to plan its action in the future. Functioning of ISO norms is based on the assumption that the quality should be achieved mainly by preventing the defectiveness, rather than removing effects."[16]

In 1997 an Act on universal health insurance was passed to reform the Polish Health Service.[17] This Act was an amendment of the Act of 1998. The Act which came into effect on January 1, 1999, implemented new principles associated with functioning of the Health Service and it precipitated the privatization of Health Services. The Act changed the bases of financing health benefits and the organization of institutions of health care. The funding scheme of health benefits from the state budget was changed to the insurance budget system, and the health-care institutions were converted from budget into independent public health-care centers. Principles of contracting health benefits were determined. New institutions established *health-insurance funds* as a payment that could cover day-to-day expenses to the majority of benefits.

An important component in the transformation of health services in Poland was the creation of independent health-care centers. These independent units covered health services liabilities for obtaining resources, managed wealth that was provided by state institutions or council offices, decided on the profit distribution as well as covered losses from own budget.[18]

An essential executive document to the Act was a *Regulation of the Department of Health and of the Social Welfare* on November 27, 1998, providing guidelines on the competition of offers for agreements for granting health benefits. The regulation determined principles of competitive selection of health benefits.[19] It also implemented a possibility of signing management contracts with managers of medical institutions and created competitions for positions of the chief nurse, superior of nurses, and the charge nurse.[20]

Health-insurance funds, which were the first institution that commercialized the health services, did not fulfill their objectives. They were mainly criticized for their underestimation of social needs in medical care. According to the experts of the Health Service:

> Health-insurance funds didn't meet with the sufficient demand for their services and hence firmly established high payment for services plus demanded fulfillment of additional conditions by insured patients. Simultaneously planning and transferring funds to health-insurance pool, wasn't monitored either regarding the amount, or the health need for performed serviced. (...) There were also over-optimistic assumptions concerning the growth in the economy, and hence amounts of paid contributions were a mistake.[21]

The amount of the insurance premium was connected with the income tax (tax return). In 1999, the unemployment started to grow, and in turn rose the number of poor who were below the higher tax-paying bracket. The jobless poor who did not receive any income were unable to pay for their medical services. To counteract the negative trends, the government established a Fund of the Work and Welfare program, as an available source to finance health needs of the poor members of society. The amount of money that was delivered into the system of the health care, however, was insufficient to cover growing needs. Additionally, the state government's decision of 1998 that reduced the contribution of state funds to health system decreased the available funds for the medical services finances. Another important component of reduction of the available funds was the way these funds were distributed. In a scale of the country, uniform model and standardized organizational structure was unproductive and inefficient.

The next problem resulted from the fact that health-insurance funds were planned without any regulations by law. Many employees and, particularly, managers of health-insurance funds did not have sufficient qualification or readiness to properly distribute and govern insurance funds.

In 1999, 13 out of 16 managers of insurance plans did not have proper education or they were not prepared to perform such type of work. Some insurance companies did not obey wage regulations. They introduced extra employee benefits and monetary rewards for their managerial staff, without justification for such granting. The lack of response to complaints directed to the funds worsened the image of the health-insurance funds. It led to a situation of disregard for patients' needs and the spread of corruption. As the data and economic estimates demonstrate for any insurance company to properly function, it needs to have up to 4–5 million of insured clients. No insurance company could present such a number; therefore by the year 2000, a few insurance companies announced bankruptcy.

> The issue of the debt is a nightmare of the Polish health care. At the time of introducing Health-Insurance Funds it amounted to the about 7 billion Polish Zloty (PLN). The only optimistic is a fact that while functioning Health-Insurance Funds hospitals learned how to estimate costs, and a privatization of rickety clinics in some cities (y) started satisfying patients. This process, determined as the beginning of medical market, was however stopped. In fact a project about the commercialization and the privatization of public healthcare centers wasn't accepted by the Seym (the Polish Parliament).[22]

Health-insurance funds were also politicized, and to some extent used to pay salaries of activists of political groups that had political clout. Such a way of appointing the managing staff and paying for their services from the health funds defeated the purpose of health reform and led to another consecutive change in the health-care system in 2003.

On April 1, 2003, the *Act on the universal health insurance at the National Health Fund* was implemented, which is in force still today. Health-insurance funds were liquidated. Those who are provided with insurance are "the people having Polish citizenship and inhabiting the territory of the Republic of Poland and foreigners who are staying in the Republic of Poland based on the card of temporary stay granting them refugee status. Insurance premiums are paid and inventoried in the Social Insurance Institution, and next they are sent to the National Health Fund"[22] which are administered funds of the Health Service that are based on an agreement with medical institutions. This fund finances health benefits as well as provides the refund of medicines funded on the basis of financial needs. The National Health Fund has 16 provincial wards. The system is financed from the compulsory health contribution of citizens which in 2011 amounts to 9% from the income of the employee.[23]

The state's current health policy is also quite severely criticized by society and the media which shocks people every now and then with information about a long period of expectation for specialist examinations or the visits at specialists. The attempt to streamline medical services has not always matched social expectations. Financial contracts for the treatment and medical advice are adjudicated every year and in principle they aren't sufficient for the entire year, particularly for the specialist health care using modern medical technologies. It causes accumulation of debt by hospitals and other medical institutions.

The attempt to conduct successful reforms in Health Services is currently being done by the health minister at the government of Civic Platform, Ewa Kopacz, who consistently attempts to introduce changes that would enable health institutions to improve the quality of health services. It is necessary however to break down the balance between the commercialization of Health Service and its accessibility to each individual member of Polish society. Introduced by the Seym at the beginning of 2011 "the Act on healing activity regards functioning of hospitals, doesn't assume compulsory converting clinics into companies; however self-government bodies which won't transform hospitals, will have to cover their financial loss within three months since the end of the term of approving the financial statement. In case of the non-compliance from it, within 12 months they will be forced to convert the hospital into the company or the budgetary authority. New hospitals will be able to be created only as companies. This act enables also to employ nurses at hospitals on contracts. Against this issue, nurses consisted in All-Polish Trade Unions of Nurses and Midwives, protested. Moreover the acts passed by the Seym provide among others for the liquidation of the medical internship, enabling patients to seek compensations without the court and implementing the e-recipe and e-referrals"[24] for the specialist treatment.

In March 2011 the Seym passed the package of health acts:

- about the refund of medicines and medical products (refund act);
- about the information system in the health care;
- revisions of acts: about patient's rights and the Spokesman of patient's rights;
- about the medical professions of doctor and the dentist; and
- about healing activity.[25]

One should emphasize that for the first time one of the patient's rights was a possibility of faster claiming of damages or satisfying for the improper treatment, without the need to initiate the legal action. Until now it was possible to only initiate legal action in civil court which very much extended the process of receiving compensation. In accordance with the new Act the compensation can be also obtained via the administrative action which shortens the time of receiving compensation by nearly seven months. However, there are some conditions stipulated in the Act that refer to the nature of compensation: "Compensations are supposed to concern only damages associated with the hospital care in Poland. So that the damage could be compensated, the provincial committee for stating about medical mistakes must decide that a mistake of the person or persons pursuing a medical profession took place. The commission won't be establishing the amount of damages. Specialists will be a member of a commission from fields of medicine and the law, of patients' organization, of the Department of Health and the Spokesman of patient's rights. The statement will have to be published within five months from the motion date. An insurance company which entered into an agreement with the hospital in which the medical mistake happened is supposed to present the proposal of the compensation. In addition, in some cases instead of the compensation, a disability pension could be also granted to a patient."[26]

In spite of the critical attitude to implemented conditions on the benefits paid to patients using retribution of cost based on the description of the Act expressed by political parties and trade unions of the Health Service[27] that oppose the Act, it should be noted that the new regulations are becoming part of a general course of the transformation and the modernization of the political and social system of Poland. Together with other reforms the reform of the health policy and health system constitutes a stable foundation for further reforms aimed at the improvement of health care in Poland.

NOTES

1. Retrieved from http://www.naukowy.pl/encyklopedia/Niko%C5%82aj_ Siemaszko. Accessed by the author on May 2, 2011.
2. Dobska M., Dobski P. (2003). *TQM total quality management in healthcare centres*, Poznań, pp. 13–15.
3. Act from August 30, 1991 about healthcare centres, Dz. U. 1991, No. 91, pos. 408.
4. For more details, see: Dobska M., Rogoziński K. (2008). *Bases of managing the healthcare centre*. Warsaw: Scientific publishing company PWN.
5. Ksykiewicz-Dorota A. (Ed.). (2004). *Bases of the nursing labour organization*. Lublin: Czelej publishing company. Also see: Dudek M. (Ed.). (2009). *Chosen areas of families' pathology*. Ryki: LSW; Dudek M. (2009). *Social nonadjustment of children with ADHD*. Warsaw: UKSW.
6. Wojtczak K., Leoński Z. (1993). *Commentary on the act on healthcare centres*, Warsaw/Poznań, p. 7. Also see: Maciejek A. (2011). *Polish Health System Service after 1989. Changes after the political-economic transformation and the attempt of reforms* (manuscript in author's possession), p. 34.
7. For more details, see: Ksykiewicz-Dorota A. (2004). *Bases ...*, op. cit. p. 31.
8. Dobska M., Dobski P. (2003). *TQM ...*, op. cit. pp. 27–29.
9. *Ibid.*
10. Dz. U. 1993, No. 76, pos. 363; Retrieved from http://isap.sejm.gov.pl/ KeyWordServlet?viewName = thasS&passName = s%C5%82u%C5%Bcba%20z drowia. Accessed by the author on May 20, 2011.
11. Retrieved from http://biesaga.info/wp-content/uploads/2009/11/1-.3.Biesaga-T.- Europejska-Konwencja-Bioetyczna.pdf. Accessed by the author on May 18, 2011.
12. Constitution of the Republic of Poland from April 2, 1997, consolidated text, Dz. U. 1997, No. 78, pos. 483.
13. Act from November 24, 1995 about the change of the scope of action of some cities and in urban zones of the public service, Dz. U. 1995, No. 141, pos. 692.
14. Dobska M., Rogoziński K. (2008). *Bases ...*, op. cit., p. 17; also see: Maciejek A. (2011). *Polish ...*, op. cit., s. 38.
15. Retrieved from http://www.cmj.org.pl/akredytacja/certyfikaty.php. Accessed by the author on May 20, 2011.
16. Retrieved from http://www.squality.com.pl/medycyna.htm. Accessed by the author on May 28, 2011.
17. Act on the universal health insurance from February 6, 1997, Dz. U. 1997. No. 28, pos. 153, with later amendment.
18. Maciejek A. (2011). *Polish ...*, op. cit., pp. 35–40.
19. Dz. U. 1998, No. 148, pos. 978, with later amendment.
20. Maciejek A. (2011). *Polish ...*, op. cit. pp. 41–45.
21. K. Mazur, A. Łukasik. (2011). Health-insurance funds and their problems in 1999–2003 years. Retrieved from http://www.biuletyn.e-gap.pl/index.php? view = artykul&artykul = 46#sub5. Accessed by the author on May 3, 2011.
22. Dobska M., Rogozinski K. (2008). *Bases ...*, op. cit. p. 20. Also see: Maciejek A. (2011). *Polish ...*, op. cit., p. 65.

23. This height has been in force from January 2007. In 2003 the rate of contribution was 8%, it then rose every year by 0.25%. In 2006 it reached the level of 8.75%, the height of 9% was assumed as the ultimate level. Retrieved from http://zus.pox.pl/zus-zdrowotne-2011.htm. Accessed by the author on May 3, 2011.

24. Also see: http://www.bip.powiatzaganski.pl/index.php?id = 260. Accessed by the author on May 15, 2011.

25. *Will Kopacz convince the President for the reform?* Retrieved from http://www.money.pl/gospodarka/wiadomosci/artykul/kopacz;przekona;prezydenta;do;reformy,133,0,802437.html. Accessed by the author on May 3, 2011.

26. *The Seym passed the government package of health.* (2011). Retrieved from http://praca.gazetaprawna.pl/artykuly/499521,sejm_uchwalil_rzadowy_pakiet_ustaw_zdrowotnych.html. Accessed by the author on May 3, 2011.

27. *Ibid.*

28. *The "Solidarity" is protesting opposite the Department of Health.* (2011). Retrieved from http://www.faktymedyczne.pl/aktualnosci_pap,list,8721452.html. Accessed by the author on May 3, 2011.

REFERENCES

Act about health care centres from August 30, 1991. Dz. U. 1991, No. 91, pos. 408.

Act about the change of the scope of action of some cities and in urban zones of the public service from November 24, 1995.

Act on the universal health insurance from February 6, 1997. Dz. U. 1997, No. 28, pos. 153, with later amendment.

Constitution of the Republic of Poland from April 2, 1997. Consolidated text, Dz. U. 1997, No. 78, pos. 483, art. 68, pp. 1–4.

Dobska, M., & Dobski, P. (2003). *TQM total quality management in healthcare centers.* Poznań: Wydawca.

Dobska, M., & Rogoziński, K. (2008). *Bases of managing the healthcare center.* Warsaw: Scientific Publishing Company PWN.

Dudek, M. (Ed.) (2009). *Chosen areas of families' pathology.* Ryki: LSW.

Dudek, M. (2009). *Social nonadjustment of children with ADHD.* Warsaw: UKSW.

Dz. U. 1993, No. 76, pos. 363.

Dz. U. 1995, No. 141, pos. 692.

Dz. U. 1998, No. 148, pos. 978, with later amendment.

http://www.naukowy.pl/encyklopedia/Niko%C5%82aj_Siemaszko. Accessed by the author on May 2, 2011.

http://www.cmj.org.pl/akredytacja/certyfikaty.php. Accessed by the author on April 8, 2011.

http://www.squality.com.pl/medycyna.htm. Accessed by the author on April 12, 2011.

http://zus.pox.pl/zus-zdrowotne-2011.htm. Accessed by the author on May 3, 2011.

http://www.bip.powiatzaganski.pl/index.php?id = 260. Accessed by the author on July 23, 2011.

http://isap.sejm.gov.pl/KeyWordServlet?viewName=thasS&passName=s%C5%82u%C5%BCb Accessed by the author on July 23, 2011.

http://biesaga.info/wp-content/uploads/2009/11/I.-3.-Biesaga-T.-Europejska-Konwencja-Bioetyczna.pdf. Accessed by the author on July 23, 2011.

http://www.cmj.org.pl/akredytacja/certyfikaty.php. Accessed by the author on January 8, 2011.

http://isap.sejm.gov.pl/DetailsServlet?id=WDU19970280153Accessed by the author on July 23, 2011.

http://isap.sejm.gov.pl/VolumeServlet?type=wdu&rok=1998&numer=148. Accessed by the author on July 23, 2011.

Ksykiewicz-Dorota, A. (Ed.) (2004). *Bases of the nursing labour organization*. Lublin: Czelej.

Maciejek, A. (2011). *Polish Health System Service after 1989. Changes after the political-economic transformation and the attempt of reforms.* Manuscript in author's possession.

Mazur, K. A., & Łukasik. (2011). Health-insurance funds and their problems in 1999–2003 years. Retrieved from http://www.biuletyn.e-gap.pl/index.php?view=artykul& artykul=46#sub5. Accessed by the author on May 3, 2011.

Sawa-Czajka, E. (2010). *The political system of Republic of Poland 1989–2010 (chosen problems)*. Polianna.

The Seym passed the government package of health. Retrieved from http://praca.gazetaprawna.pl/ artykuly/499521,sejm_uchwalil_rzadowy_pakiet_ustaw_zdrowotnych.html. Accessed by the author on May 3, 2011.

The "Solidarity" is protesting opposite the Department of Health. Retrieved from http:// www.faktymedyczne.pl/aktualnosci_pap,list,8721452.html. Accessed by the author on May 3, 2011.

Will Kopacz convince the President for the reform? Retrieved from http://www.money.pl/gospodarka/ wiadomosci/artykul/kopacz;przekona;prezydenta;do;reformy,133,0,802437.html. Accessed by the author on May 3, 2011.

Włodarczyk, W. C. (1996). *Health policy in the democratic society* (pp. 320, 322). Łódź: University Medical Vesalius.

Wojtczak, K., & Leoński, K. (1993). *Commentary on the act on healthcare centers*. Warsaw: Wydawca.

THE NUTRITION AND HEALTH OF WOMEN AND CHILDREN IN THE AFTERMATH OF NATURAL DISASTERS

Sitora Khakimova

ABSTRACT

Natural disasters have an enormous impact on the lives and well-being of people in many parts of the world. When a disaster occurs, it causes massive damage to people's livelihoods. Although a household is automatically disrupted after experiencing a natural disaster (floods, earthquakes, mudslides, etc.), the accessibility of food commodities is often the most negatively impacted. Since pre-disaster periods are already challenging in the context of providing sufficient food within poverty-stricken areas, natural disasters leave a trail of vulnerable and disadvantaged people who cannot acquire an adequate amount of nutritious food necessary for survival. The inability to maintain consumption levels exposes households to food insecurities – insecurities experienced particularly by women, who head households. Women are more susceptible to food scarcity and lose the ability to sustain their families' livelihood due to the loss of seeds, livestock, and food, in general. Natural cataclysms, however, not only hamper access to nutritious food, but also considerably affect women's and children's health conditions. In countries like Tajikistan, there is a small body of research that

Democracies: Challenges to Societal Health
Research in Political Sociology, Volume 19, 71–87
ISSN: 0895-9935/doi:10.1108/S0895-9935(2011)0000019009

assesses the impact of hazardous events on women's and children's health and nutrition in the aftermath of disasters. This study seeks to provide insights into the access of balanced diets to families in post-disaster situations and analyzes how disasters impact the health of affected people.

INTRODUCTION

Natural disasters, such as floods, mudslides, earthquakes, droughts, and other climate change hazards, can have significant negative impacts and effects on the lives of poor and marginalized populations around the world (Carter, Little, Mogues, & Negatu, 2005; Gulligan & Hoddinott, 2007). Yet, countries, cities, and communities vary considerably in their degree of susceptibility to environmental shocks. Alarmingly, more and more people are becoming vulnerable to the consequences of catastrophic occurrences. The loss of income due to the flooding of arable land, damaged food crops, and reduced agricultural production may bring serious challenges to many households and put families' well-being at high risk for insecurities (Menghestab, 2005; Micahel, Peter, Tewodaj, & Workneh, 2007). The failure to access nutritious food brings additional constraints to already vulnerable and impoverished households. As referenced above, disaster leads to food insecurity (Mearns & Norton, 2010), social instability, and long-term health problems in some settings while also leading to damage or destruction of related livelihoods (Eric & Thomas, 2007).

   Although many impoverished people continue to try to extricate themselves from poverty-induced hunger and improve their livelihoods, environmental hazards hinder their progress toward self-reliance (FSTS, 2010), resulting in immediate increases in poverty and scarcity of food (Carter et al., 2005). Pyles and others have looked into the accessibility of households to food during disasters and complex emergencies, and concluded that access to food is a significant challenge for poverty-stricken families (Pyles, Kulkarni, & Lein, 2008). This shows that the burden of climate change is likely to have more durable effects on less well-off families, limiting their access to nutritious, healthy food. If flood events occur quite often in the same communities, it reduces people's power to bounce back before another flood hits. This automatically results in an increase in poverty and chronic food insecurity among a marginalized population (Tom, Thomas, & Kattie, 2007). From the affected women's point of view, disaster events hamper their livelihood strategies and leave them and their families with few options to combat increased poverty (Tom et al., 2007).

The food consumption and livelihood of affected families are significantly exacerbated when families are forced to relocate to a temporary camp or shelter of some kind. Families may find themselves in a position of having poor access to adequate food to feed their children. An empirical study by Pyles et al. shows that families experience increased food shortage when they are displaced in the aftermath of a disaster (Pyles et al., 2008). Furthermore, a research study in India shows that the relocation of families not only increases women's lists of duties, but also reduces their capacity to control food commodities and revenues (Schwoebel & Menon, 2004). Multiple losses occur due to relocation, and the overall damage to and inadequate availability of nutritious food lead to food insecurity in households. The World Food Summit of 1996 defined food security in the following terms: "it exists when all people, at all times, have physical and economic access to sufficient, safe and nutritious food that meets their dietary needs and food preferences for an active and healthy life."

Zakeri defines food insecurity as "limited or uncertain availability of nutritionally adequate and safe food or limited or uncertain ability to acquire acceptable food in socially acceptable ways" (Zakeri, 2006). "When a person's livelihood is secure, he is food secure" (Kerren, 2008). The loss of kitchen gardens, agricultural land, and livestock places considerable strains on already vulnerable families during recovery and resettlement processes (Jalol, 2009). This significantly increases the chance of families to become trapped in an insecurity cycle. According to the World Food Program Assessment in Tajikistan, "women-headed households are markedly more likely to be food insecure than male-headed households during emergency situations" (WFP, 2008). A study among flood victims in Malaysia found that female-headed households and households in which the head family member is over 50 years of age are the most vulnerable groups in the event of disasters (Ngai & Dennis, 1996). Similar research in Honduras and Nicaragua has deduced that both sexes can be vulnerable to the negative effects of environmental shocks due to biological reasons, such as physical disability and age status. For women, this includes pregnancy and lactation (Patricia & Elizabeth, 2000). Women's susceptibility to food insecurity is noticeable in multiple ways: they do not have access to equal levels of health care as men; they are more likely to be denied relief aid or compensation for any material losses if a male family member(s) is not present to navigate the available aid channels (Hamilton & Halvorson, 2007).

A number of research studies reveal that women mostly retain the traditional female responsibility of providing food and water for their family members, protecting the meager belongings of the family, and taking care of the sick, as well as preserving seeds and storing food during post-disaster events. Yet, in addition to performing multiple duties, women-headed households often remain behind when the flow of food aid reaches affected communities. Momsen (2004) claims that women are often the most vulnerable group during post-disaster events, as they possess inadequate resources to recover as well as poor social standing to be able to receive the entitled food items (Momsen, 2004). Tanesia (2007) claims that Indonesian women without male relatives are often left out during the distribution of aid due to their inability to fight for assistance. She uses the case of Jogjakarta as an example, where after waiting long hours for aid coordinators to distribute food, many women left with nothing since only the physically strongest had access by struggling and jostling for the food (Tanesia, 2007). A study of Darfur camp refugees also reached the same conclusion. Women without a husband or male relative are often the last to receive assistance (Mench, 2008). A case study in Afghanistan (Savage, Delesgues, Martin, & Ulfat, 2007) exemplifies that women victims hardly gain access to aid. The study reveals that much humanitarian aid fails to reach the intended recipients, since relief distribution mainly occurs among kinship groups or aid workers. The people who benefit the most are those who have relatives who are in charge of the distribution of resources (Savage et al., 2007). This leaves most people unable to provide for themselves and their families, while the control and distribution of food remains in the hands of the powerful. Based on this evidence, women-headed households are found to be the most vulnerable population group in disaster periods due to their limited access to quality food items in the aftermath of disasters. This leads to a domino effect of a poor nutritional state leading to the eventual deterioration of their health condition.

Women's and children's poor access to nutritious food and potable water and poor hygiene practices in the aftermath of disasters lead to various diseases that affect their health status negatively. According to the World Health Organization, floods and mudslides have the potential to increase the transmission of infective diseases. The factors that contribute to health deterioration are population displacement, the loss of clean drinking water, poor sanitation, inadequate food supplies, lack of immunization, and restricted access to health care (WHO, 2003). When affected people are faced with food scarcity, this leads to a lowering of their immunity and increases their chances of becoming infected with measles, malaria, or tuberculosis (Wright & Vesala-Husemann, 2006). Wright and Vesala-Husemann note that "if further deterioration in nutritional status, through inability to eat is not treated by nutritional intervention or medical care, this cycle continues ultimately leading to death" (Wright & Vesala-Husemann, 2006). Natural disasters are very likely to create serious obstacles for attaining the Millennium Development Goals (MDGs) for combating diseases. For example,

- Disasters exacerbate women's and children's access to a healthy and balanced diet (MDG1).
- Disasters cause malnutrition resulting in poor health and weaken the immunity of children and women (MDG4&5).
- Disasters enhance the outbreak of communicative and vector-borne diseases, for example, malaria and diarrhea following floods and mudslides (MDG4,5&6).

Despite similarities in the degree of food insecurity and poor health of people cross-culturally, the examination of access to food and adequate health services remains necessary for the design of future relief interventions. This study attempts to provide insight into women's access to food and their health condition in rural Tajikistan. By means of information obtained through phone and individual interviews with women in the Khuroson and Kulob districts in the Khatlon region of Tajikistan, this analysis provides an overall understanding of women's and their families' health conditions and nutrition status following disasters.

TAJIKISTAN AND NATURAL DISASTERS

Tajikistan is a small and landlocked country in Central Asia (143,100 square miles) with a population of 7,627,200 (CIA, 2011). Ninety-three percent of the geographical area is covered with mountains and only 6.52 percent of the territory is suitable for agriculture. Tajikistan has the lowest income rate among all of the former Soviet Union states with a GDP per capita of $879 and a gross domestic product average of $6,831 billion (GF, 2011). The largest sector of the economy is dominated by the production of cotton, grains, and vegetables; however, geographical constraints lead to less-advanced transportation means that, in turn, lead to a failure to attract investors for large-scale industrial projects (Jones, Black, & Skeldon, 2007).

Tajikistan encountered tremendous economic challenges following the dissolution of the Soviet Union, which resulted in a withdrawal of subsidies from Moscow. The country had not only undergone a shift from a market-led economy and the withdrawal of subsidies from Moscow (Kanji, 2002), but also had to face the breakup of states, which induced power struggles between Communists and Islamist fundamentalists that has erupted into one of the most violent post-Soviet conflicts so far (Haarr, 2007). The withdrawal of Soviet subsidies and the destruction caused by civil wars resulted in economic stagnation. This resulted in a sharp decline in agricultural production and a stagnation in the industrial sector and influenced the overall economic scheme due to a concomitant lack in salaries, payments, pensions, and aid (Jones et al., 2007).

Despite recent signs of recovery, Tajikistan still faces significant challenges in rebuilding its economic and social structures. The country remains the poorest post-Soviet republic and is ranked only 112th out of the 169 countries on the United Nations Human Development Index (HDI, 2010). Through to the end of the Soviet era, Tajikistan had one of the lowest standards of living among the other Soviet Union countries. According to local experts, 5 million Tajik people live below the poverty line, which is 70 percent of the population (Gafforov, 2011), while 18 percent fall under the extreme poverty level (CIA, 2011). Poverty is especially widespread in rural areas, as 75 percent of the people in those areas live below the poverty line (UNIFEM, 2010).

In addition to existing challenges, the country frequently encounters unstable climatic conditions. Tajikistan is prone to many types of hazards, particularly floods, mudflows, earthquakes, landslides, and droughts (ADRC, 2006). These natural disasters cause great damage both to the economy and the lives of the people, especially those who live in mountainous areas that are more prone to disaster (Government of Republic of Tajikistan, 2005). It is estimated that 85 percent of Tajikistan's surface is prone to mudflows, and 32 percent of the area is located in the high mudflow-risk area. In case of heavy rainfalls, which tend to occur in spring, the mountainous part of the country experiences mudslides and floods, which devastate the livelihood of people (SoE, 2003).

Unusually heavy rainfall in Tajikistan during the months of April and May 2009 caused severe flooding and mudflows in 40 out of the 58 districts of rural Tajikistan (CAP, 2009). The calamities led to the loss of lives of 26 individuals and negatively impacted 12,000 people (Reliefweb, 2011). This weather-related shock caused significant damage to households in the Khuroson and Kulob districts in the Khatlon region of Tajikistan. Households in these districts are situated in disaster-prone areas. When floods occurred in Khuroson in April and May 2009, it caused the complete devastation of four villages, directly affecting 3,400 people (REACT, 2009). Families were forced to relocate due to the mudslides that completely destroyed their houses. The affected families had no other choice but to temporarily live with relatives in neighboring districts (Majidov, 2010) or stay in nearby schools and mosques that had been converted into temporary shelters in order to house some of the families (Reliefweb, 2011). In the case of the Kulob floods, livelihoods were destroyed and the water washed away 4,500 people's belongings (Majidov, 2010). Since the mudslides and flooding occurred in the middle of night (Majidov, 2010), people were unable to prevent the loss of most or all of their belongings and livestock.

The floods and mudslides washed away land, newly planted crops, seeds, and livestock, which was a huge loss to households for whom family income was heavily dependent on the amount of food produced (Reliefweb, 2011). The agricultural lands and crops were buried under the flow of mud and rocks and led to huge economic losses and hardships for rural households. The loss of kitchen gardens, agricultural land, and livestock placed considerable strain on already vulnerable families during the recovery and resettlement processes (Sharipov, 2009a, 2009b).

These hardships left many families in Khatlon with scarce resources and food supplies, which increased their vulnerability to future calamities (Walker & Lynch, 2011). Undoubtedly, these environmental disasters caused significant damage to the livelihood of people in both districts, but the outcome particularly affected women-headed households. Women-headed households are often the most vulnerable to these events and tend to suffer poverty over longer periods of time (Oxfam, 2011). In the southern part of Tajikistan, the majority of rural males are away from their families, working as labor migrants in former Soviet Union countries, while the women are alone in their struggles to access an adequate amount of food and take care of their families in the aftermath of disasters. These women are extremely vulnerable when disastrous events devastate their livelihoods, deplete their food supplies, and, in addition, lead to deteriorated health conditions for themselves and their families.

To date, there has been a very limited amount of research that analyzes the impact of natural disasters on the nutritional aspects and health conditions of women and their families in post-disaster periods in Tajikistan. Recently, although a significant number of researchers have discussed the impact of disasters and the damage they cause, virtually no research has been done that looks at the health of women and children, including their access to balanced diets in post-disaster periods in rural Tajikistan. The main objectives of this study are to understand the health condition of women and children following disasters, including their access to healthy food in post-disaster periods. The outcomes of this study will clearly fill a gap in the limited literature on the impact of disasters on health issues and will help analyze the amount of access people have to adequate amounts of food within Tajikistan and the Central Asian communities. The findings of this study will also be significant for the purposes of program development by local NGOs and international organizations working on the issues of food security and the health of rural populations. As environmental cataclysms are ongoing events in Tajikistan that cause a loss of food and the deterioration of health conditions, a better understanding of people's experiences and needs is crucial for the development and implementation of future effective relief strategies.

METHOD

This section introduces the methods that have been used to conduct this research study. This exploratory study uses a qualitative research method to provide an overall understanding of the situation of women in the aftermath of disasters in Tajikistan and identifies challenges faced by women and how their needs are disregarded by various stakeholders.

Data for this study has been collected in two ways: phone interviews and individual/or face-to-face conversations. Due to the distance between the target group and the researcher, phone interviews were selected to engage with the women from the Kulob districts. According to Dapzury and Pallavi, phone interviews yield information that is compatible with face-to-face contact and allows researchers to build some level of trust with the subjects. A total of eight women in the Kulob district were interviewed via phone in May 2010. Individual interviews were conducted during a field visit to the Khuroson district in June–July 2010. Eight women from different affected households were randomly selected and interviewed for the study.

The research questions were developed in English, and later translated into the Tajik language. However, before the process of data collection began, research questions were field tested with a number of women who were demographically similar to the research sample. Two randomly selected women[1] who were willing to participate in the process were interviewed using the research questions. After the interview, the feedback from the participants helped to restructure two particular questions. Specifically, the volunteers had difficulties in understanding these two questions because of the use of formal language; therefore, it proved necessary to alter the wording of these questions. Further, pretesting was useful in identifying the amount of time needed to conduct an interview, which ranged between 30–40 minutes.

Before the subjects were asked to participate in the interview, the women had been familiarized with the study by means of an introductory letter. The subjects were then given one day to think about the acceptance of the invitation. As soon as they expressed their willingness to participate in the interview, the interviews were scheduled at their convenience. The only piece of equipment used for this study was a tape recorder that all participants were made aware of. Patton (1990) describes this technique for data collection as absolutely necessary, while Lincoln and Guba (1985) recommend refraining from recordings except in the case of extraordinary circumstances (qtd. in Hoepfl, 1997). The recording technique was applied in this study because it has the advantage of capturing the conversation and conveniently allows for the safeguarding of important information. Prior to starting each individual interview, the subjects were informed that the conversation was recorded for the purpose of accuracy and would later be used to document the research findings. In addition, in order to maintain confidentiality, the participants signed an informed consent form stating their agreement to being recorded. In the case of phone interviews, women's oral consent was received prior to the interview.

RESULTS

Profile of the Target Group

The age of the subjects who participated in this study varied between 28 and 60 years. Twelve-and-a-half percent of the respondents were divorced, while 87.5 percent were married. Thirty-one percent of the subjects were from nuclear families, the remaining 69 percent of the respondents lived with their extended families in multigenerational households. Data on education indicates that 56.3 percent of the women had received secondary education; however, 43.7 percent of the interviewed women merely had an incomplete primary education. Nearly 12 percent of the women were employed by public institutions (medical care, education, and other services), while 88 percent were engaged in agriculture. Agriculture is the principal economic activity for the households in the target areas. A large percentage of the women worked on other people's farms or cotton fields, or bartered their labor for dried cotton stalks.[2]

Damage of Livelihood and the Access of Women to Food

The vast majority of respondents reported that the quantity of their family's food was heavily dependent on their garden plots. Nearly 87.5 percent of the respondents generally grow multiple agricultural crops to have enough food stocked up until the next planting season; 12.5 percent of the respondents did not own sufficient land to grow their own food. Since 87.5 percent of the families grew their own food in their family plots, they experienced crop damage from the floods and mudslides of 2009 and 2010. The damage was so severe that it destroyed newly planted spring seedlings. Crop loss in the early spring resulted in considerably more difficult access to sufficient food all year round. The remaining 12.5 percent of the correspondents were employed on other people's farms, where they were given a small share of land to grow their own food. However, this group of respondents also reported substantial crop losses, which limited their access to food and decreased their food supplies. This decrease in yields led to a substantial increase in the challenge to meet the dietary needs of their families. Twenty-five percent of the respondents also stated that prior to the flood they had a few cows that were kept for their milk and other dairy products; however, the livestock were either killed by the flood or sold by the families to cover immediate expenses in the aftermath of the flood.

When asked to describe their access to food in the post-disaster period, all respondents reported that the level of household food stocks was completely depleted following the disaster, including wheat stocks. This meant that the dramatic loss in food such as wheat flour,[3] which is the basis of the rural Tajik diet, created threats for already vulnerable households. The outcome of the question of whether families had enough to feed themselves elicited varied responses; however, in most cases women reported going hungry or consuming less in order to provide more food for their children. About 43.7 percent of the women stated that due to the shortage of food in post-disaster periods, they were compelled to cut down on the number of their meals. These women confessed that the fear of having inconsistent access to food dictated this reduction in their own intake. As an illustration, out of this 43.75 percent, 18.75 percent of the women reported that they had been eating only bread and tea with sugar for the duration of 3–4 weeks, while another 25 percent of the respondents strived to consume less food. Twenty-five respondents reported going hungry during the day, giving their food to younger children. A large number of women, 56.25 percent, stated that they had only two meals a day: bread and tea and later in the evening a hot meal. This hot meal typically consisted of a soup of potatoes, onions, and macaroni; a diet with a limited nutritional value. In answer to the question of whether the quality of food was the same as in the pre-disaster period, the respondents identified the quality of their food as significantly lower. In the pre-disaster period, 62.5 percent of the respondents reported including at least meat and dairy products to their intake at least twice a week; however, in the post-disaster period families had to exclude the consumption of beef. Nearly 93.75 percent of the respondents identified their food as not being nutritious enough to remain healthy and prevent the outbreak of diseases.

Half of the respondents, mostly from the Khuroson district, reported receiving some type of humanitarian assistance from the World Food Program, Save the Children, or the Red Crescent/Cross. According to the respondents, these agencies assisted affected households with different food items such as wheat flour, vegetable oil, and lentils, as well as nonfood commodities, such as donated clothing and temporary shelters. Women respondents were very appreciative of the agencies' timely response to the affected households. Nevertheless, according to some women's feedback, access to wheat flour, oil, and lentils did not reduce the food shortage or eliminate the challenges that the people faced in providing food for their families. In order to prepare meals, families needed additional cooking supplements, which they did not have the money to buy. Due to having large families, the distributed commodities (wheat flour, lentils, and vegetable oil) were only sufficient for two-and-a-half months. Only two respondents (12.5 percent) from the Kulob district complained about being deprived of food assistance. These two women were not included in the distribution list. As per the women, they experienced the same degree of damage as did their neighbors. However, when food assistance did reach the distribution point, they were not able to access the food commodities. These women experienced a greater impact from the disaster due to their food loss and their inability to access food commodities in the post-disaster period. Almost every interviewed woman recalled the support of friends, people living in neighboring areas, and family who united to render support; they mostly provided hot meals to the affected households while they temporarily resided in summer camps or shelters.

In addition to the loss of crops, for many rural families in Tajikistan, access to available potable water is a key stress point. According to some interviewees, in the aftermath of the disaster families had inadequate access to potable and irrigation water. Many families have not had access to irrigation water since disaster struck their areas in 2009. Access to clean water still remains a challenge for families in the Khuroson district. Women reported that there was poor access to a safe source of drinking water. Without access to running water, rural households are unable to grow food or produce yields that can be compared to the circumstances before the natural disasters struck. Most of the respondents continue to face difficulties in accessing water, which decreases their capacity to grow their own food.

Deterioration of Health in Post-Disaster Periods

All the respondents complained about the deterioration of their health conditions, including that of their family members, in the post-disaster period. Poor health has been particularly noticeable among women, elderly people, and children. Women and elderly people experienced high blood pressure, which constantly hampered their mobility. In total, 68.7 percent of the respondents complained about experiencing frequent high blood pressure in the aftermath of the flooding. Some mentioned having severe headaches, while a quarter of the respondents reported feeling fatigued and suffered a loss of energy. Although the vast majority of the respondents noticed a deterioration in their health, they did not seek help or medical care. Women reported that they did not seek treatment because they did not feel the problem was serious enough to warrant professional attention. From the conversation with the respondents, it is apparent that despite the high and seemingly stable rate of health problems in women affected by the flood, only a small proportion sought medical care. Women paid less attention to their own health and physical condition, prioritizing the needs of other family members. One woman confessed that when her children were sick in the aftermath of the flood, she cared less about her own condition.

Symptoms of stress, such as nervousness and insomnia, were observed immediately following the disaster. Sixty-two-and-a-half percent of the women complained that they felt anxious and suffered from insomnia for the duration of 2–3 months. These respondents reported feeling a constant fear of another flood in which they would be unable to rescue their children. Women experienced posttraumatic stress symptoms that affected their sleep habits. In one case, a woman had daydreams in which she relived the disastrous event as if it were recurring. However, emotional stress symptoms due to the disaster were largely ignored by the respondents, as none of them approached psychosocial services. They felt it was unnecessary to deal with this because stress was assumed to be a short-term condition.

Further, the overcrowded living conditions and poor water provisions and sanitation in the temporary settlements increased the number of sick children. Women reported being busy taking care of sick children. According to the respondents, damage to water and sewage systems had a great impact on the health of their family members. Due to the lack of access to clean potable water, an outbreak of communicable diseases emerged among the children. While parents were busy extracting their belongings from under layers of mud, children were left without proper supervision; as a result, they drank water from unsafe sources. Multiple factors contributed to the outbreak of infectious diseases. A large majority of the respondents, 87.5 percent of the women, reported having at least one or two sick children infected with diarrhea or typhoid. These infectious diseases soon began to spread to other family members. Moreover, women mentioned that exposure to the cold, contaminated flood waters, and damp conditions resulted in colds, coughs, flu, and throat infections among children. When asked if medical assistance was available for affected families in their districts, 31.5 percent of the respondents from the Khuroson district confirmed the availability of health centers in the temporary shelters. To combat further spreading of disease, families were supplied with medicines, while women in the Kulob district had limited access to health services. A few significant differences emerged between the women in the Khuroson and Kulob districts with regard to the accessibility of health services. Thirty-seven-and-a-half percent of the respondents from the Kulob district reported that health centers or services were not available in the affected areas in the post-disaster period, whereas only 12.5 percent of the respondents mentioned that local health providers distributed pills for children for diarrhea and other communicable diseases.

DISCUSSION AND CONCLUSION

The evidence presented in this chapter suggests that besides social and material losses, disastrous events have an enormous impact on the health of children and women and hampered the access of families to quality food items. When the women were asked about the effects of the flooding on their food consumption and their health condition, they were asked to think back to events that had happened a year earlier. Since the floods and mudslides of 2009 and 2010 were such prominent events for the communities in the Khuroson and Kulob districts, the respondents did not have difficulty in reporting how the floods affected their food consumption and contributed to their health deterioration.

The interviews and the discussions with the women in the two districts in Tajikistan show that women had to reduce their food consumption for a period of 3–4 weeks. For instance, women were worried about not having enough food or failing to provide an adequate amount of food for their children, thus cutting down on their own intake. During the discussions with the women, it was confirmed that prior to the disaster, the food of the affected families had a limited nutritional value; however, in the aftermath of the disaster the quality of their food significantly worsened. This finding indicates that these families had a limited ability to access meat and dairy products, which resulted in diets with an imbalanced nutritional value and increased the food insecurity of these families.

The provision of basic food items, such as wheat flour, vegetable oil, and lentils by various international agencies was essential and was viewed as desired support in post-disaster times. However, the availability of these commodities did not fully mitigate the increased food shortages faced by many families. It is important to note that these households lost their entire food supply and crops after the floods. The immediate assistance from NGOs and various stakeholders was therefore greatly welcomed by the affected people. The interviews also indicate that families received support from extended families, friends, and people living outside their communities. The support from these groups of people and other sources helped them to overcome the destitution brought on by the environmental disasters.

The data on the health conditions of these people reveals that even though women had poor health outcomes in the aftermath of the flooding, they showed little concern about their own condition. Only the women in Khuroson had access to health services, which were located in the vicinity of their shelters. Although medication was available for sick children and people, there was a lack of counseling services for women who complained of anxiety, insomnia, and loss of energy. High blood pressure, weakened immunity, and stress may lower women's ability to handle their multiple responsibilities in post-disaster periods. A women's health status affects not only her own performance, but also influences other aspects of her family's well-being, particularly when women do not seek or do not receive timely care for any diseases or traumas experienced due to disasters. Health services in disaster-affected settings failed to immediately respond to the psychological needs of these women.

Another important indicator of the more vulnerable position of women in post-disaster periods is that women went hungry in order to give more food to their children; this restriction had a negative impact on their day-to-day performance. Women complained about a lack of energy and fatigue during the entire post-disaster period. Poor health and inadequate nutrition jeopardize women's health. The inability to access quality health care and a balanced diet reduces women's capacity to perform their multiple productive and reproductive responsibilities. Another factor that contributed to the deterioration of the respondents' health were the living conditions of the women and children. Findings reveal that people lived in temporary shelters that were not equipped with proper sanitation facilities and potable water. Children consumed water from the river or drains, and this resulted in an increased number of sick children.

In the absence of empirical research on the impact of the floods in Tajikistan, the results of this recent study may provide useful information concerning the access to food and health of women and children following floods. Such knowledge and information are significant for various stakeholders, NGOs, and government authorities in order to comprehend fully the needs of affected people in post-disaster periods. The findings presented in this chapter may help stakeholders to design appropriate programs and interventions with regard to future occurrences of natural disasters that can help alleviate the hardships of affected people.

NOTES

1. These two women dwell in a village, and one of them works at the local school. When I asked whether they would like to participate in the field-testing of my questions, the replies were positive. They preferred not to disclose their names.
2. Rural households use dried cotton stalks for fuel during the cold season.
3. Wheat flour is used to make bread, which is a staple food for Tajik families. For instance, a family consisting of five members may consume two bags (220 lbs.) of wheat flour a month. Two bags of wheat flour cost 260 Tajik Somoni (55.99 USD).

REFERENCES

ADRC. (2006). *Country report for Asian disaster reduction center*. Tajikistan: ADRC.

CAP. (2009). *Tajikistan-food security*. Consolidated Appeal. Dushanbe, Tajikistan: United Nations.

Carter, M., Little, P., Mogues, T., & Negatu, W. (2005). Poverty traps and natural disasters in Ethiopia and Honduras. *World Development, 35*(5), 835–840.

CIA. (2011). The world fact book. Retrieved from https://www.cia.gov/library/publications/the-world-factbook/geos/ti.html. Accessed on June 14, 2011 from Central Intelligence Agency.

Dapzury, V., & Pallavi, S. *Interview as a method for qualitative research*. Southern Cross University and the Southern Cross Institute of Action Research (SCIAR).

Eric, N., & Thomas, P. (2007). The gendered nature of natural disasters: The impact of catastrophic events on the gender gap in life expectancy, 1981–2002. *Annals of the Association of American Geographers, 97*(3), 551–556.

Food Security Technical Secretariat. (2010, October). Food security situation in Southern Sudan. *Southern Sudan Food Security Updates*, Vol 012.

Gafforov, I. (2011, April 26). Tajikistan – Suicide found as a method for solving the problem. Retrieved from CentraAsia: http://www.centrasia.ru/newsA.php?st=1303807200. Accessed on May 20, 2011.

GF. (2011, June). Tajikistan country report. Retrieved from Global Finance: http://www.gfmag. com/gdp-data-country-reports/165-tajikistan-gdp-country-report.html#axzz1UJWsoenO. Accessed on August 7, 2011.

Government of Republic of Tajikistan. (2005, June). *Report and action plan on building national capacity to implement commitments of the republic of Tajikistan on global environmental convention.* Retrieved form http://www.untj.org/undrmp/undac/docs/bld_capcty_global_ environm_converntions_eng.pdf

Gulligan, D., & Hoddinott, J. (2007). Is there persistence in the impact of emergency food aid? Evidence on consumption, food security and assets in rural Ethiopia. *American Journal of Agricultural Economics, 89*(2), 225–226.

Haarr, R. (2007). Wife abuse in Tajikistan. *Feminist Criminology, 2*(3), 246.

Hamilton, J., & Halvorson, S. (2007, November). The 2005 Kashmir earthquake: A perspective on women's experiences. *Mountain Research and Development, 27*(4), 296–301.

Hoepfl, M. (1997). Choosing qualitative research: A primer for technology education researchers. *Journal of Technology Education, 9*(1), 52.

International Human Development Indicators. (2010). *Tajikistan – country profile of human development indicators.* Retrieved from http://hdrstats.undp.org/en/countries/profiles/ TJK.html

Jalol, S. (2009). *Khuroson mudslide: Situation analysis report.* Dushanbe, Tajikistan: Save the Children.

Jones, L., Black, R., & Skeldon, R. (2007). *Migration and poverty reduction in Tajikistan.* Working Paper C11. Institute for Development Studies, Sussex Center for Migration Research. Available at http://www.dfid.gov.uk/r4d/PDF/Outputs/MigrationGlobPov/ WP-C11.pdf

Kanji, N. (2002). Trading and trade-offs: Women's livelihoods in Gorno-Badakhshan, Tajikistan. *Development in Practice, 12*(2), 139.

Kerren, H. (2008). *Slow-onset disasters: Drought and food and livelihoods insecurity. Learning from previous relief and recovery responses.* ALNAP Lessons Paper 5.

Lincoln, Y. S., & Guba, E. G. (1985). *Naturalistic inquiry.* Beverly Hills, CA: Sage Publications, Inc.

Majidov, S. (2010, May 26). Severe flooding in Tajikistan. Retrieved from Central Asia-Caucasus Institute: http://www.cacianalyst.org/?q = node/5337. Accessed on July 07, 2011.

Mearns, R., & Norton, A. (2010). *Social dimensions of climate change: Equity and vulnerability in a warming world.* Washington, DC: The World Bank.

Mench, D. (2008). Change for women's sake. *Undergraduate Research Journal, 1*(2), 9–14.

Menghestab, H. (2005). Weather patterns, food security and humanitarian responses in sub-Saharan Africa. *Philosophical Transactions of the Royal Society, 360*(1436), 2169–2171.

Micahel, C., Peter, L., Tewodaj, M., & Workneh, N. (2007). Poverty traps and natural disaster in Ethiopia and Honduras. *World Development, 35*(5), 835–856.

Momsen, J. (2004). *Gender and development.* London and New York, USA: Routledge.

New and Expanded Opportunities for Vulnerable Groups in India. Contract No. GEW-I-00-02-00016-00-80

Ngai, C. W., & Dennis, P. (1996). Response to dynamic flood hazard factors in peninsular Malaysia. *The Geographical Journal, 162*(3), 313–325.

Oxfam. (2011). *Climate change: Beyond coping. Women smallholder farmers in Tajikistan. Experiences of climate change and adaptation. Oxfam Field Research.* Dushanbe, Tajikistan: Oxfam.

Patricia, D., & Elizabeth, S. (2000). *Gender and post-disaster reconstruction: The case of Hurricane Mitch in Honduras and Nicaragua.* The World Bank Gender Team in Latin America and the Caribbean.

Patton, M. Q. (1990). *Qualitative evaluation and research methods* (2nd ed.). Newbury Park, CA: Sage Publications, Inc.

Pyles, L., Kulkarni, S., & Lein, L. (2008). Economic survival strategies and food insecurity: The case of Hurricane Katrina in New Orleans. *Journal of Social Service Research, 34*(3), 43–53.

REACT. (2009). *Overview of damage and needs caused by disasters in Tajikistan.* Dushanbe, Tajikistan: UNDP.

Reliefweb. (2011). *Briefing kit for UN country team in Tajikistan + appeal.* Dushanbe, Tajikistan: REACT.

Savage, K., Delesgues, L., Martin, E., & Ulfat, G. (2007). *Corruption perceptions and risks in humanitarian assistance: An Afghanistan case study.* London, UK: Humanitarian Policy Group; Overseas Development Institute.

Schwoebel, M. H., & Menon, G. (2004). *Mainstreaming gender in disaster management support project* (A report for the women in development IQC task order). India: Chemonics International Inc.

Sharipov, J. (2009a). *Food security.* Dushanbe, Tajikistan: Save the Children.

Sharipov, J. (2009b). *Situational analysis report.* Kulob, Tajikistan: Save the Children.

SoE, S. O. (March 03, 2003). Natural disasters. Retrieved from Tajikistan 2002 State of the Environment Report: http://enrin.grida.no/htmls/tadjik/soe2001/eng/htmls/disas/state.htm. Accessed on August 03, 2011.

Tanesia, A. (2007). *Women, community radio, and post disaster recovery process.* Indonesia: Isis International.

Tom, M., Thomas, T., & Kattie, L. (2007). We know what we need: South Asian speak out on climate change adaptation. University of Sussex, UK. Bangladesh, India, Nepal: Institute of Development Studies (IDS).

UNIFEM. (2010). *Country gender profile – Republic of Tajikistan.* Dushanbe, Tajikistan: United Nations Fund for Women.

Walker, L., & Lynch, W. (2011). *Reaching the tipping point in southern Tajikistan. Nutrition and food security assessment for Khatlon and GBAO regions. With special focus on the districts of Jilikul, Qumsangir, Baljuvon, Temurmalik, Muminobod, Vanj and Darvoz.* Dushanbe, Tajikistan: Save the Children.

WFP. (2008). *Emergency food security assessment in urban areas of Tajikistan. A food security, livelihoods and nutrition assessment.* Dushanbe, Tajikistan: Government of Tajikistan.

WHO. (2003). *Climate change and human health.* Geneva: World Health Organization.

Wright, M., & Vesala-Husemann, M. (2006). Nutrition and disaster preparedness: Vulnerability, building capacities: Malnutrition and nutrition-focused responses and preparedness. Retrieved from Medscape Today: http://www.medscape.com/viewarticle/546014_5. Accessed on August 13, 2011.

Zakeri, A. (2006). *Livelihood strategies of food-insecure poor, female-headed families in Alabama's black belt.* Discussion paper series. UK Center for Poverty Research, UK.

DOMESTIC VIOLENCE AGAINST WOMEN IN RURAL RAJASTHAN, INDIA: A SOCIOLOGICAL ANALYSIS

Nirupama Prakash

ABSTRACT

Domestic violence is one of the crimes against women which is linked to their disadvantageous position in the society. Internationally, one in three women have been beaten or abused by a member of her own family.

Though violence against women in the family is a global phenomenon, yet its ramifications are more complex and its intensity much greater in India. The status of women fits into a vicious circle of mutually reinforcing gender inequalities and patriarchal practices in Rajasthan.

The present study was conducted in two villages near Pilani, Rajasthan during January–June 2009. Main objectives of the study were to explore the incidence, type, and cause of violence among women and to examine the awareness level of "Prevention of Domestic Violence Act 2005." Simple random sampling technique was used. Respondents were married women within the age group of 15–50 years. A total of 150 women were interviewed.

Democracies: Challenges to Societal Health
Research in Political Sociology, Volume 19, 89–102
Copyright © 2011 by Emerald Group Publishing Limited
All rights of reproduction in any form reserved
ISSN: 0895-9935/doi:10.1108/S0895-9935(2011)0000019010

stically significant relationship was found between violence and wo... n's age, caste, structure of family, literacy level of women, husband's level of education, and husband's alcohol consumption. Not a single case of violence was reported to the police.

INTRODUCTION

Gender-based violence is currently recognized as a major issue on the international human rights agenda. This involves both men and women in which the female is usually the victim, and is derived from unequal power relationship between men and women and directed specifically against women. It is sustained by a culture of silence. It encompasses a wide range of human rights violations, including sexual abuse of children, rape, domestic violence, sexual assault and harassment, trafficking of women and girls, and several harmful traditional practices (http://www.unfpa.org/gender/violence.htm).

Gender-based violence reflects and reinforces inequities between men and women and compromises the health, dignity, security, and autonomy of its victims. It leaves deep psychological scars, damages the health of women and girls in general, including their reproductive and sexual health. (http://www.unfpa.org/gender/violence.htm).

The Declaration on the Elimination of Violence Against Women, adopted by the United Nations General Assembly in 1993 defines violence against women as "any act of gender based violence that results in, or is likely to result in physical, sexual, or psychological harm or suffering to women, including threats of such acts, coercion or arbitrary deprivation of liberty, whether occurring in public or private life." It encompasses, but is not limited to, physical, sexual, and psychological violence occurring in the family, including battering, sexual abuse of female children in the household, dowry-related violence, marital rape, female genital mutilation and other traditional practices harmful to women, nonspousal violence and violence related to exploitation; physical, sexual, and psychological violence occurring within the general community, including rape, sexual harassment, and intimidation at work, in educational institutions, and elsewhere; trafficking in women and forced prostitution (Panda, 2004).

In situations where domestic violence prevails, causative factors generally are subordinate status of women combined with sociocultural norms that are inclined toward patriarchy and masculinity. Lack of legal protection, particularly within the sanctity of the home is also a strong factor in perpetuating violence against women. Lack of economic resources underpins women's vulnerability to violence. Lifestyle of men such as smoking, alcoholism, and drugs promote men to commit domestic violence. In some cases, sons of violent men raised in patriarchal family structure that encourages traditional gender role are more likely to abuse their intimate partners (http://www.isical.ac.in/~wemp/Papers/PaperManasRanjanPradhanAnd HariharSahoo.doc).

It has been observed that mostly domestic violence cases are left unrecorded and underreported. Generally women are reluctant to report about these incidents because of shame, fear of their husbands and in-laws, lack of awareness about their legal rights on one hand and their economic dependence on the other hand. Even if a woman dares to file a report against such violence, she may not get proper attention.

The issue of gender-based violence has to be analyzed in the larger sociocultural framework.

GENDER AND SOCIETY

The term gender is used to refer to behavioral differences between males and females that are culturally based and socially learned. Cultures differ widely in their norms and values regarding gender roles, the normative expectations concerning appropriately "masculine" or "feminine" behavior in a particular culture. Terms "male" and "female" are used for sex differences that are biological in origin. Terms "masculine" and "feminine" refer to the corresponding culturally specific gender differences that are social in origin (Appelbaum & Chambliss, 1995).

Global comparisons show that, by and large, societies do not consistently define most tasks as either feminine or masculine. With industrialization the importance of muscle power declines, so people have even more options and gender differences are further reduced. Thus, gender is simply too variable across cultures to be considered a simple expression of biology. Instead, as with many other elements of culture, what it means to be female and male is mostly a creation of society.

Considerable research points to the fact that young children tend to form single-sex play groups. Peer groups teach additional lessons about gender. Boys favor team sports with complex rules and clear objectives such as scoring a run or making a touchdown. Because such games nearly always have winners and losers, they reinforce masculine traits of aggression and control. Girls too play team sports. But, girls also play hopscotch, jump rope, or simply talk, sing, or dance.

These activities have few rules, and rarely is "victory" the ultimate goal. Instead of teaching girls to be competitive, female peer groups promote the interpersonal skills of communication and cooperation, presumably the basis for girls' future roles as wives and mothers. Boys reason according to abstract principles. For them, "rightness" amounts to "playing by the rules." Girls, on the other hand, consider morality a matter of responsibility to others. Thus, the games we play offer important lessons for our later lives (Macionis, 2006). Sexuality may refer to sexuality (biology)/sex or sexuality (gender)/gender identity. Gender identity is a person's own sense of identification as male or female. The term is intended to distinguish this psychological association, from physiological and sociological aspects of gender.

Culture is defined as way of life. Culture is divided into material culture and nonmaterial culture. Material culture includes innovations, products, tools/technologies, and information and communication technologies (ICTs), whereas nonmaterial culture refers to beliefs, values, customs, and language common to a group. ICT can be used as an important tool to bring about change in the mind-set, thus reducing gender inequities.

REVIEW OF LITERATURE

Domestic violence has become a major issue in life of women, not only nationally but also internationally. It crosses boundaries of all cultures and regions. Hence numbers of studies have been conducted on this issue.

According to the Bureau of Justice Statistics (USA), 1995, women are about six times as likely as men to experience intimate partner violence. Percent of women surveyed (national survey) who were ever physically assaulted by an intimate partner was Bardosa (30%), Canada (29%), New Zealand (35%), Switzerland (21%), and United States (22%). Some surveys in specific places report figure as high as 50–70% of women surveyed who were ever physically assaulted by an intimate partner. Others including survey in the Philippines and Paraguay reported figure as low as 10%. In India it was found to be 66% (Statistics, USA).

Though violence against women in the family is a global phenomenon, yet its ramifications are more complex and its intensity much greater in India. Much water has flown down the river Ganges since India achieved independence fighting with the weapon of nonviolence. The land of Buddha and Gandhi in spite of proclaiming the efficacy of nonviolence still remains gripped with violence in almost all fields.

Violent and destructive behaviors are not inherent in the animal nature of human beings. Rather such behaviors tend to occur where supportive social structures are absent and people are engulfed in fear and anxiety. According to the National Family Health Survey, India 2005–2006 (NFHS-3), overall 37% Indian women face domestic violence. Slapping is the most common act of physical violence by husbands. More than 34% said their husbands slapped while 15% said their husbands pulled their hair or twisted their arms. Around 14% of the women had things thrown at them. Domestic violence depicts widespread violence in almost all the states in India. Spousal violence varies greatly by state. The prevalence of physical or sexual violence is 6% in Himachal Pradesh, 13% in Jammu and Kashmir, 46% in Madhya Pradesh and Rajasthan. Even the protective law for women has not proved successful to impart justice to women. Only 2% of the abused women have ever sought institutional help. This is a matter of great concern in the country where women have been accorded respectful status since ancient times.

However, in last two decades a number of state-sponsored initiatives have been introduced to eradicate the problem of domestic violence against women. Special cells have been established to provide services to countless women facing violence. These cells act on the premises that violence against women is not a private matter, and is not just the responsibility of the woman to address. It enables a woman to challenge her partner and her family, and makes them part of the problem-solving process (http://www.tiss.edu/specialcell-documentation%2006.pdf).

As per *The Protection of Women from Domestic Violence Act, 2005*, any act, conduct, omission or commission that harms or injures or has the potential to harm or injure will be considered domestic violence by the law.

A recent article in *Times of India* states that as per ruling of Bombay HC on August 17, 2009, a court hearing on domestic violence case need not wait for a report filed by the protection officer before awarding interim compensation. Earlier under the Domestic Violence Act, 2005, a woman or a protection officer or a third party could file a complaint alleging abuse before the magistrate. The magistrate after hearing the parties could pass an interim order asking the man to pay compensation or monthly maintenance for the injuries caused to the woman. The Act had a clause which stated that before passing such an order the magistrate shall take into consideration any domestic incidence report received from the protection officer. On the basis of this Act when a trial court is required to pass an order, it keeps on waiting for the report of the protection officer which entails delay. This delay has now been avoided resulting in relief to battered women (*Times of India*, 2009a).

A study conducted by Panda (2004) in three rural and three urban settings in Thiruvananthapuram district of Kerala (South India) tried to explore the prevalence of domestic violence and the causative factors responsible for it. A total of 500 households (300 rural and 200 urban) were selected. Respondents belonging to the age group of 15–49 years were interviewed. The study found that out of total respondents, 35.7% women reported experiencing physical violence and 64.9% women reported experiencing psychological violence at least once in their married life. The study further highlighted that physical as well as psychological violence were reported comparatively less by urban as compared to rural women. The study concluded that lack of ownership of property by a woman, lack of social support, husband's excessive consumption of alcohol, and experience of violence in a woman's family during her childhood (i.e., witnessing father beating mother) were the major factors causing domestic violence.

A study conducted among married women in rural Gujarat explores the magnitude, onset, forms of violence as well as the reasons for occurrence of violence. A total of 346 married women were interviewed. The data revealed that two-thirds of the women had undergone some form of psychological, physical, or sexual abuse. The causative factors for violence were the failure to perform duties and responsibilities, economic stress, inadequate dowry, alcohol use, and hierarchical gender relations. Study found that women from the nuclear families reported more violence than women living in joint families (Burton, Duvvury, Rajan, & Varia, 1999).

RAJASTHAN CONTEXT

Rajasthan, the largest state of India is a vibrant, exotic state where tradition and royal glory meet in a beautiful display of colors. It represents an unusual diversity in its various forms such as people, customs, culture, costumes, music, manners, dialects, or cuisine (http://www.webindia123.com/Rajasthan/index.htm). The status of women fits into a vicious circle of mutually reinforcing gender inequalities and patriarchal practices in Rajasthan. Generally women in Rajasthan are viewed as an economic liability in natal home and a burden in the marital home (http://www.cuts-international.org/securing_gender_justice.htm).

In majority of districts in Rajasthan, women still face enormous obstacles in their search for redress when they suffer abuse in the name of custom or tradition. When the perpetrators of violence are men within the family, a greater pressure is exerted on women to maintain the silence (Mathur, 2004).

Many factors coalesce dramatically to make the position of women in Rajasthan a desperate one. Ancient traditions, religion, caste-based patriarchy, the economic effects of global capitalism combine with environmental stress factors make the way forward extremely complex. Patriarchy, discriminatory customs and values, caste-based discrimination, high illiteracy and high rates of poverty seem pervasive. Despite all efforts toward social justice, women continue to be perceived as burdens. Some of the factors contributing to this are sex ratio – there are 910 women for every 1,000 males in the population of Rajasthan (regional differences show Dholpur and Jaisalmer districts to be the worst at 795/810, respectively) – female infanticide, anemia, poor nutrition, maternal mortality (558 per 100,000), child deaths from poor nutrition and water-related diseases. Eighty percent of all women of childbearing age suffer from anemia; infant deaths are 79/1,000; the maternal mortality rates are among the highest in the world. Women and girl-children are caught in a cycle of malnutrition. Sati and child marriage are age-old customs in Rajasthan. Incidences of sexual abuse and domestic violence are high. The state has one of the lowest rates for female literacy in India. Recognizing all this, the state has initiated various schemes for empowerment of women. Academic institutions, Centre for Women Studies, and NGOs in Rajasthan are also working in this direction. Women in rural Rajasthan are now voicing their views to live in dignity which means meeting the basic needs, freedom from violence, and access to justice. So the whole life cycle of discrimination against rural women begins to be transformed (Grey, 2007).

A theoretical study undertaken in rural Rajasthan examined how cultural contexts and norms affected gender violence. The goal of the study was to identify collective driven solution that could deter the increased rate of violence against women. It concluded that strategies for countering gender violence must emerge from women's collective and shared experience of both subordination and empowerment (Mathur, 2004).

As reported in *Times of India*, more than 40% girls in Rajasthan marry below the age of 18 in at least 13 districts, including the capital city Jaipur. Among the married women, more than 45% suffer from all kinds of physical, mental, and sexual violence. More than 40% girls in the state do not complete their education. They also do not have any means of livelihood and thus are easy prey to maternal mortality and domestic violence. As far as domestic violence is concerned, the NFHS data points out some startling facts

Interestingly, government reports point out that more than 85% women have reportedly said that husband are perpetrators of violence. As per the findings, more than 50% of married women in the age group of 15–18 feel that husbands are right in perpetuating violence. Age of women at marriage and education has a direct link to violence (*Times of India*, 2009b).

Even though some studies in Rajasthan have been conducted on domestic violence not much information is available on this issue in villages near Pilani, Rajasthan. Hence, the present study "A Sociological Study on Domestic Violence Against Women in Villages Near Pilani, Rajasthan" has been conducted which tries to explore the extent and types of domestic violence that are prevalent in villages around Pilani and factors responsible for such violence. Further the study attempts to suggest some measures to reduce its prevalence in the community.

Area of Study

This study was conducted in two villages namely, Jherli and Raila. These villages are approximately 11 km from Pilani, which falls under the district Jhunjhunu in Shekhawati region of Rajasthan. Shekhawati region includes the administrative districts of Churu, Jhunjhunu, and Sikar. Both these villages are part of Jherli Grampanchayat.

Time Frame: January–July, 2009

Objectives

1. To examine the prevalence of domestic violence against women in two selected villages.
2. To study the nature of violence and its causes.
3. To examine the link between social variables and domestic violence against women.
4. To explore the awareness level of Protection from Domestic Violence Act, 2005, among women.
5. To suggest suitable measures for reducing the prevalence of domestic violence against women.

Methodology

Data for this study was collected from two villages, that is, Jherli and Raila, near Pilani, Rajasthan. Village Sarapanch was contacted to collect information about number of households and population size of these two villages. Simple random sampling procedure was followed for drawing the sample. A total of 150 women were selected from these two villages.

The respondents were married women within the age group of 15–50 years, constituting mothers-in-law, daughters-in-law, and married daughters. Out of 150 respondents, 77.33% (116) were daughters-in-law, 20.66% (31) were mothers-in-law, and rest 2% (3) were married daughters. Primary data was collected by covering houses in 25 lanes (15 lanes in Jherli village and 10 lanes in Raila village) with the help of a structured interview schedule.

Questions related to demographic profile of respondents (caste and age), structure of family, source of income, educational qualification, age at marriage, marital status, number of children, detailed experiences of violence (physical, psychological, sexual) before and after marriage, dowry-related issues, injuries due to violence, medical treatment received, access to finances, help from any organization, husbands' alcohol consumption, educational and occupational background of husbands, and awareness about Domestic Violence Act, 2005.

Respondents were given the freedom to withdraw at any stage of the interview. Data was analyzed by Software package in Social Science (SPSS), simple frequency analysis, cross tabulation, and Chi-square test. The study revealed that there were 21 women who suffered violence out of the sample size of 150. Participant observation revealed that 11 respondents did not open up with the real story of their marital life out of fear of their husbands and in-laws.

Data Analysis/Discussion

Data analysis reveals that out of 150 respondents, 14% (21) had experienced violence, 72.7% (109) belonged to the joint family system, and rest 27.3% (41) were from nuclear family. Most of the violent cases were reported from the joint family system.

Among the 21 cases of violence, 13 were reported from the joint family and rests 8 were from nuclear families. In these families as the violent activities of husbands were supported by their family members, respondents had to face not only the violent behavior of their husbands but also of their in-laws.

Out of the total respondents interviewed, 51.3% (77) belonged to Harijan caste, that is, the lowest caste and rest belonged to Brahmin, Jaat, Rajput, Meena, and Jhangir. Out of 21 reported violent cases, most of the cases, that is, 17 cases, were reported from Harijans and rest 4 cases were from the

Meena caste. Not a single case of violence was found among Brahmins, Jaats, Rajputs, and Jhangirs.

Violence was more prevalent among the age group of 15–30 and this group mostly constituted of daughters-in-law. Out of 21 respondents experiencing violence, 11 were from this age group. The study further highlights that education level of the respondents in these villages was not at a satisfactory level in comparison to their husbands' education. Out of the total number of respondents, only 48% (72) were literate out of which 13.3% (20) were educated up to primary class and 30.7% (46) had their education up to middle class. On the other hand, 71.3% (107) husbands of the respondents' were literate and out of which 48.7% (73) were qualified up to middle class and 12.7% (19) were educated up to higher class. The study shows a significant relationship between the education of the respondents and violence experienced by them. It has also been observed that illiterate women are facing more violence from their husbands in comparison to literate women. Out of 21 respondents experiencing violence, 18 were illiterate. Out of the same number, in 12 cases husbands were literate and in 9 cases they were illiterate.

After excluding 21 cases of violence, out of 129 respondents 52.7% (68) were literate and 47.3% (61) were illiterate and 75.2% (97) of respondents' husbands were literate and rest 24.8% (32) were illiterate. This clearly shows that among the educated group the occurrence of violence is almost negligible. As per the Chi-square test, there is a significant relationship between the education of the respondents and violent behavior of their husbands toward them. If a woman has proper education she can stand up against any misbehavior directed toward her.

Consumption of alcohol was also found in these areas; 32% (48) of the respondents' husbands were alcoholic and 20% (30) of them consumed alcohol almost everyday. Again out of those alcoholic husbands (30), 14% (21) behaved violently with their intimate partners. The Chi-square test also shows a significant relationship between the alcohol consumption of the husbands and their violent behavior. Moreover, 5.3% (8) alcoholic husbands also behaved violently toward their children. There are 21 violent cases in the study and husbands related to these cases were all alcoholics. Out of 21 respondents experiencing violence, 9.3% (14) of them got injured during such violence and only 1.3% (2) had received medical treatment and rest did not get any due to the fear of their husbands and in-laws as well as due to financial problems. Majority of the affected respondents stated that their husbands were spending more than half of their income on alcohol and after consuming alcohol they showed more sign of violence.

Findings of the study imply that alcohol is the main cause for the violent behavior of a person. Study reveals that employment does not have significant relationship with violence in the family. Out of 21 violent cases, in 2 cases husbands were unemployed and rest 19 were employed. Of the total 150 respondents, in 136 cases, husbands were employed and only 14 were unemployed. Out of the employed husbands, 55.3% (83) were daily wage workers, 9.3% (14) were businessmen, 12.7% (19) were engaged in agriculture, and 1 was a shareholder. Study also shows that violence is more among the daily wage workers. Out of 21 violent cases, majority of husbands (18) were daily wage workers.

Out of 21 respondents (experiencing violence), 13 (8.7%) were beaten and slapped frequently by their husbands and in-laws, 4 (2.7%) were only beaten, 3 (2%) were slapped, and rest 1 (.7%) had to tolerate abusive words of her husband and in-laws. Out of 21 respondents experiencing violence, 18 (12.0%) were pressurized for sex against their will out of which 10 (6.7%) were pressurized almost everyday and 8 (5.3%) were pressurized occasionally. Of 21 respondents facing violence, 3 (2.0%) were tortured for dowry by their husbands and in-laws, whereas 2 (1.3%) were tortured by their husbands only for bringing more dowry.

The study finds no relationship between respondents' experience of violence before marriage and existing violence experience after marriage. Out of the total violent cases, only three respondents had that experience before marriage. Study clearly states that out of the total respondents, only 15.3% (23) were aware of the Domestic Violence Act and the majority 84.7% (127) did not have any knowledge about this Act. Out of 21 violence experiencing respondents, none of them had knowledge about the Domestic Violence Act, 2005. That is why the respondents did not have any idea about their own legal rights. This is the main reason for not reporting a single case of violence to the police and also for not consulting with any local NGO/ Institute. The fear of their husbands and in-laws, lack of economic independence, and fear of police and society did not allow them to raise their voice against injustice.

From the Victim's Heart

Case Study 1
Bimla, a 24-year old lady, belongs to a Harijan family. Her husband is a daily wage worker. Both Bimla and her husband are not literate. During the interview she frankly speaks against her husband. As she has two daughters,

her husband tortures her a lot both physically and psychologically. Many a times her kids are also beaten by her husband. She complains that her husband spends his whole earning on alcohol. She is left with no money to take care of her kids. Finding no other alternative, now she is living with her parents for the past eight months. During this period her husband never tried to contact her. Now she is looking for work to earn something to take care of her daughters.

Case Study 2
Vimlesh is 20 years old and **Manish** is 40 years old. Both of them are sisters and belong to a Harijan family. Their marriage took place in one family (with brothers). They said that both the brothers were daily wage workers. They were heavy alcoholics and tortured them severely. Both the sisters have no kids. The financial decision of the family was controlled by their mother-in-law. They were frequently insulted and beaten by their husbands with sticks and shoes and got deep wounds and scratches on their bodies. Manish was hospitalized after the violent behavior of her husband led to her broken arm. She was subsequently looked after by her elder sister. Their mother-in-law also supported the husbands. They were even forced by their husband and mother-in-law to bring more dowry. Under such circumstances, both the sisters had applied for divorce from their husbands. It has been 12 months since Vimlesh got divorce from her husband. She is continuing her study now. Manish's case is in court. But she is still in dilemma whether or not she wants the separation.

Case Study 3
Santosh a 50-year-old mother-in-law from Meena caste is living in a joint family. Agriculture is their main source of income. She got married at a very young age. She has seven children, i.e., five daughters and two sons. Her husband is an alcoholic and behaves violently with her. Patience has some limitation. Out of frustration sometimes she also dares to slap her husband. Frequent arguments often arise between them over financial matter, not cooking properly, and not attending to household chores. She further stated that her father also had the same attitude toward her mother.

The case studies noted above and many others which were recorded invariably tell the same story. Poor economic condition, lack of education, alcohol consumption of the husbands, lack of awareness among women about their legal rights, and economic dependence are the main causes of domestic violence in these villages.

CONCLUSION

The study finds a statistically significant relationship between violence and age, caste, structure of family, husband's type of employment, education level of women, and husband's alcohol consumption. Analysis of the data affirms that husbands' alcohol consumption and lack of proper education among respondents (victim) are the main causes of domestic violence against women. Moreover, out of 21 violent cases, not a single case was reported to the police and not even consulted by any NGO.

As study reveals, fear of husband and in-laws, lack of confidence, lack of proper education, lack of information about legal rights, and legal cost involved in the legal system had made these women reluctant to report incidences of violence suffered by them. It has been noted that though domestic violence is prevalent in this part of rural Rajasthan, yet it is not highly prevalent in the two villages undertaken for study. Data analysis revealed only 21 cases of domestic violence out of 150 sample size.

These two villages are situated only 10–12 km distance from the campuses of Birla Institute of Science & Technology (BITS) and Central Electronics Engineering Research Institute (CEERI), Pilani. The overall conducive environment with educational institutes in close proximity of the villages may have a positive impact.

Various workshops, social development projects, training programs for women, and gender sensitization programs are continuously undertaken by different organizations such as Centre for Women Studies, Nirman and NSS group of BITS, Pilani for the upliftment of rural population. These initiatives work toward to bring about behavioral changes and shift in the mind-set of stereotypical gender roles. This helps in combating evils such as domestic violence against women.

SUGGESTIONS

A. Based on the study
  - Empowerment of women through education and their increased access to financial services.
  - Counseling of husbands against alcohol consumption.
  - Awareness and advocacy campaigns for Prevention of Domestic Violence Act.
  - Mobile courts should be introduced as an effective strategy for reaching out to victims especially in the rural areas.

B. General suggestions
- Women's participation should be increased in decision-making bodies.
- There should be a separate wing of police dealing with women's issues, attached to all police stations and should be excluded from any other duty. Some states have already initiated this exercise; this should be replicated in other states as well.
- NGOs working in different fields should be made proactive to the issues of domestic violence so that prompt assistance could be rendered to the victims.
- ICTs could give a major boost to the economic, political, and social empowerment of rural women, and the promotion of gender equality. ICTs can help in combating gender-based violence.

REFERENCES

Appelbaum, R. P., & Chambliss, W. J. (1995). *Sociology*. New York, NY: Harper Collins College Publishers.

Burton, B., Duvvury, N., Rajan, A., & Varia, N. (1999). *Violence against women in India: Evidence from rural Gujarat*. International Center for Research on Women [ICRW], pp. 9–17. Retrieved from http://www.popline.org/docs/1383/159581.html

Ending Widespread Violence Against Women. Retrieved from http://www.unfpa.org/gender/violence.htm

Grey, M. (2007). *Women's struggle in rural Rajasthan: Seeking a life of dignity*. Retrieved from http://www.wellsforindia.org/pdf/empowerment.pdf

Indian States and Union Territories: Rajasthan. Retrieved from http://www.webindia123.com/Rajasthan/index.htm

Interventions at Special Cells. Retrieved from http://www.tiss.edu/specialcell-documentation%2006.pdf

Macionis, J. (2006). *Sociology*. Delhi: Pearson Education.

Mathur, K. (2004). *Countering gender violence*. New Delhi: Sage Publication.

Panda, P. K. (2004). *Domestic violence against women in Kerala*. Discussion Paper no. 86. Kerala Research Programme on Local Level Development, Centre for Development Studies, Thiruvananthapuram.

Sahoo, H., & Pradhan, M. R. *Domestic violence in India: An empirical analysis*. Retrieved from http://www.isical.ac.in/~wemp/Papers/PaperManasRanjanPradhanAndHariharSahoo.doc

Statistics, USA. Retrieved from http://en.wikipedia.org/wiki/Domestic_violence

Times of India. (2009a). 40% girls in Rajasthan marry before 18. Shekhawati – The land of multi-hued frescoes. UNICEF. *Times of India*, March 17. Retrieved from http://www.Rajasthanunlimited.com/shekhawati.html

Times of India. (2009b). Domestic violence victim get HC relief. *Times of India*, August 19.

WOMEN AND DOMESTIC VIOLENCE: A CASE STUDY IN RURAL SRI LANKA

Seela Aladuwaka and Ram Alagan

ABSTRACT

Violence against women remains a significant barrier to securing human-centered development goals. Domestic violence in particular has limited options in almost every sphere of women's lives and in most community space. It also compromises the healthy development and well-being of their children and families. Yet, domestic violence is widespread in all regions, classes, and cultures. Wife beating is the most common form of family violence, and it poses a threat to the quality of women's lives in nearly every culture and society (Penn & Nardos, 2003). Victims of violence are often silent because they are helpless. Social and legal barriers continue to make it difficult to collect accurate data and sufficient evidence for domestic violence. In patriarchal societies in Asia, such as Sri Lanka, women face many difficulties due to domestic violence. This chapter identifies diverse problems and harassment faced by women in their domestic life in Kandy District in rural Sri Lanka. It focuses on problems women face in their youth, married life, and, in some cases, divorce. The qualitative study focuses on understanding the nature of the problem, the reason for domestic violence, and providing some conclusion from the material gathered from the study.

Democracies: Challenges to Societal Health
Research in Political Sociology, Volume 19, 103–120
Copyright © 2011 by Emerald Group Publishing Limited
All rights of reproduction in any form reserved
ISSN: 0895-9935/doi:10.1108/S0895-9935(2011)0000019011

INTRODUCTION

Violence against women remains a significant barrier to securing human-centered development goals. Domestic violence in particular has limited women's options in almost every sphere of their lives and in most community space. It also compromises the healthy development and well-being of their children and families. Domestic violence is a health, legal, economic, educational, developmental, and human rights problem. It has serious consequences in terms of development. Violence prevents women from participating fully in different areas of their lives – family, community, and society – and energies that might be directed toward social good and development are curtailed (Commission on Human Rights, 1995). Violence against women prevents them realizing their full potential yet, domestic violence is widespread in all regions, classes, and cultures. Wife beating is the most common form of family violence and poses a threat to the quality of women's lives in nearly every culture and society (Penn & Nardos, 2003).

Victims of violence are often silent because they are helpless. Social and legal barriers continue to make it difficult to collect accurate data and sufficient evidence on domestic violence. In patriarchal societies in Asia, such as Sri Lanka, women face many difficulties due to domestic violence. According to the 2006 survey by the Ministry of Child Development and Women's Empowerment in Sri Lanka, more than 60% of women in Sri Lanka face domestic violence, and 44% of pregnant women are subject to such violence. It is a widespread problem in the country. Domestic violence has reached the top in Sri Lanka by leaving all the other forms of violence far behind (*Nirmanee Bulletin*, 2003).

This chapter identifies diverse problems and harassment faced by women in their domestic life in the Kandy District of rural Sri Lanka. The chapter is divided into three main sections. The first section discusses literature on violence against women to formulate the conceptual approach to this research. The second section describes the case study that focuses on the problems women face in their youth, married life, and, in some cases, divorce. The qualitative study focuses on understanding the nature of the problem and the reasons for domestic violence. The last section provides some conclusions from the research and some recommendations to assist victims of domestic violence.

Violence Against Women: Definitions

According to the United Nations Commission Human Rights 1997 Report on Special Rapporteur on Violence Against Women, "domestic violence is defined as violence that occurs within the private sphere, generally between individuals who are related through intimacy, blood, or law." The report recognized domestic violence as a gender-specific crime, perpetrated by men against women, and as a powerful tool of oppression (Human Rights Commission, 1997). Therefore, violence against women in general, and domestic violence in particular, serve as essential components in societies that oppress women, since violence against women not only derives from but also sustains the dominant gender stereotypes and is used to control them in one space traditionally dominated by women, the home (Human Rights Commission, 1997).

Domestic violence has been broadly defined in Article 2 in the United Nations Declaration on the Elimination of Violence Against Women, "domestic violence as encompassing, but not being limited to physical, sexual, and psychological violence occurring in the family, including battering, sexual abuse of female children in the household, dowry-related violence, marital rape, female genital mutilation and other traditional practices harmful to women, non-spousal violence and violence related to exploitation" (Human Rights Commission, 1997). This chapter utilizes this broader definition of domestic violence that looks at various difficulties women face in their domestic sphere.

CONCEPTUAL FRAMEWORK

Domestic Violence as a Violation of Human Rights

This research utilizes human rights approach as a theoretical framework to examine domestic violence against women. The human rights approach helps to frame the issues of violence against women as a serious phenomenon and to encourage necessary measures designed to alleviate violence against them. In her preliminary report, the United Nations Special Rapporteur outlined in detail the international human rights standards with regard to violence against women (Commission on Human Rights, 1995). It stated that domestic violence – violence that occurs within the domestic sphere perpetrated by both private and state actors – constitutes a violation of the human rights of women. Thus, "violence such as wife beating is not an individual, isolated, or aberrant act, but a social license, a duty or sign of masculinity, deeply ingrained in culture, widely practiced, denied and completely or largely immune from legal sanction" (Commission on Human

Rights, 1995). Domestic violence, therefore, is considered as a human rights concern rather than as a mere domestic criminal justice concern.

The main barrier to preventing domestic violence is the separation of private–public issues. Domestic violence occurs at home and it limits women's security at home. Taking actions against domestic violence becomes difficult because it is tolerated by society and state as a "private/personal issue occurring in the private sphere." Thus, it was not recognized as problem until recently, even though it is a development, heath, human rights, and societal problem at large. Therefore, the notion of private–public issues has been challenged by the human rights approach because it justifies inaction by state and society and continues to subordinate women. Many began to criticize human rights as gendered and demanded to include gender-specific violence in the Human Rights Agenda (Bunch, 1995; Fenster, 1999; Peters & Wolper, 1994).

The women's rights as a human rights framework became one of the main themes in the Fourth World Conference on Women in Beijing. This conference incorporated a vast range of issues that are related to women's rights and argued that "women's rights are human rights." This phrase was first used in the Vienna Human Rights conference, and it raised the fact that violence against women is one of the most prominent human rights abuses women experience.

In December 1993, as a consequence of the World Conference on Human Rights in Vienna in June 1993, the United Nations General Assembly adopted a landmark resolution on gender violence called the Declaration on the Elimination of Violence Against Women. This declaration defines for the first time what constitutes an act of violence against women and calls on governments and the international community to take specific measures to prevent such acts. It defined violence as "any act of gender based violence that result in, or is likely to result in, physical, sexual or psychological harm or suffering to women, including the threat of such acts, coercion or arbitrary deprivation of liberty, in both public or private life" (Commission on Human Rights, 1995). Violence against women forced them into subordinate positions to men. Therefore, under international human rights law, governments are not only obliged to refrain from committing human rights violations but also to prevent and respond to human rights abuses without discrimination.

The Convention on the Elimination of All Forms of Discrimination against Women (CEDAW), in Article 2, requires states parties to "pursue by all appropriate means and without delay a policy of eliminating discrimination against women," which includes the duty "to refrain from engaging in any act or practice of discrimination against women and to ensure that public authorities and institutions shall act in conformity with this obligation" and "to take all appropriate measures, including legislation, to modify or abolish existing laws, regulations, customs and practices which constitute discrimination against women." Many countries however, fail to bring strong measures to end violence against women, though it is a common problem.

As is stated in the Preamble to the United Nations Declaration on the Elimination of Violence against Women, "violence against women is a manifestation of historically unequal power relations between men and women" (United Nations, 1993). Thus, violence is a historical process. The oppression of women is therefore related to politics, requiring an analysis of the institutions of the state and society, the conditioning and socialization of individuals, and the nature of economic and social exploitation (Human Rights Commission, 1997). Since the roots of female subordination lie in historical power relations within society, the institutions of state and civil society must accept responsibility for female subordination, including violence against women. Powers dynamics and women's subordination were clearly linked. Women become victims of violence because of power and control over their lives in many ways. Historical norms support male dominance within the household. These norms are so strong that many victims do not seek public help because they think battering is a private matter (Langan & Innes, 1986). An analysis of power relations challenges private–public notions, and a human rights approach will be useful to understand the problems of domestic violence. Therefore, it is important to identify this as a critical issue to be raised and addressed publicly and encourage society to condemn acts of domestic violence and try to prevent them from happening in the first place.

CASE STUDY FROM KANDY DISTRICT

While Sri Lankan society places high value on the institution of the family, domestic violence has emerged as a key area of violence against women in the country. Despite the fact that most often societal and cultural pressures prevent many victims from making such incidents public, the monitoring of recent newspaper reports has revealed that these incidents occur with disturbing regularity (Women and Media Collective, Colombo, 1998). It is important to bring attention to this issue, and this study is an attempt to bring attention to the problem through a primary investigation.

Objective of the Study

The main objective of this study is to identify the diverse problems women face due to domestic violence. The study looks at women's domestic violence problems in their youth, married life, and marriage breakdown. The second objective is to recommend policies based on the findings.

Sample and Research Methods

Forty women, whose experiences touched on the issues relevant to the study, were selected with the help of the government agent, prominent villagers, and with the researcher's familiarity with the area. Twenty-nine (77.5%) of these women were harassed at home, while eleven women (22.5%) were divorced or separated. Another three who were raped, were also included in the sample, although information regarding them was not obtained from the victims themselves.

Qualitative research methods were employed in this study. Although a structured format was prepared to collect the field data, no attempt was made to administer a questionnaire to the respondents. Instead, data was collected through informal conversations and the material was subsequently slotted into the information sheet. A certain amount of cross-checking of the information supplied was possible by talking to the neighbors of the respondents, a few respected village elders, and the Village Officer (*Grama Sevaka*). As the information sought was of a very personal and sensitive nature, it was felt that recording responses in the presence of the interviewees would inhibit the free expression of their feelings.

Research Area

This study is about rural Sri Lanka and the area selected is not an isolated traditional rural locality. It is situated not very far from the city and can be described as a rural locality with an admixture of urban influences. Five villages of the Pahatha Hevaheta AGA division in the Kandy District were selected for the field study (see Fig. 1). These villages have few infrastructural facilities and are mostly underdeveloped. The lack of transport, water, sanitary, and other basic facilities continues to cause severe strain on the lives of the people of this particular village.

The major occupation is agriculture with employment in small-scale personal enterprises coming a close second. Women are mostly involved in

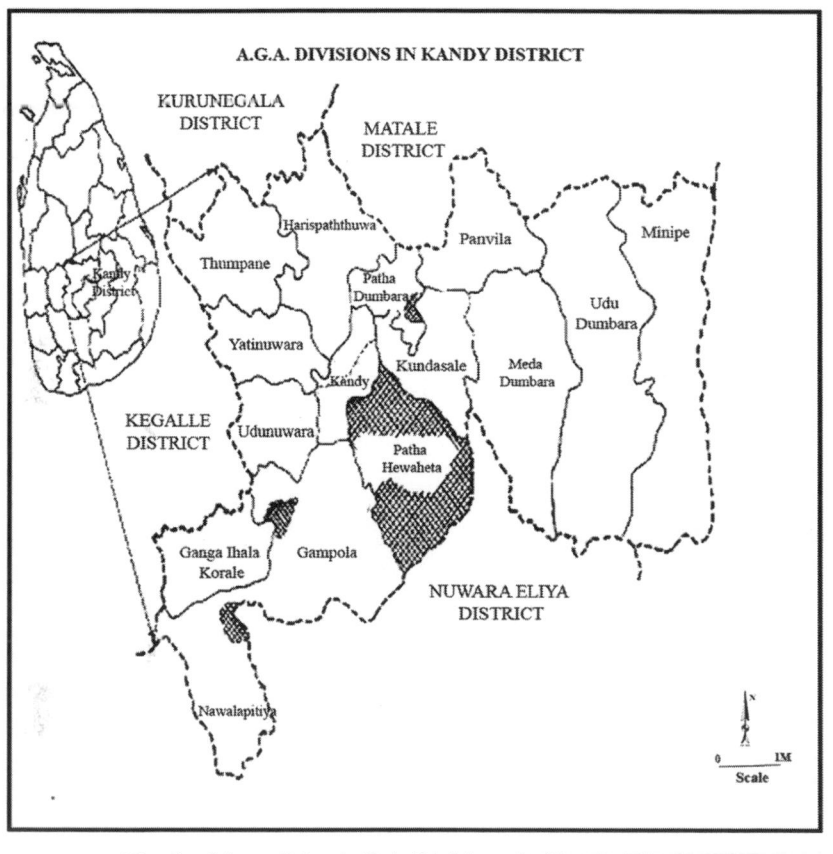

Fig. 1. Map of the A.G.A Divisions in Kandy District.

agriculture and home-based income generating ventures such as selling of cooked food. A fair number of women work as daily-paid laborers. Nearly 70% of the families belong to the low-income group, and poverty is a major factor that dominates the lives of these people.

Description of the Sample

The majority of the women in the sample are under the age category 26–35 and 36–45. Generally, the level of education of the respondents was low: six had no education at all and five had studied up to grade five. The level of

education of 19 was between grades five and nine. Six had studied up to
GCE Ordinary Level (O/L) examination and only one had studied further.
Twenty-two women out of the sample of 40 were housewives and some were
self-employed. As for the employment situation of the husbands of the
respondents, it was seen that seven were government servants, which is
interesting to note as not a single women in the sample worked in a
government sector job.

Family income of the respondents was very low, as fourteen families
received less than 1,500 rupees (about $15) per month. It was noticed that
there were no large families in the sample. Twenty-seven families had less
than five children, twelve families had three children, and nine had two
children. There was only one respondent who had nine children. The
standard of housing was not satisfactory. Twenty-five respondents lived in
their own houses and nine lived with their parents, while three lived in
rented houses. One respondent lived in a wattle and daub hut on
government land. Marital status is interesting to note. With respect to
marital status, 28 respondents were legally married and nine were separated
or divorced. They were not legally married but lived together and had
children.

Findings from the Study

Wife Battering

It was identified from the study that 29 women had faced domestic violence
in the sample we surveyed. In the majority of cases it involved assault. Of
this number, 12 women seemed to face intensive assault daily and it involved
bodily injury. In the case of other women facing domestic violence although
not receiving injuries, it appeared they faced assault frequently. There were
12 such women in our sample and they could expect their husbands to be
violent to them at any time. It was identified that five women faced rare
domestic violence, and these assaults according to their testimony were not
so severe. There were instances where women had to seek medical treatment
after such assaults. There were four women who said that they had to be
admitted to hospital after being assaulted by their husbands.

The reactions of the victims to these forms of domestic violence were
varied. Sixteen women felt that they were harassed physically as well as
mentally, while five women felt intensive mental harassment. Eight women
did not feel depressed about the harassment. These figures indicate that the
large majority of women in our sample feel that they were harassed both

physically and mentally. In our interviews we saw that they were severely depressed about their plight. One of these women was assaulted by her husband when she was in an advanced stage of pregnancy and she had to be hospitalized. She delivered the child while in the hospital and being treated for the injuries. She described to us the intense harassment she faced in the hands of her husband. Such cases indicate severe physical and mental trauma.

In our survey we also came across women who were not so much physically harassed, but who felt more mentally depressed because of their situation. Five women in our sample belonged to this category. There were several causes for it. The fact that they felt increasing disharmony in the family affecting the education of the children, feelings of shame in facing society, the belief that the family will never prosper because of the husband's behavior, and feelings of future insecurity were the causes indicated by these women at the interviews.

Some women facing domestic violence have a different attitude to their plight. Although they undergo many types of harassment in the hands of their husbands, they do not seem to be sad or depressed about their condition. They appear to be able to ignore these experiences and also appear to feel that it is the women's lot to undergo such harassment. It seems women in Asiatic societies, including Sri Lanka, accept the traditional belief in fate. Many women appear to tolerate this harassment due to their desire to save the marriage at all costs. They are unwilling to bother their parents or their sisters and brothers with their problems and they also fear the social stigma attached to a woman who has been deserted by her husband. These factors seem to make them go through a marriage that they feel their fate has destined for them.

There is however a group of women who do not seem to be prepared to tolerate their condition any longer and are eager to find a solution. Some of them have sought police protection. Two women stated that they had complained to the police or the Village Officer (*Grama Sevaka*) about the harassment they undergo. What they expected from these authorities was for them to intervene on their behalf and advise their husbands to mend their ways. But it is significant that the vast majority of women are unwilling to take such a step. Upon inquiry we found that the women prefer not to give publicity to their plight. Many women appear unwilling to talk about their problems with others, which includes law-enforcing authorities. This characteristic seems to be tied up with feelings of shame and self-respect among the rural women in Sinhalese society.

Eight women in our sample appeared to have made a personal effort to bring about an improvement in their situation by seeking employment.

Women faced with domestic violence also face many economic difficulties. They have found employment to fulfill the needs of their children, relieving them of some amount of emotional strain.

A significant feature that emerged in our interviews was the strong attachment women felt for their children and family members, despite the harassment they faced. Women who are subjected to daily harassment seem to tolerate it because of their attachment to the family. Ten women in our sample stated that each time they were severely harassed they would decide to leave their families and go away but that they would change their minds subsequently. Of them four women had on several occasions gone back to their parents and eventually returned to their families. Such instances indicate that the strong attachment to the family cause many women endure their harassment.

In our attempts to identify the causes for domestic violence we found that several factors contributed to this situation. Often these factors are interconnected and it is difficult to separate one factor from another. If we are to classify them we can do so under five headings (see Fig. 2). These figures indicate that alcoholism is a major factor in domestic violence. Often several factors become interconnected. For example, an alcoholic usually shows little concern about the economic necessities of the family. The facts revealed by one woman in an interview are worth noting in this connection.

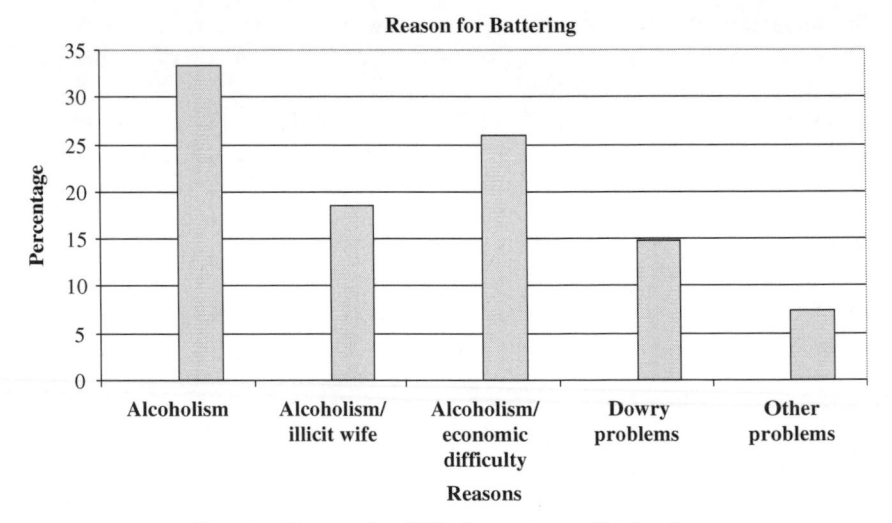

Fig. 2.   Reason for Wife Battering in Sri Lanka.

The husband in this instance was a government employee who was receiving a substantial monthly salary, which the wife thought, was sufficient to maintain the family. But because he spends the money on excessive drinking, money for domestic needs has to be borrowed over and over again. As these debts are often not paid back, the wife faces immense difficulties. Furthermore, she stated that the husband harasses her often under the influence of liquor. He has now lost his job and the family has no regular means of support. The little money they get sometimes is spent by him on liquor and according to her he assaults her and blames her for his plight. He seems to have no concern about the present needs or the future of the three children. In our interviews we found that there are many such husbands who neglect their children.

According to several women we interviewed, the harassment they face in the hands of their husbands is due to the involvement of these husbands with other women. There were five women in our sample who fell into this category. The women seem to get assaulted when they try to question them or advise them about these illicit affairs. One wife described how she got married under compulsion by her parents and now her husband harasses her frequently while having an open affair with another woman. She seems to live with great difficulty, having to maintain six children because her husband gives them very little money. She supplies cooked food to a restaurant and thereby earns some money for the children's education. The husband, who visits her rarely, assaults her inhumanely. These assaults have been of frequent occurrence and affect their three children adversely. According to her six-year-old daughter, when they notice their father coming home, they stop their studies and go to bed. Children exposed to such situation could be neglected and abused. Furthermore, studies found that children who experience violence in childhood tend to develop the risks of committing violence in adulthood (Hotaling & Sugarman, 1986).

The harassment faced by many women can be traced to the economic background in which they live. Some of the husbands spent a part of their earnings on liquor. This practice was noticed among a few of the daily-paid laborers. Another case of economic hardship is of a couple with seven children who live in a small house consisting of two rooms. The wife, in this case, stated that the husband's daily earnings were barely enough for one meal for the nine of them. Such problems lead to tensions and end in her being subjected to violence by the husband.

Poverty is a significant factor that seems to lie at the root of many domestic conflicts. Of our sample of 40 respondents, 16 belong to the very low-income group. Arguments about money or the lack of it often lead to domestic conflict.

In our survey, we came across wives who faced harassment due to dowry problems and interference by the relatives of the husband. There were two women who faced violence because of dowry problems. Both of them had married against the wishes of their parents and when confronted by economic difficulties the husbands bring up the question of dowry. Arguments end with the wives being assaulted. The husbands in both cases are addicted to drinking and they appear to use the issue of dowry as provocation for assault. One of these women lives with her mother-in-law who according to her encourages her son to assault the wife over the issue of dowry.

The relative educational level of the respondents and their husbands appear to have a bearing on family conflict as they present themselves in this investigation. In families where the wife is more educated than the husband, the wife's superior status has an indirect effect on conjugal relationships. In our sample, ten women were found to have higher educational qualifications than their husbands, four of them having passed the GCE O/L examination. In these households, the women are not ready to accept their traditional subordinate role and the men, in turn, resent the advice, wishes, and suggestions of their wives. This attitude of the men perhaps from a feeling of inferiority could be interpreted as an unconscious attempt to bring down the status of their spouses. This leads to domestic strain and conflict. One of the women among our interviewees passed the GCE O/L examination and even acquired working knowledge of English. Although she is very keen to seek employment, her husband is severely opposed to it. Any attempt on her part to advise him or the children meets with abuse, and arguments often end with assault.

Couples who have little or no education, are equally disadvantaged but for different reasons. Very poor social awareness causes conflict, and wife battery in such situations were starkly noticeable. According to our information, these men act on sudden provocation and are more prone to listen to tales that often results in the physical assault of their wives.

Separation, Alimony, and Maintenance
In this survey, an attempt was made to investigate the question of maintenance where there is a breakdown of marriage. Of the forty women interviewed eleven were facing this problem. Two out of these eleven were women who had not entered legal marriage.

It is clear that four women out of eleven in this category did not attempt to obtain maintenance. Their views reflect the fact that they left their husbands due to deep resentment and that they disliked having any communication with them. Their main concern was to leave the husbands, and having done so they do not expect any alimony or maintenance from them. Upon inquiry, whether they could manage without such compensation, we found that these women try very hard to do so by their personal efforts. Two women in this category have gone to the Middle East to earn an income to maintain their children. They have also received help from their parents and are now planning to embark on business ventures. Another woman who did not receive any maintenance from her husband works in a stone quarry in the area to bring up her children. When we inquired why she did not attempt to obtain alimony and maintenance, she replied that she had managed for 15 years without such help and that soon her children who are now grown up will be able to help her.

We also came across women who were legally separated and were receiving maintenance. Two women in this category stated that the money they receive is not adequate for their needs. We also met two women who tried unsuccessfully to obtain compensation. One woman who was promised Rs. 200.00 ($20) per month did not receive it regularly. Her attempts to recover this money led to the disappearance of her husband and now she is planning to go to the Middle East so that she could provide for the future of her child. In the case of another woman, the husband took the children along with him when he left her. Her attempts to obtain maintenance have failed.

Two women in our survey are facing a peculiar situation because they are not legally married. Both have children and their attempts to obtain any form of maintenance have failed. Since the women entered this situation against the wishes of their parents they do not seem to get any help from that quarter either. These women face severe difficulty. One of them goes to work as a laborer. She is forced to take her child to work.

There are many instances where women who are separated from the husbands receive support from their parents or brothers. It is a frequent occurrence for the daughter or sister to return home after the break-up of her marriage and receive help. We could identify six such women in our sample. A mother who takes care of her three grandchildren and daughter, who is separated, felt that one has to somehow find ways and means of meeting such situations. The brother of this woman is also helping her and the children because she receives no maintenance. The woman explained that due to alcoholism and other problems, the husband is not in a position to give her maintenance.

Reasons for Separation

In our survey, we found several causes for separation from legal husbands. They may be categorized as follows:

(a) Assault and harassment due to addiction to liquor.
(b) Involvement with another woman and consequent problems.
(c) Husband leaving without informing the wife.

As indicated above, four women have decided to live away from their husbands because of the harassment they faced from their liquor-addicted men. The women took this decision due to the intense harassment they underwent and because they were completely disappointed with the husbands who cared neither for them nor for their children. Another woman who lives separately with her three children stated that she took this decision because her husband was having affairs with several other women.

It was also necessary to find out about second marriages of the women whose first marriage had broken down. Of the 11 we interviewed, 4 had "remarried." These were not legal marriages; however, three first marriages in all these cases were legal and the women are now living with other men without legally going through a divorce. Three of these women have not obtained any form of maintenance.

The women mentioned that their second "marriage" was for obtaining protection for themselves and for their children. But two of these women have grown up daughters. Two other women who have small children said that they wanted their children to have fathers. One woman who is living with a man much younger than her said that she separated from her first husband because of the harassment she underwent, as he was living with another woman. Now, this woman seems to be harassed by her second husband in front of her grown up daughter. The man is heavily addicted to liquor and the woman's plight appeared to be worse now than during her first marriage. She is very worried about her daughter and she stated that the only solution to her present condition is committing suicide. Another woman feels guilty that her parents have to undergo many difficulties because of the breakdown of her marriage.

A major problem faced by separated women seems to be that of obtaining alimony and maintenance. It appears that these rural women with little or no education are unaware of their rights in this regard. For example, one woman who has been separated from her husband for 17 years did not know that she was entitled for maintenance. Only a year ago she initiated action in this regard when she was advised to do so.

With regard to the women who had been legally separated with arrangements for maintenance, we noted that this was possible not because of their own initiative but because of a knowledgeable person in their family. Women without such support usually become helpless and fall into great difficulty. Among the women who receive maintenance, there are some who are faced with difficulties in obtaining it on time. Usually, the money they receive is inadequate and although the need is there to have it increased there are many difficulties in getting it done. Even women who are in great need of maintenance find it difficult to initiate action because that again involves money. They become despondent and give up all hope of getting alimony and maintenance. Thus, lack of knowledge and lack of economic strength to fight for their rights make the lives of lot of these women difficult.

In the area under survey we came to know of three rape cases. But there was no possibility of interviewing the victims. The information was supplied by the government officer of the area, and one incident is said to have occurred while two women aged 18–20 were returning home one night after a ceremony in a school. Two unknown men had committed the offence on these women. The women had informed their parents about it and a complaint had been lodged. But the offenders could not be traced and there was no possibility of pursuing the case any further. It is possible that there are other cases of rape of women in this area. However, fear of publicity and the consequent social stigma usually compel women to suffer in silence.

CONCLUSION

The purpose of this survey was to obtain an understanding of domestic violence, separation, and alimony and maintenance in a rural society in Sri Lanka. The study suggests that women are subject to violence in their own homes and they are often helpless. We can arrive at several conclusions from the material we gathered; however, for a more complete picture we need a more exhaustive survey. The present survey was a very impressionistic one, the following conclusions can be drawn from this study: (a) lack of mutual understanding between husband and wife seems to lead to domestic violence and separation, (b) the women under survey often face domestic violence because of the alcoholism of their husbands, (c) marriage at an early age leading to immature attitudes, lack of economic means, and lack of education appear to lead to alcoholism because liquor is seen as a means of escape from problems, and (d) the general attitude of the women appears to be one of stoic tolerance of their sad lot. Women's main aim seems to be the provision of a safe future for their children.

It is possible that women are often in a sad plight because they are unaware of their rights as well. Many women who consider their husbands as the decision-makers in the family seem to be ignorant of their rights. It will be greatly beneficial if women are educated about their rights. This appears particularly necessary in the case of rural women. We came across several women who had become destitute because of the breakdown of their marriages. The fact that they could not resort to legal means to solve their problems was largely due to their unawareness about their rights. The lack of suitable means of receiving advice in such cases in rural areas appears to be a severe shortcoming.

Furthermore, while the necessity is there to obtain legal separation and maintenance, the fear of the legal process has made them depressed. Thus, it is clear that some organizational means should be made available for such women. Rural women in particular need family counseling. An organization such as "Women in Need" has been providing a great service for battered women for long period. Women in rural areas lack knowledge about such organizations and thus women cannot benefit from services and counseling provided by such organizations. Furthermore, counseling centers are located in urban areas and women in rural areas have limited access to those places. Shelters for battered women are limited and do not exist in rural areas in the country. Even if counseling and shelters are available in nearby towns, it is very clear that these rural women are completely unaware of the existence of such institutions.

Despite the growing visibility of such crimes committed against women within the sanctity of marriage and the family, the country did not have a specific law that addresses the issue of domestic violence except the Penal Code. Women subjected to domestic violence can prosecute a perpetrator under general Penal Code provisions that deal with murder, assault, grievous hurt, etc. When Sri Lanka's Penal Code was amended in 1995 the definition of grievous hurt was extended. However, these crimes articulated in the Penal Code are not gender specific and are applicable to both men and women. Violence inflicted on women in the domestic sphere, however, is gendered and determined by unequal power relations and socialization that is discriminatory toward women (Law and Society Trust, Annual publication in Sri Lanka, 1999). In March, 1993, the government of Sri Lanka adopted women charters that incorporate many of the provision of CEWDA. After a long wait, the Domestic Violence Act was introduced in 2005, and it gave legislation recognition to the problems related to domestic violence. It has given protection order by law, which is a vital element of prevention of domestic violence where any person with fear of violence can seek protection order.

This important act is, however, yet to receive more publicity. The vast majority of women are unaware of such legal remedies to the problems they face due to domestic violence. It is vital that more women and men get educated about the act; especially this information has to reach grassroots level, and specifically rural women. Domestic violence is discriminatory against women, and the state therefore has a duty not to discriminate against women as well as protect their rights to safety and security of person.

Recognizing that economic deprivation and isolation are often significant aspects of domestic violence, states should ensure women's economic empowerment through increased job opportunities for women, as well as equal rights to property, inheritance, and family income. As the human rights approach indicates, the state has a responsibility to prevent this type of crime against women. The government of Sri Lanka agrees to the international convention of prevention of all types of violence against women, yet effective preventive mechanisms are yet to be adopted and implemented.

Domestic violence is not a private issue even when it happens at home. As pointed out by Bunch and Carrillo, "the home is most dangerous place for women and frequently the site of cruelty and torture" (Bunch & Carrillo, 1991). Thus, an issue of domestic violence is a serious concern and it is a societal issue, women's rights issue, and developmental issue. It affects every aspect of a women's life as well as well as children's lives. It is vital to understand the complexity of the problems in domestic violence as it is more often related to intimate relationships. Hooks asserts that "feminists calling attention to the reality of violence in intimate relationships must compel people to take the issue seriously as such violence seems to be daily on the increase" (Hooks, 2007, p. 257). Women globally suffer from violence at their own home, mostly by their loved ones. As stated by Hooks, "the process by which women recover from the experiences of being hit by a loved one is a complicated and multifaceted one, an area where there must be much more feminist study and research" (Hooks, 2007, p. 274). It is evident from this preliminary research that women face various difficulties due to violence that occur in their own homes, and immediate and proper attention must be given to prevent it. Especially, that these problems continue as a major problem in Sri Lanka today, for example, the recent 2011 court case brought by a young female member of Sri Lankan parliament who was battered by her husband. The member initiated discussion within the Parliament on the topic of domestic violence and its prevention. Recognition of this critical issue at the state level is imperative, and preventive measures should be taken at every level.

REFERENCES

Bunch, B., & Carrillo, R. (1991). *Gender violence: A Development and human rights issue.* New Brunswick, NJ: Center for Women's Global Leadership Douglass College.

Bunch, C. (1995). Beijing, backlash, and the future of women's human rights. *Health and Human Rights, 1*(4), 449–453.

Commission on Human Rights. (1995). *Preliminary report by the UN Special Rapporteur on violence against women,* Ms. Radika Coomaraswamy. Technical Report no. UN Doc. E/CN.4/1995/42. United Nations, New York.

Nirmanee Bulletin. (2003). *Domestic violence against women in Sri Lanka. Nirmanee Bulletin.* Retrieved from http://www.nirmanee.org/graphics/domestic_violence_against_Wo men.pdf

Fenster, T. (1999). *Gender, planning and human rights.* New York, NY: Routledge.

Hooks, B. (2007). Violence in intimate relationships: A feminist perspective. In: L. O'Toole (Ed.), *Gender violence.* New York, NY: New York University Press.

Hotaling, G. T., & Sugarman, D. B. (1986). An analysis of risk markers in husband to wife violence: The current state of knowledge. *Violence and Victims, 1*(2), 101–122.

Human Rights Commission. (1997). *Report of the Special Rapporteur on violence against women.* Retrieved from http://www.eurowrc.org/06.contributions/1.contrib_en/35.contrib.en.htm

Langan, P. A., & Innes, C. A. (1986). *Preventing domestic violence against women.* Washington, DC: Bureau of Justice Statistics, US Department of Justice.

Law and Society Trust. (1999). *Annual publication 1999.* Colombo, Sri Lanka.

Penn, M. L., & Nardos, R. (2003). *Overcoming violence against women and girls.* Oxford: Rowman and Littefield Publishing Inc.

Peters, J., & Wolper, A. (1994). *Women's rights, human rights: International feminist perspectives.* New York, NY: Routledge.

United Nations. (1993). *Declaration on the elimination of violence against women.* Retrieved from http://www.un.org/documents/ga/res/48/a48r104.htm

Women and Media Collective. (1998). *Women's Rights Watch,* 1st, 2nd, 3rd and 4th Quarters, The Women and Media Collective, Colombo, Sri Lanka. Retrieved from http:// hei.unige.ch/humanrts/commission/thematic52/53-wom.htm

NATURAL DISASTER, GENDER, AND CHALLENGES: LESSONS FROM ASIAN TSUNAMI

Ram Alagan and Seela Aladuwaka

ABSTRACT

Although gender dimensions have been widely discussed in social research, many disaster relief and recovery programs still ignore gender needs and gender discrepancies. Specially, in a disaster situation, certain cultures and governments have a lack of mind-set and skills to focus on women's needs adequately although it requires much more investigation. During natural disasters, females face unprecedented challenges than men, because they are vulnerable and marginalized – socially, culturally, economically, and politically. To overcome these challenges, it is strongly suggested that a multifaceted decision-making process is practiced.

This chapter explains challenges for women in a natural disaster situation and discusses how to overcome difficulties and rebuild livelihoods of a vulnerable population in Sri Lankan society. The 2004 tsunami claimed over 40,000 lives, displaced about 1.0 million from their homes, and caused severe damage to the physical infrastructure and the damage estimated was well over US $1.5 billion. As the female population face unprecedented challenges, it is suggested that gender needs and gender discrepancies require thorough investigation. This chapter presents a study based on needs assessment carried out in tsunami impact communities in East

Democracies: Challenges to Societal Health
Research in Political Sociology, Volume 19, 121–132
Copyright © 2011 by Emerald Group Publishing Limited
All rights of reproduction in any form reserved
ISSN: 0895-9935/doi:10.1108/S0895-9935(2011)0000019012

and South Sri Lanka in 2005 and outlines the lessons learned on how
women and men operate and anticipate post-disaster relief and recovery.
Using participatory mapping methodology (e.g., narratives, ethnographic
observations, community mappings, key informant interviews, focus group
interviews, and other qualitative methods) this study suggests effective
techniques to incorporate gender needs in a natural disaster situation.

Keywords: Gender needs; natural disaster; participatory mapping

INTRODUCTION

Social relations, including gender, are weakened by conflict and natural
disaster (Hyndman, 2008). To overcome disaster relief and recoveries, it is
strongly suggested that a multifaceted decision-making process is introduced. Regrettably, many disaster relief and projects ignore gender needs
and gender discrepancies. Different cultures and governments do not have
the mind-set and skills to adequately focus on women's needs in a disaster
situation. Enarson (2000) states that gender relations as well as natural
disasters are socially constructed under different geographic, cultural,
politico-economic, and social conditions and have complex social consequences for women and men. As stated by Enarson, women and men have
different types of challenges in post-disaster periods; especially women face
gender marginalization. This special report explains challenges for women
in a natural disaster situation and discusses how to overcome challenges in
rebuilding the livelihood of vulnerable populations (women and children) in
Sri Lankan societies.

ASIAN TSUNAMI: 2004 DECEMBER

In recent years, natural disaster relief and recovery issues have become vital
concerns in many countries. Sri Lanka is an island situated in the Indian
Ocean. The island is surrounded by nearly 1,600 km of rich coastline. The
2004 tsunami struck the coast and claimed over 40,000 lives, displaced about
1.0 million from their homes, and caused severe destruction to the physical
infrastructure and estimated the damage over US $1.5 billion. In recent
history, Sri Lanka has never faced a natural disaster of this magnitude. Tens

of thousands of houses and business places were washed away. A number of towns and villages were completely wiped out. Infrastructure like roads, schools, power, and water was devastated. Thousands of women and children lost their lives and faced severe recovery challenges due to lack of proper planning strategies. To reconstruct such large-scale damage, rehabilitation planning programs required adequate skills and expertise (such as gender-based planning), disaster management, data, coordination, collaboration, and communication among decision-making institutions. Unfortunately, in Sri Lanka, it has not been well thought-out to implement, mitigate, or measure the multifaceted natural disaster situation especially on valuable communities. Although seven years have passed, disaster relief and recovery continues to be a slow and difficult process in many impact communities due to lack of coordination, collaboration, and communication among government and local institutions. In addition, the 30-year conflict between the government and terrorist groups (ended in May 2009) in the northern and eastern parts of the country left tsunami impact groups with more challenges in disaster recovery planning. In both situations, (such as human-made war and natural disasters) women and children faced unprecedented challenges because they are poor, do not have power to make decisions, and do not have access to information and services. Thus, it is profoundly important to recognize the role of women and children in societies and to initiate programs of support during critical times.

To incorporate gender needs, a gender vulnerability awareness program of the disaster could be highly effective. A gender vulnerability program could bring women and men's participation in decision-making. The Center for Environmental Studies (CES) and International Center for Ethnic Studies (ICES, 2005) in Sri Lanka have employed multifaceted disaster assessments during the 2004 tsunami. A gender vulnerability study is one of the programs for identifying varied needs in different communities. As described, impact women groups were marginalized in pre- and post-disaster relief, and recoveries programs as women were not considered as important players in decision-making. Fig. 1 displays the magnitude of the disaster in Kalmunai and Fig. 2 illustrates gender vulnerability assessment in Kalmunai (Eastern Province) in Sri Lanka. Studies carried out on need assessments in tsunami impact communities in 2005 by ICES, Kandy, Sri Lanka, and CES, University of Peradeniya, Sri Lanka, specifically developed questionnaires and qualitative methods such as focus group interviews and community mapping to learn how women and men operate and anticipate pre- and post-disaster relief and recoveries. As field research highlighted, coastal communities especially, women participants described their emotion of threats,

Fig. 1.   A Scene from the 2004 Tsunami Disaster in Kinniya, Sri Lanka.
Source: Ram Alagan, Field Survey (2005).

Fig. 2.   Incorporating Gender in Disaster Recovery Planning in Kinniya, Sri Lanka.
Source: Ram Alagan, Field Survey (2005).

vulnerability, and marginalization in pre- and post-disaster. According to impact women groups, the cultural and societal (Muslim and Tamil) factors have restricted women to engage in the social, physical, and coastal activities. Thus, women including young girls were not prepared to take immediate action during disasters like tsunami. Alternatively, men and boys were fully allowed to take part in any activity in the coastal areas. Because men had open access to the sea and experience in water-related activities, it has been highlighted that men's social behaviors and expectations were different from women. During CES and ICES disaster vulnerability study, men described different feelings and, specifically, job-related disaster recovery issues. It was clearly underlined that due to social and cultural gaps between women and men, both groups behaved differently and articulated that they have specific needs. Figs 1 and 2 explain the importance of skilled research programs to capture vulnerability of women and men in disaster situations.

GENDER AND DISASTERS

In recent years, the world has been facing more and more regular and intense disasters, both natural and man-made, with devastating impacts (Dasgupta, Şiriner, & Sarathi, 2010). Although, gender planning is considered as one of the core domains of social justice and sustainable development, many societies have still been unsuccessful in implementing reasonable decision-making for women in natural disaster relief and recoveries. Dasgupta further illustrates that, in disasters, women play an important role in providing economic, health, and mental assistance to the family and society in post-disaster recovery activities and at the same time enthusiastically and willingly participate in disaster prevention programs. However, for the most part, women's role in disaster recovery has been neglected or marginalized. Since disasters create more damage on women's lives than on men, it is important to develop programs that support women as they are vulnerable than others. Enarson (2000, 2006) states that gender is also seen as an aspect of women's lives more than of men's and as derivative of social class, that is, women are disaster victims because they are poor, and disaster is closely related to women than men in terms of relief and recovery challenges (such as women are facing more challenges for survival – increased work burden and disproportionate burden). Enarson further describes that arising in disagreement to the foremost technocratic emergency management approach, vulnerability theory (Blaikei, Cannon, Davis, & Wisner, 2004; Fordham, 1999) and feminist theory (Enarson, 2000;

Jagger & Rothenberg, 1984) suggest an alternative approach that linking social justice and gender equality to disaster mitigation through sustainable development is inevitably important. Wisner (1993) explains that vulnerability is in combination with the occurrence of a natural disaster. Poverty is one of the main aspects of vulnerability (Momsen, 2010). Wisner further underlines that, women on their own are even more vulnerable and may find it especially difficult to get loans for rebuilding and reestablishing a viable livelihood.

GENDER PLANNING AND MARGINALIZATION

Although there were several local and international organizations engaged in the Sri Lankan tsunami post-disaster recovery, projects often failed to understand the importance of gender relations in people's lives in traditional societies and formulate policies without appreciating local cultural practices and institutions, resulting in loss of traditional sources of status and power of women. In almost every disaster area in Sri Lanka, the lessons learned were the lack of understanding of gender role in a disaster situation. The limited skills have created unprecedented impact in women's lives to overcome post-disaster relief and recoveries. One example, the amount of donations (in dollars) and enthusiasm came from international and local NGOs to support tsunami relief and recovery; if done properly, with more careful planning, (according to local culture and societal beliefs) the country could have achieved a great relief, recovery, and enhanced women lives much more satisfactorily. Unfortunately, as described before, most of the disaster relief and recovery plans did not have the right skills and experts to understand and incorporate the local reality (especially women's participation, and motivation) in disaster relief and recovery decision-making. This situation affects the well-being of women; results in their oppression, violation of rights, and freedom; and puts at risk their comprehensive development and survival. The gender impact of natural disaster reflects the position of women in different cultures, and women generally have less access to resources and less representation at all level of decision-making (Momsen, 2010). Unequal access of women to resources and power and their representation in decision-making process is particularly critical in emergency situations. Thus, it is vital for integrating the gender perspective into all natural disaster-related policies and decision-making processes giving due consideration to the cultural, economic, political, and social differences. But the truth of the challenge is how to implement the theoretical arguments (gender planning and vulnerability theories) over technocratic emergency management approach in real world practice where most of the decisions are highly patriarchal.

SRI LANKAN POST-TSUNAMI RECOVERY AND GENDER PLANNING

Several main actors (government of Sri Lanka and local and international NGOs) have been engaged in the 2004 tsunami disaster relief and recovery planning. Ariyabandu (2005) reveals that several main actors were lacking in competence and skills to engage or consult women participants in disaster recovery plans. Ariyabandu further articulates that many institutions did not have any knowledge on gender planning in the rebuilding process. Also, it was evident that plans such as livelihood recovery, capacity building, and resettlement suffered without proper gender planning and expert knowledge. A number of research programs highlighting many relief and recovery plans were developed without sufficient comprehensive gender focus. Ariyabandu explains that many relief and recovery programs pinpointed that the institutions responsible for capacity building and planning were often not equipped with people with the required skills. It was evident in this study as well. The situation in a number of institutions working in the disaster areas suffered without skills in gender planning. On one hand, it was a chaotic situation to manage the large-scale damage for a country with limited skills. Thus, many implementing institutions were often staffed with technical men rather than personnel with socioeconomic skills to face the situation, most importantly, awareness of gender planning. On the other hand, predomi nantly and traditionally planning practices in Sri Lanka are based on male perception and domination. This was one of the main reasons for most of the post-disaster planning institutions being staffed with men than women. In such a situation, it is a major concern about how pre- and post-disaster planning could be seen from women's eyes than of the men. Sri Lankan post-disaster planning mainly focused on physical construction. While men (technical staff members) were engaged in physical construction and structural aspects, capability of the related socioeconomic and cultural aspects were often neglected or did not get a prominent focus. Such a situation has impacted mainly women and children as their needs and desires were not met. This led to further marginalization and gender-based gaps in disaster relief and recovery planning.

GENDER-BASED POST-DISASTER RECOVERY PLAN

In disaster situation, gender issues have become a vital concern. Thus, gender issues are important for policy formulation that makes development more sustainable. The gender perspective acknowledges that men and women have different roles, activities, and responsibilities in the society and they are socially constructed and determined. These socially created perceptions and roles have negatively impacted women more than men and created more unequaled states for women in societies in a particular disaster situation. To explore the unequaled states and marginalization, the research has involved a series of studies by the CES and ICES, Sri Lanka, in tsunami affected regions.

A team of socioeconomic and Geographic Information Systems (GIS)[1] experts visited a number of affected districts; Southern Province (Hambantota, Matara, and Galle), Western Province (Kalutara), and Eastern Province (Ampara, Batticaloa, and Trincomalee). Field surveys and gender-based study in two tsunami impact districts – Hambantota and Trincomalee – will be discussed here. There were a number of local and international institutions that employed diverse research techniques (qualitative and quantitative) and GIS in the tsunami disaster areas to explore social and physical damage. Mostly, the application of GIS helped to gather information and identify the location of damage. In other words, the function of GIS was limited to a traditional application for disaster mapping. Further, the ability of GIS has not been used to initiate a robust system to support a collaborative approach and gender planning for disaster relief and recovery. This study incorporates GIS as a participatory mapping technique to understand gender differences in tsunami recovery process.

In Hambantota and Kinniya, four local government divisions were surveyed. The CES and ICES have implemented mixed methodologies (gender planning and participatory GIS (PGIS)[2]) to capture required relief and recovery issues from the disaster. Since women deal with a number of challenges, the CES and ICES prioritized their goals using GIS as participatory mapping technique to capture women's needs in post-disaster relief and recovery. Basic mapping tools and participatory mapping guidance were provided to impact groups (women and men) separately, and they were invited to describe their priorities in post-disaster relief and recovery plan. Each group was separated in the exercise to identify the gender discrepancy. With the facilitation of the research team, maps were drawn with impact group's own initiatives. Interestingly, both groups had provided information with absolutely different requirements to be fulfilled in the post-disaster relief and recovery planning (Fig. 3). Fig. 3 illustrates occasions where women and men participated in GIS-based gender participatory mapping.

According to PGIS survey, the following information was prioritized by women's groups in Hambantota (Southern Province) (Table 1).

In Trincomalee District (Eastern Province), two local governmental divisions were surveyed to explore disaster recovery. To capture gender priorities, PGIS mapping was conducted in two different local communities in Kinniya (Figs. 4 and 5). PGIS has been employed to explore the post-disaster relief and recovery plan from the communities. Fascinatingly, once again women's groups highlighted their differences than the men. The following chart explains the differences between women and men in terms of disaster recovery needs (Table 2).

It is important to recognize that women's needs are different than men's, and it requires careful attention in policy planning. As Enarson (1998, 2000) states, seeing disasters "through women's eyes" is extremely vital and it raises a new set of questions, concerns, and planning issues for planners for

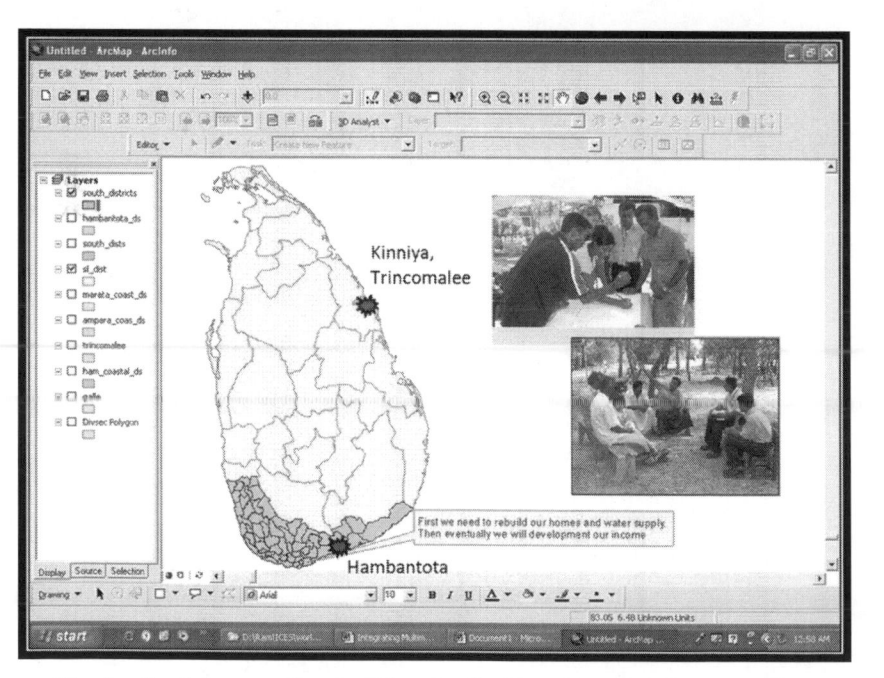

Fig. 3. Participatory Gender Mapping for Post-Tsunami Recovery Plan.
Source: Ram Alagan, Filed Survey (2005).

Table 1.   Identifying Gender Priorities for Post-Tsunami Disaster Relief
and Recovery in Hambantota, Sri Lanka, 2005.

Women Priorities	Men Priorities
• Resettlement sites in interior • Rebuild basic infrastructure facilities • Rebuild religious places • Family protection • Rebuild schools • Rebuild health facilities • Rebuild community integration	• Resettlement sites in sea side • Job protection • Rebuild marketing • Rebuild sports complex • Rebuild fishing facilities • Rebuild schools • Rebuild health facilities • Rebuild youth facilities

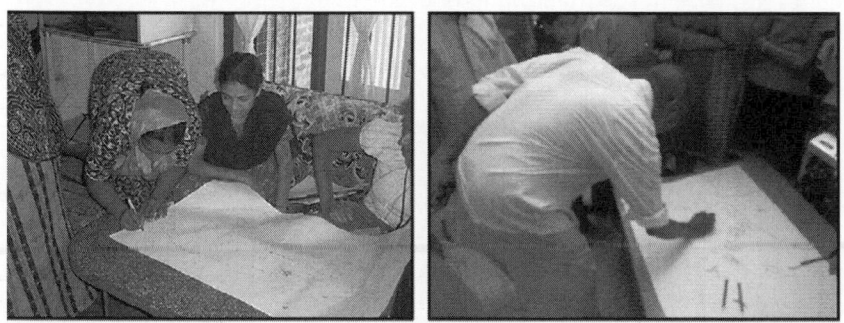

(a)   (b)

Figs. 4a and b. Post-Tsunami Participatory Gender Mapping in Kinniya,
Trincomalee. *Source*: Ram Alagan, Field Survey (2005).

identifying critical system gaps and brings gender centrally into development
and disaster recovery plans. Women are more concerned on protection of
children and families, while men are more interested to rebuild job
protection. On one hand, it is imperative to recognize that job security is
vital to support the livelihood of family. On the other hand, it is also
fundamental to comprehend that women's needs are different and pivotal to
build a family organization. Thus, it is strongly suggested that disaster relief
and recovery plans need diverse gender-based methodologies to capture the
gender difference, preference, and needs. Figs. 4 and 5 illustrate gender
participation in participatory mapping for post-disaster relief and recovery
planning in Kinniya.

Table 2. Identifying Gender Priorities for Post-Tsunami Disaster Relief and Recovery in Kalmunai, Sri Lanka, 2005.

Women Priorities	Men Priorities
• Resettlement sites in interior	• Resettlement sites in sea side
• Family protection	• Job protection
• Sanitary supplies and privacy	• Rebuild marketing
• Culturally appropriate opportunities for worship	• Rebuild sports complex
• Rebuild schools	• Rebuild transportation facilities
• Rebuild religious places	• Rebuild schools
• Rebuild health facilities	• Rebuild fishing facilities
• Rebuild community integration	• Rebuild health facilities
	• Rebuild youth facilities

In addition, it is vital to develop research methods to incorporate gender identities. The ways in which CES and ICES have provided opportunities to women and men differently have created gender differences in post-disaster relief and recovery plan through participatory mapping exercise. The PGIS has also supported planners to explore the differences and acted accordingly in post-disaster relief and recovery planning and policy formulation.

Above distinctions highlight that it is vital to recognize that gender differences need to be documented. Moreover, the patriarchal decision-making practices are lacking in identifying the reality of gender differences and gender equality in a post-disaster situation. In this context, there are a number of post-disaster recovery planning issues that need to be developed. First, develop a set of gender-based issues that are essential in major disaster recovery policy planning. Second, integrate effectively gender analysis in disaster planning at the grassroots and institutional levels. Third, recognize the gender gap in policy planning and establish an immediate action plan for a change. Fourth, identify the basic needs, technical skills, and capacities for gender integration at the planning, implementation, and monitoring stages. Fifth and finally, introduce a cross-cultural research agenda on gender and natural disasters.

NOTES

1. Geographic Information System (GIS) is a system of hardware, software, and data for capturing, managing, analyzing, and displaying all forms of geographically referenced information. GIS also allows people to view, review, understand, question, interpret, and visualize spatial and nonspatial information in many ways

that reveal spatial relationships, patterns, and trends in the form of maps, reports, and graphs. In addition, GIS supports communities and decision-makers to answer questions and solve problems by looking at spatial data in a way that is understood and easily shared.

2. This research employed Participatory Geographic Information Systems (PGIS) methodology. PGIS employs a number of innovative participatory approaches such as two-dimensional GIS, three-dimensional GIS, community mapping, global positioning systems, and diverse participatory workshops. These methods seek to enhance people's access to project data, improve representation, integrate multiple realities, empower local communities, and effectively incorporate local knowledge. PGIS approach also supports initiatives from bottom-up decision-making rather than top-down or male perception.

REFERENCES

Ariyabandu, M. (2005). Gender issues in tsunami recovery panning. In *Tsunami, gender, and recovery*. Online special issue for international day for gender risk reduction. Southasiadisaster.net, 2005.

Blaikei, P., Cannon, T., Davis, I., & Wisner, B. (2004). *At risk: Natural hazards, people's vulnerability and disasters* (2nd ed.). New York, NY: Routledge.

Dasgupta, S., Şiriner, İ., & Sarathi, P. (2010). *Women's encounter with disaster*. Kolkata, India, and London: Frontpage Publication Ltd.

Enarson, E. (1998). Through women's eyes: A gendered research agenda for social science. *Journal of Disaster Studies, Policy and Management, 22*(2).

Enarson, E. (2000). Gender and natural disasters, ILO (International Labour Organization). In: *Focus Programme on Crisis Response, and Reconstruction*. Geneva. Retrieved from http://www.ilo.org/public/english/employment/recon/crisis/download/criswp1.pdf.

Enarson, E. (2006). Gender shapes the social worlds within which natural events occur. An executive summary. In: *Understanding gender differential impacts of tsunami and gender mainstreaming strategies in tsunami response in Tamil Nadu*. Oxfam America and Anawin Trust.

Fordham, M. (1999). The intersection of gender and social class in disaster: Balancing resilience and vulnerability. *International Journal of Mass Emergencies and Disasters, 17*(1), 15–36.

Hyndman, J. (2008). Feminism, conflict and disasters in post-tsunami Sri Lanka. *Gender, Technology and Development, 12*, 101–121.

International Center for Ethnic Studies (ICES) (2005). Qualitative assessment survey of tsunami and non-tsunami villages. Report submitted to World Vision, Sri Lanka.

Jagger, A., & Rothenberg, P. (Eds.). (1984). *Feminist frameworks: Alternative theoretical accounts of the relations between women and men*. New York, NY: McGraw-Hill.

Momsen, J. (2010). *Gender and development* (2nd ed.). London: Rutledge.

Wisner, B. (1993). Disaster vulnerability: Scale, power, and daily life. *Geojournal, 30*(2), 127–140.

THE DECLINING HEALTH STATUS AS FUELLED BY ILLUSORY INTERNAL MIGRATION IN SUB-SAHARAN AFRICA: IS THERE ANY FUTURE?☆

Rasel Madaha and Barbara Wejnert

ABSTRACT

This study reveals that despite the negative effects of migration, the Tanzanian government has not done enough to address migration-related health issues. This is owing to inadequate data or information about effects of migration in the country. Dodoma region, the focus of this study, is selected for its migration-inducing factors as they relate to the declining health status of its inhabitants. Harsh climatic conditions causing irregular and inadequate rainfall and prolonged drought have led to a severe decline of the health of the poor. The region is entirely dependent on subsistence

☆This chapter was also presented at International Research Committee on Disasters (IRCD) Researchers Meeting, organized by them. A partnership between the International Sociological Association's International Research Committee on Disasters and the Natural Hazards Centre on Tuesday, July 12 through Wednesday, July 13, 2011, Omni Interlocken Resort, Broomfield, Colorado, USA. Many thanks to the participants of the conference for sharing useful comments.

Democracies: Challenges to Societal Health
Research in Political Sociology, Volume 19, 133–159
Copyright © 2011 by Emerald Group Publishing Limited
All rights of reproduction in any form reserved
ISSN: 0895-9935/doi:10.1108/S0895-9935(2011)0000019013

agriculture and livestock production. The small-scale production is locally practiced at household level. Extreme poverty motivates rural people to migrate to cities with the main migrant groups being middle school (about 13 to 15 years old) and high school dropouts (15 to 18 years old), and youth including young parents (18 to 35 years old). The rural-urban migration conjoined with harsh climatic conditions significantly downsizes local population, available agricultural labor force, and further endangers food security. More importantly, however, due to exposure to HIV in the cities, most migrants who are unable to find city jobs return home terminally ill with HIV/AIDS, which further adds to impoverishment of rural families and to downsizing of rural population.

INTRODUCTION

Studies on migration have become popular lately as new topics of migration evolve; among them are the separation of migration studies according to typology of international migration or immigration and local urban-rural migration. In modern times, both forms of migration are linked to a broader economic development, social change, political organization, and cultural systems, and hence, it is essential to link the study of migration with development, cultural, economic, and political processes, and these processes of countries complex dynamics (UNESCO, 2008).

Immigration

The current world population of 6.5 billion that is growing by 1.2 percent annually is estimated to cross 9 billion by 2050. This increase largely comprises of youth of less developed countries that are considered as "the South" (Wallerstein, 1999, 2001) and this visible increase is predicted to continue in the imminent future. Under these circumstances, international migration (in fact immigration) to the well-developed Western countries of "the North" (Wallerstein, 1999, 2001) is expected, especially because population growth in poorer countries coincides with static or declining population growth rates and population aging in the North. The pressure on existing public sector pension systems and social welfare programs in the developed countries is expected to fuel immigration (Aderanti, 1991; Dalen, Groenewold, & Schoorl, 2003) from the places where there is no scarcity of human resources in the global South to demanding human resources in countries of the global North. The immigration from African countries that are poor, have low socioeconomic conditions, low wages, high-levels of unemployment, and lack economic opportunity, has already started and will continue in the near future. In addition to economic factors, various political factors, such as war, and social factors, such as tribal stigma, creating fertile grounds for immigration (NIDI, 2008) also contribute to the factor. It includes within Africa and outside of the African continent. International migration has attracted the attention of many scholars across the fields of sociology, anthropology, political science, and economy (Disaster Control Priorities Project, 2007). Much less scholarly attentions are devoted to local migrations and their patterns.

Migration

In most general terms, migration is a movement of people within a country, predominantly from villages to cities that often involves a prolonged change of place of residence. The complexity of migration comes from the fact that it is a continuous, often repeated process rather than a single event, and it is difficult to collect data on. The data is limited to that of census data to provide information on issues such as fertility and mortality. The available census data on migration also presents serious limitations for possible analyses because census data that has been available for many countries has been inadequate to allow full analysis of migration profiles for given groups of migrants as well as their latitudinal movement within the society (Aderanti, 1991; CBASSE, 2008; IUSSP, 1998; Jackson, 1969; URT, 2008a). Jackson also believes that research results on migration are incoherent due to diverse methodologies used by scholars representing various disciplines in social science (Jackson, 1969). Lack of unified, standardized and a comprehensive data source, and uniform methodological approach make migration study difficult to conduct.

This study focuses on migration processes in Tanzania and their effects on population's health status in Mvumi and Chilonwa Divisions of Chamwino district in the Dodoma region. The study effects of migration on the health of the population living in Tanzania is also studied. We specifically try to answer the following question: How does internal migration decline health status of rural inhabitants in Sub-Saharan Africa and Tanzania in particular? We argue that in Tanzania, similarly to other Sub-Saharan countries, rural-urban migration is harmful to migrants as the majority fail to find better living opportunities in cities and return to villages with no resources. Unfortunately not being prepared for life in cities, many migrants are engaged in sexual practices (either as sex-workers or as their clients) and come to villages infected with communicable diseases. Current trends in Tanzania and Dodoma region, in particular, attest to a possibility of the significant decrease of the size of rural population in the near future due to rapid increase of HIV and malaria infections contracted by migrants moving to cities to look for jobs. The inability to find employment in cities and acquired illness further adds to the impoverishment of rural families and crippling of rural lives because they weaken rural agricultural labor and add burden to families of sick migrants. We argue that migration requires greater focus in future studies and calls for the attention of policy makers.

As is the case of most publicly available statistical data, the migration data for Tanzania is inadequate. We conduct the study using mixed methods that combine content analyses of existing statistical data with data from conducted field interviews in villages of Tanzania.

METHODOLOGY

For this study we have selected content analysis of relevant documents and reports following specific guidelines described in literature on the analysis of existing documents (Berg, 1998; Insch, Moore, & Murphy, 1997; Krippendorff, 2004; Neuman, 1994; Silverman, 1993; Woodrum, 1984). In most general terms, content analysis involves systematic identification, classification, and analysis of information relevant to a particular study. For this chapter, documentary information proved to be most useful. According to Yin (2009, pp. 101–105), the kinds of documents that can be used for case studies include letters, memoranda, e-mail correspondence, personal diaries, calendar, personal notes, agenda, announcements, minutes of meetings, written reports of events, proposals, progress reports, formal studies, news clippings, and other articles appearing in the mass media or in community newspapers. Specifically, this study draws experience from two unpublished case studies titled the Role of Food Security Groups' Networks in Poverty Reduction: A case study of Chamwino District, Dodoma region, Tanzania (unpublished MA dissertation of Madaha), and Territory diagnosis and market opportunity identification in Chilonwa and Mvumi divisions in Dodoma region, Tanzania, and Mkuyuni Division in Morogoro region, Tanzania (unpublished consultancy Madaha for LVIA). The two studies employed both quantitative and qualitative data collection methods. A survey questionnaire was used to collect quantitative data, whereas focus group discussion, observations, review of documents from government and NGOs, in-depth interviews, community meetings, and resource mapping served as tools to collect qualitative data. The two reports are supplemented by data from other similar unpublished case studies such as government and NGOs reports. After the two reports were produced, we updated the prior data by sets of new in-depth interviews, observations, review of archival documents, and documents from government and NGOs. Thus, we extended quantitative data available from Tanzania National Census, 2002, by collecting detailed information about life experience of rural-urban migrants.

REGION OF STUDY

Data for this study was obtained from Mvumi and Chilonwa Divisions of Chamwino district, Dodoma region, Tanzania. Dodoma (see Fig. 1) is one of the regions of Tanzania.

The region covers an area of $41,310 \, km^2$ and has 1,698,996 inhabitants (census of August 2002). The region is the 12th largest in Tanzania and it covers about 5 percent of the mainland of the country (not counting the islands). The capital of the region is the city of Dodoma. The region lies at $4°–7°$ latitude South and $35°–37°$ longitude East. Much of the region is a plateau rising gradually from some 830 m in Bahi Swamps to 2,000 m above sea level in the highlands north of Kondoa. The region is almost entirely dependent on agriculture and livestock production practiced locally, largely at the household level despite harsh climatic conditions. There is small-scale processing of agricultural and livestock products. Agriculture is characterized by low productivity resulting from low and erratic rainfall, high evapotranspiration, and low moisture-holding capacity. These conditions compounded by poor farming practice and overgrazing make the region susceptible to extensive soil erosion. The main staples grown in the region include sorghum, bulrush millet, cassava, and maize, while major cash crops are groundnuts, sunflower, simsim and to a lesser extent castor, and pigeon peas. In the late 1970s and early 1980s, grapes and paddy emerged as important cash and food crops respectively. Livestock is the second contributor to the regional economy. The region ranks third in the country in terms of livestock number including cattle, goats, and sheep, however, only a small proportion of the population own livestock. Poultry and piggery farming for commercial purposes are mainly confined to urban and

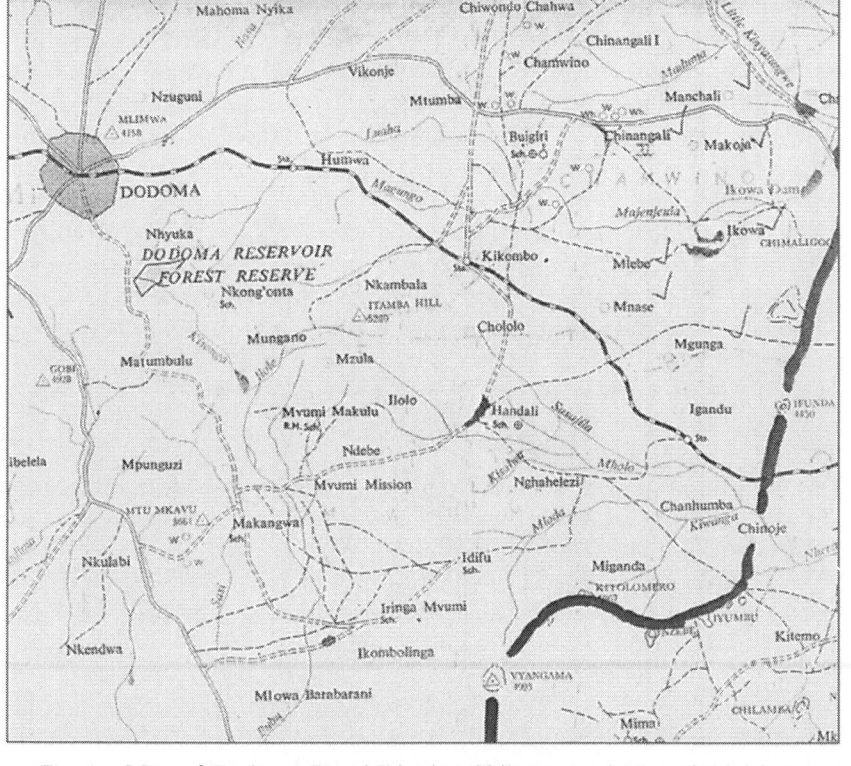

Fig. 1. Map of Dodoma Rural District: Chilonwa and Mvumi Divisions.
Source: Dodoma Rural District.

semi-urban trading centers of the region. In addition, abundant local
chicken production abounds in the region, which is stimulated by high
demand in the Dar es Salaam market (URT, 2008b).

Natural resources include forestry, wildlife, beekeeping, fishing, and
mining but access to them is limited to only a few people. Products such as
timber, logs, poles, wildlife, honey beeswax, fish, salt, and gold are locally
harvested. However, the sector's contribution to the economy of the region
is minimal because of poor technological capacities. Apart from a few small-
scale processing industries such as oil extraction, carpentry, pottery,
blacksmith, and wood carving, whose operation are mostly confined to
urban and trading centers, industrial sector is yet to take shape in the region.

In the Dodoma region of Tanzania, agricultural production used to account for about half of the national income, three-quarters of merchandise exports, while recently the service industry accounts for the largest portion of the nation's income (Research and Analysis Working Group, 2009) providing employment opportunities to about 80 percent of Tanzanians. Agriculture is linked with the nonfarming sector through linkages to agro-processing, consumption, and export. It also provides raw materials to industries and a market for manufactured goods. Agriculture in Tanzania is dominated by smallholder farmers (peasants) cultivating an average farm between 0.9 hectares and 3.0 hectares each. About 70 percent of Tanzania's crop area is cultivated by hand-hoe, 20 percent by ox plough, and 10 percent by tractor. It is rain-fed agriculture. Food crop production dominates the agriculture economy – 5.1 million hectares are cultivated annually, of which 85 percent is under food crops. Moreover, agricultural GDP has grown at 3.3 percent per year since 1985, the main food crops at 3.5 percent and export crops at 5.4 percent per year (URT, 2008a, 2008b). Women constitute the main part of agricultural labor force, even though they do not benefit much from their contribution – this should be an area for further research. Importantly, the major constraint facing the agriculture sector is the falling labor and land productivity due to application of poor technology, dependence on unreliable rain, and presence of irregular weather conditions (CIA, 2004; URT, 2008b). Simply put, Tanzania is fed by agriculture, which heavily depends on manual labor as opposed to mechanized one. Undoubtedly, mechanized agriculture is capable of producing huge quantities of food for a particular country but this is largely absent in Tanzania.

OVERVIEW OF MIGRATION IN TANZANIA

In Tanzania, the net migration is 1.9 migrants out of 1,000 people. Currently the Tanzanian population is 38,478,000. International migrants, 52.2 percent of which are women, make 2.1 percent of Tanzanian population. The current rising trend of international migration in Tanzania can be attributed to many factors including rapid globalization, advancement in transport, communication and technology, deteriorating political, socioeconomic and environmental conditions, demographic factors, and armed conflicts. The patterns of international migration flows are mixed, complex, and challenging (URT, 2008a, 2008c). For example, in Tanzania, there is an increase in the vulnerability to human trafficking among the Tanzanian population: the country has been identified as a country of origin, transit, and destination for trafficked persons. Trafficking in Tanzania is mostly internal; for instance, girls and boys are trafficked from rural to urban areas for the purpose of domestic labor, commercial agriculture, fishing and mining industries, and child prostitution. On the international level, women are mostly trafficked out of the country for prostitution and/or domestic work (IOM, 2008).

The world has experienced urbanization over the years but the huge rise in the number of people moving to towns and cities is a recent phenomenon. In 1950, less than one – in three people lived in urban areas. The world had just two so-called "mega cities" with populations in excess of 10 million: New York and Tokyo. Today, there are at least 20. Greater Tokyo, the world's biggest city, has expanded from 13 million residents in 1950, to today's figure of 35 million (IFPRI, 2008). A similar situation is also happening in Tanzania where migration to urban areas has continued unabated and increased during the program of government decentralization and the creation of new provincial capitals in the 1970s. Since the economic liberalization in the 1980s, rural to urban migration has become more permanent with migrants investing profits in ventures in or near the towns rather than remitting them to their areas of origin (Black, Hilker, & Pooley, 2004).

Data on migration is missing in the key documents of Tanzanian government. Thus, for example, migration is mentioned only once in the National Strategy for Growth and Reduction of Poverty (NSGRP)[1] and the government's latest report, Poverty and Human Development Report, 2007, does not include data on migration. The only available quantitative data are from the Tanzania Main statistical table pages 363–364 that reports on migration of people from their birth place to various other regions across the country but not on rural-urban or seasonal migration. The 2002 National Census data do not include any information on the reason why people migrate from one place to another nor what the outcomes of their movement are (National Bureau of Statistics, 2006). Likewise, scholarly explanations of the causes and effects of migration in Dodoma are also very limited. However, there are some case studies that have covered Southern, Northern, and Western regions but these studies mainly report on refugees who migrate from neighboring countries such as Rwanda, Burundi and Democratic Republic of Congo to Tanzania (Black et al., 2004; Lerise, 2001). Moreover, there are limited available statistical data that discuss the effect of migration on the health of the population in Tanzania.

Despite the Tanzanian government's awareness of massive rural-urban migration, there are visibly limited governmental programs that could help migrant workers. The supply of new houses in urban areas is outstripped by massive rural-urban migration, and where such housing is available, it is of low quality, in a poor environment, and with inadequate or no access to clean water, electricity, roads, and sewerage lines and its impact on urban planning little has been done to address migration (Vice-President's Office, 2005). There is little recognition of the living conditions and quality of housing in rural areas. Nonetheless, living conditions are the main stimulants of migration.

There is no program that addresses the negative outcomes of migration. The Tanzanian government claims that fertility and mortality (URT, 2008a) are the most important population concerns. Yet, the effects of migration on the Tanzanian economy cannot be underestimated especially because agricultural production is based on manual labor as mechanized agriculture is largely absent, therefore any negative outcomes of migration on rural labor force or health of rural population poses serious consequences for the future of the nation. Other effects of migration such as increasing poverty of migrants and their families, potential ethnic conflict of migrants out of their place of origin also pose economic and political challenges for policy makers (African Union, 2008). Since migrants are not a homogenous group, in addition to the same basic needs they also have needs that are specific to their groupings (URT, 2008c), thus the government of the United Republic of Tanzania should welcome international dialogue on migration and the opportunity it has provided for putting the issue of migration and development on the worldwide agenda.

MIGRATION PUSH AND PULL FACTORS IN CENTRAL TANZANIA

One of the most commonly known theoretical concepts in migration research is the so-called push-pull model for the explanation of the causes of migration: the push-pull framework gives insight into the different forces at work to explain migration (African Union, 2008). In its most limited form, the push-pull model consists of a number of negative or push factors that cause people to move away, in combination with a number of positive or pull factors that attract migrants in a region. Lists of push factors include elements as economic, social, and political hardships in the poorer regions or countries, while the pull factors include the comparative advantages in the richer regions or countries. Combinations of push and pull factors would then determine the size and direction of flows (Portes & Böröcz,

1989). The fundamental assumption is that the more disadvantaged a place is, the more likely it will be to produce migration. The general criticism is that such models do not explain why migration from some regions is high, while migration from other regions is not the same or not to the same extent, or why within regions some people move and others stay.

A discussion on push and pull factors of the two regions is important as it will shed light on the key discussion on the effects of migration on agricultural production. The push–pull factors identified in this study are geographical locations, characteristic of local population, transport, financial services, agro-ecology and productive assets, household food security, social and organizational assets, and the relationship between community and neighboring villages.

Migration Pull and Push Factor in Mvumi and Chilonwa Divisions, Dodoma

Generally, the living conditions in Mvumi and Chilonwa divisions as well as the rest of Dodoma region are harsh as they force people to migrate rather than make them immigrate into the region. Agricultural production in the region is, by and large, carried out at household level. Crop production is estimated to engage 85 percent of the total regional labor force and is a major contributor to the Regional Domestic Product. However, the development of the agricultural sector is besieged by a number of constraints that include unpredictable rainfall, poor tillage, and inadequate input support (URT, 2008b). Because there is no clear line for push and pull factors – what pushes people out today, may pull them back tomorrow – the discussion on push-pull factors incorporates characteristics of local population, transport, financial services, food security, local agricultural production, social and organizational network, and interrelations with neighboring villages.

Local Population
Mvumi and Chilonwa are regions of Chamwino district in Dodoma, Tanzania. The main ethnic group is Gogo. However, in trade centers like Chalinze, Mvumi Makulu, and Mvumi Mission there is a mixture of other Tanzanian ethnic groups. Mvumi region has a total population of 65,000 people as per the 2002 census. On the other hand, the population of Chilonwa region is 57,690. In the two districts, the average size of the family is 6–9 members and in some villages a relevant percentage of household (25 percent) are families of single mothers.

Both the regions dominate agricultural production and small-scale livestock keeping. Part of the region is under forest reserve policy managed by Tanzanian government, which contributes to scarcity of land that could be utilized for cultivation and pasture which encourages migration out of this region – the push factor (LVIA, 2005).

Transport

The main road runs through Mvumi division in the direction of Dodoma and to the asphalt road – Dodoma to Dar es Salaam. It is a well-built road (Mvumi-Dodoma-Dar es Salaam) as it is passable by daily public transport throughout the year. Also a number of lorries of 3–6 tons capacity owned by business people who collect agricultural products during the harvesting time from May to July pass this road. Nevertheless, minor roads which link different villages of the division are not easily passable throughout the year. On these roads, only four-wheelers can travel during the rainy season. Chilonwa region has similar road infrastructure (Madaha, 2006).

In addition to bus and car transportation that is possible on the main roads, local transport is organized using oxen and ox-cart, which are owned by farmers, but these are very few. Consequently, transportation cost is relatively high. Poor roads, high transportation cost, and absence of reliable inexpensive means of transportation add to the push away factor.

Financial Services

Both divisions lack essential financial services – there is no bank or any Savings and Credit Cooperatives (SACCOS) at village and division level (Madaha, 2006). Thus, majority of the rural population in the region does not have access to banks to receive credits to purchase agricultural land that is needed to boost agricultural production. At the same time, the rural population is too poor to purchase land by cash, without credit (URT, 2008b). Consequently, absence of those services inhibits increase of agricultural production and an increase of farmers' income. One of the keys to farmers' success is availability of financial services.

Household Food Security

Majority of people in the divisions are affected by transient food insecurity and a large percentage of them is chronically underfed. For instance, in the years 2005 and 2006, food situation was good for the medium- and high-class (see Table 1) for the whole season. However, farmers of lower class, even if rainfall was relatively abundant, suffered from shortage of food.

Table 1. Wealth Ranking at Mvumi Division 2005.

Wealth Rank: Mvumi Division		
Lower	Definition	Poor clothing quality and dirty
		House standard is poor: *tembe* type of very low quality
		Unable to assist their children for school materials and some of them are not able even to complete standard seven
		Not in a position to contribute and paying for health services
		Deeply involved in wage labor
		Not able to pay for pure water: usage of unsafe water
		Able to own and manage only 1–2 acres but not effectively
		Number of meals is once per day
	Percent	30
Medium	Definition	They are able to send their children to primary school and few of them can manage to send the children to secondary school
		They are able to contribute and pay for the health services
		Their houses are good; some are roofed by iron sheet
		They are able to keep even small animal like pigs, goats, and chicken
		Number of meals is twice per day
		They own small shops for giving service to their colleague at the village
		Able to own about 2–5 acres and manage it and getting good harvest
		They are able to own even a bicycle and radio
	Percent	60
High	Definition	They are able to own at least one pair of oxen
		Able to own about 5–10 acres of land and they are in a position to manage it and get good harvest
		They are able to get three meals per day
		Good standard of house and clothing materials
	Percent	10

To avoid hunger and starvation poor people work as laborers on others' fields and do not get time to cultivate their own plots. They work as agricultural labors within and outside their areas, mainly in Kongwa district, in divisions of Zoissa, Hogoro, Songambele, and Mkoka. The main activity of laborers is tillage, planting, and weeding (Madaha, 2007). After the rainy season, these laborers also work as hired hands in harvesting and maize threshing. During good years, when there is adequate rainfall, only 10 percent of the population works as hired hands outside their villages, while the rest of them work within the village for wealthy people. Because they work on fields owned by others, the plots owned by hired hands are not cultivated and do not produce any income. Even during good, rainy years these farmers have no time to engage in agricultural production at their plots and steadily become more dependent on sale of their labor and less on the production from cultivation of their own land. Since manual labor is inexpensive in comparison to gains from own agricultural production, the farmers who are hired hands increasingly become poorer.

During drought years, as much as 50 percent of the total population – among the lower and the medium class – are forced to work as hired hands. Especially in Mvumi division, there is only a small area of land that is available for cultivation as the larger area is under government forest reserve since 1986, the Dodoma Land Rehabilitation Program (HADO: a Swahili acronym for *Hifadhi Ardhi Dodoma*). The low and the medium classes of this region, thus, have limited land available for cultivation. The enactment of forest reserve forced livestock keepers to move livestock out of the division as part of an important land rehabilitation program. Forest reservation was necessary because overgrazing and over cropping threatened to deplete all of the scarce forests in the division. The program has introduced the concept of partnership management to ensure that natural resources are productively utilized and sustainably managed. In Tanzania this program is still at a very limited level (Nkwilima, 1999).

At this point, the number of livestock in the division is small because there is no grazing. Also, livestock keeping is not popular in the division since Chief Mazengo, one of the traditional leaders of Mvumi Gogos, used to refuse promotion of livestock raising in the area. Lack of grazing land added to the cost of livestock keeping, and particularly expensive is keeping oxen, which in turn affects crop production (Madaha, 2006). Therefore, food insecurity is one of the main factors forcing people out of the divisions. Food insecurity and poverty leads to dropouts from secondary school as families cannot afford to pay school fees. For example, in *Ndehwe* village in 2004, about 32 pupils were selected to join secondary school but only 10 managed to pay the school fees and the rest could not continue their education (Madaha, 2006).

Agro-ecology and Productive Assets
Mvumi and Chilonwa divisions are semidry areas – rainfall is around 400 to 500 mm per annum. In few years, that is, 1979, 1987, 1991, and 2001 harvest was in plenty due to sufficient rainfall. However, such periods are rare and unpredictable: the vagaries of weather (i.e., the amount, reliability, and distribution of rainfall) constrain production of crops grown in the division. Accordingly, majority of farmers in fertile areas, hesitate to increase production because of unpredictable rainfall. About 60 percent of agricultural

production is dependent on the hand-hoe resulting into poor tiling capacity, low soil conservation, low water conservation and low labor productivity. Worst is, only a few progressive farmers have access to fertilizer, pesticides, and improved seeds. Consequently, agricultural production is limited, but naturally produced (URT, 2008b).

On the other hand, the soil allows production of a variety of crops – a great proposition of the soil, in the divisions, is sandy, suitable for millets, groundnuts, and bambara nuts. Another is the red clay soil, suitable for growing maize, tomatoes, and sesame. Food crops include sorghum (marcia and pato variety), millet, maize, cassava, pigeon peas, and sweet potatoes. Millet is mainly consumed for stiff porridge (*ugali in swahili*) and local beer production. Similarly, maize is the most important cereal used for *ugali* and commercial use. Sorghum is the second most important cereal and it is mainly traded, together with maize during the good years. Both cereals have conservation problems as opposed to millet as they are susceptible to many pests. Cassava, on the other hand, is cultivated mainly for home consumption.

Cash crops (see Table 2) are leguminous crops (bambara nuts, pigeon peas), sesame, sugarcane, grape, mangoes, papaya, tomatoes, and sunflower (Madaha, 2006). It has to be noted that the main cash crops are sesame, groundnuts, and sunflower. However, due to the low price, sunflower production has been reduced. Leguminous crops such as pigeon peas are consumed as a fresh vegetable and are sold when ripe. Likewise, bambara nuts make a big part of protein source for home consumption (Madaha, 2007).

Table 2.   Area Cultivated in Mvumi Division 2005.

Type of Crop	Size Cultivated in Hectare
Brush finger millet (Uwele)	428.2
Maize	505.7
Cassava	160
Sorghum	70.3
Sweet potatoes	16.3
Groundnuts	552.8
Sunflower seeds	4.47
Grape	29
Simsim	40.1
Leguminous	186.67
Other	325.46
Total	2,319

The divisions have a tradition of selling agricultural products to generate income for household needs. The markets for the agricultural products are Dodoma town and the city of Dar es Salaam. Marketing information is mainly available at the market place in Dodoma and Kibaigwa towns when agricultural products have already been transported (see Table 3). As a result, the bargaining power of the farmer selling their produce is very limited. Mobile phone network covers major part of the division but has not yet been fully utilized. Better access to information about sales and marketing would assist farmers and help them to increase their bargaining power (Madaha, 2006).

Agricultural products obtained in the divisions are traded mainly through middleman from in or outside the divisions. Only few farmers are able to transport their products, especially groundnuts, directly to Dar es Salaam city, which is the largest city in Tanzania and serves as the market for agricultural products from different parts of Tanzania.

Social and Organizational Assets
From 1965 to 1970, Mvumi division was home to four functional rural cooperative societies cultivating cereals, groundnuts, and also involved in castor oil and wax production as well as commercialization of the products. This happened at a time when there was social cohesion and initiative in both the political and the economical sectors: the cooperatives were controlled by the government who used them to achieve its policy objectives that were often not approved by the local citizens (Madaha, 2006).

Likewise, the presence of the Anglican Church (Dioceses of Central Tanganyika-DCT) has been important in the area, with the foundation of a village center called Mvumi Mission, which takes the name of the DCT initiative. The church offered important social services like a referral hospital and a small airport; the two still exist to date. Until few years ago, the development program was active in several villages near the mission and among others with a program of keeping cattle for milk production with limited availability of pasture areas.

Similarly, in the past, the government supported promotion of farmers groups: the promotion was mainly through provision of credit for petty business (farm and nonfarm), tree seedling production for HADO program, and livestock keeping (zero grazing and small animals). Moreover, honey production was successfully promoted with support of the international aid. There was a group of 40 farmers dealing with beekeeping. Only one farmer remained (renamed herein Stephine Kayunga) after the NGO phased out. The farmer owns about 200 local hives with a capacity of 20 liter of honey per

Table 3. Production and Marketing Data in Mvumi and Chilonwa Divisions 2005.

Type of Crop	Unit	Lower Price TAS/Tin (18–20 kg) Season Min.	Max.	Month	Higher Price TAS/Tin (18–20 kg) Season Min.	Max.	Month	Production Capacity Per Acre	Acres Owned	Cropping System
Millet	TAS/tin	500	800	June–July	2,500	4,000	December–January	2–3 bags	1–3	Monocropping
Sorghum	TAS/tin	1,000		June–July	2,000	2,000	December	6–12 bags	3	Monocropping
Maize	TAS/tin	1,500	2,000	June–July	2,500	3,000	December–March	6–12 bags	3	Monocropping
Groundnuts	TAS/tin	1,200		April–October	3,000	3,000	December–January	6–8 bags	3	Mixed cropping
Simsim	TAS/kg	450		June	700	700	July–December	10–12 bags	1–3	Monocropping
Sunflower seeds	TAS/kg	250		June–August	500	500	October–December	4 bags	1	Monocropping
Grapes	TAS/kg	300		March	500	700	September–October	One tan	1–2	Monocropping
Chicken	Unit	800						10–30		Monocropping
Choya	TAS/kg	200	2,000	June	2,500	3,000	October			
Sugarcane	TAS/acre	200,000								Just scattered in the field

hive per annum. The farmer's main market is in Dodoma town. To date, Mvumi division has only a few farmers groups and most of them are poorly managed, both administratively and financially, with no prospect of future development. Majority of the groups failed after the beginning and the eventual repayment of the credit. The limited number of farmers' groups reflects the insufficiency of governmental programs. New interventions need to focus on the weaknesses of prior developments to be sustainable (Madaha, 2006).

In contrast with Mvumi division, the division of Chilonwa has six cereal banks, locally known as *"Benki Mazao,"* operating in Mgunga, Chalinze, Manchali, Makoja, Mnasse, and Chinangali villages. These banks provide food security credits to be repaid in agricultural products, mainly in sorghum, and a commercial credit to be repaid in cash. While the food security credit is largely or completely repaid by all cereal banks, the cash credit is less demanded. Yet, community leaders of the cereal banks claim that the commercial function of the bank is important for the local economy. This might hold true for maize, not sorghum, which is valued in many places of Tanzania for its deliciousness (when used as *ugali*). To regain funds cereal banks need to sell the repaid sorghum in the market at a competitive price and to reduce storage costs. However, the banks' workers have limited knowledge about market mechanisms and processes that operate during trade transactions. Among other problems is limited knowledge about the demand for type of crop (crop variety and timing), poor knowledge on quality issues and relative know-how (purity, selection, conservation etc.), and lack of updated information and communication on market prices (Madaha, 2007). Established banks are economic assets for communities, they act as reducers of migration and need to be better utilized in the future. Most modifications need to be done in areas such as cereal storage, commercialization of crops, and management skills.

Relationship Between Community and Neighboring Villages
In the time of food shortage, farmers are able to get credit from their fellow villagers. The credit is paid on the following agricultural season with an interest of 50 percent (Madaha, 2007). Such credit is only given to those of the medium class (see Table 1) but not to the lower class who are incapable of repaying the credits. Credit can also be obtained by people from neighboring villages, when the borrower can have a guarantor for the credit to be taken. Generally speaking, credit has a very high interest rate and contributes to the poverty cycle. However, the situation can be addressed by the formation of SACCOs that offer financial services suitable for rural areas.

THE EFFECTS OF MIGRATION ON HEALTH STATUS

By all measures, rural population in Sub-Saharan Africa and Tanzania, in particular, is unhealthy if we take into account the World Health Organization's (WHO) definition.[2] Promoting and protecting health, as revealed by WHO (2010), is essential to human welfare and sustained economic and social development. More than three decades ago, the Alma-Ata Declaration signatories recognized that the population's health contributes both to a better quality of life for people and also to global peace and security. In Tanzania, many health risks are an outcome of migration. Migration in Tanzania is not a new phenomenon as the history of rural-rural and rural-urban migration dates from precolonial and colonial period, when labor was recruited from neighboring countries to provide a workforce for plantation agriculture. Nevertheless, in postindependence Tanzania, following a Marxist socialist development path, long-distance rural to rural migration slowed due to a policy focus on community level farming. However, seasonal labor migration still takes place in rural areas as extra labor is required during harvesting, for example, to what were communal sisal farms near the coast. In southern Tanzania, research suggests that male migration to save and invest in rural areas is also common, although such investment is unlikely to have significant returns. In northern Tanzania, however, opportunities for migration appear to be especially important for marginalized women who migrate permanently to urban and semi-urban areas in search of employment (Black et al., 2004). In contrast, the situation in Central Tanzania, the focus of this study, is unique because throughout the year people move out of villages temporarily either in search for food or to seek better living conditions. In other words, migration in the area is circular and seasonal, rather than permanent, and thus it is difficult to depict its effect on health of individuals.

Consequently, the complexity of migration patterns underscores the need for case studies to thoroughly understand the effects of migration. The overall increases in circular and temporary migration suggest that migration is part of wider household strategies that involve multi-activity – including farming and nonfarming income sources – over multiple locations. According to Bah et al. (2003), migrant members contribute to their households' welfare and return on a regular basis. A study of rural-urban linkages in Mali, Nigeria, and Tanzania suggests that about 50 percent of rural households in the study areas have at least one migrant member, with peaks of up to 80 percent in drought-prone areas like central Tanzania (Bah et al., 2003). As our study reveals, however, many of those who migrate, often contract diseases such as HIV contributing almost nothing to the household income.

Effects of Migration in Mvumi and Chilonwa Divisions, Dodoma Region

In Dodoma region, groups that commonly migrate are school dropouts (about 13 to 15 years old), primary school alumni or seventh-grade leavers (15–18 years old), youths (18–35 years old both farmers and businessmen), farmers-parents (fathers and mothers), and government employees (Madaha, 2006).

Movement Out

Majority of the migrants are school dropouts and seventh-grade graduates. They often seek employment by migrating to nearby cities and towns. The main destinations are usually the city of Dar es Salaam and Dodoma and Morogoro towns. The city of Dar es Salaam is the destination for the majority of migrants who search for employment. Some of them temporarily live with their relatives in the city and if it happens that they find a job they settle permanently. Others without relatives in the city leave the village searching for employment and return to their villages if they do not find employment. Their situation is much worse since they do not have a place to stay; they often live as temporary couples with lack of food, accommodation, and often contract HIV.

Similarly, school dropouts migrate throughout the year, they leave studying before the completion of primary school education. Many seventh-grade leavers migrate immediately after completing standard seven. Standard seven leavers are the majority of youth migrants; they migrate to urban areas in the months of November, December, and January (soon after standard seven examinations). Most of the youths who migrate to urban areas usually lack essential skills to secure a reliable employment. Also, rural youth grow up in a culture that does not typically support entrepreneurship hence they can only find unskilled, low paid jobs such as housekeeping or shop keeping. Often the earned income is insufficient to meet their basic needs.

Some of the dropouts become petty businessmen known as "Marching guys," *Wamachinga* in Kiswahili because they sell commodities on foot from one place to another. The activity is not safe, involves confrontations with the police (the activity is illegal) who seize their properties compelling them to start again. Often times, they use of drugs, which largely increases their risk of contracting HIV. Some school dropouts and seventh-grade leavers engage in petty theft, armed robbery, drug abuse, and unprotected prostitution or unsafe sex. Such crimes often lead to contraction of HIV/ AIDS and many social ills like family crises, mental disease, imprisonment, and deaths (URT, 2007). Unemployment is the main challenge facing the youth in Tanzania. For example, 700,000 youths from primary, secondary, and higher learning institutions enter the labor force annually but only 40,000 can find employment in any formal sector of the economy (Shaidi, 2008; URT, 2007). Therefore, youth constitute 60 percent of all the people who are unemployed. As the Tanzania Poverty and Human Development Report (2007) shows, finding work is more difficult in cities where unemployment for Tanzanians aged 18–34 is 41.4 percent than in villages where the unemployment rate is 8.6 percent. Unskilled youth migration to urban areas very rarely ends with profitable employment.

Parents (husbands, wives, and single parents) constitute another category of migrants. On the one hand, housewives go to neighboring villages to do petty businesses such as selling of agricultural products or food vending. They frequently travel to markets in Dodoma and Morogoro towns to sell their products (especially groundnuts and simsim). This is particularly frequent after the harvest season from July to October. Although majority of them have already harvested all their crops, there is still need to prepare land for the new season (August–September) and sowing of seeds (October– November). Housewives usually leave their villages with a specific business, which is usually selling the products from their field, and return when their work is done (Madaha, 2007). On the other hand, husbands (heads of households) normally move out of their villages from September to November, a period in which land preparation and sowing is being done. They usually travel to nearby urban areas (Kongwa, Dodoma, and Dar es Salaam) to look for temporary employment because in many cases their harvest is not sufficient to feed the family for the whole year. Also, husbands more frequently become involved in short-term relationships with other women, contracting diseases such as HIV. The spread of HIV infection leads to a frequent contraction of HIV by rural population migrating to work in cities. The migrants return to villages after becoming ill with AIDS adding burden instead of help to farmers families.

The seasonal migration of husbands usually brings less benefit to families than the migration of wives. In most cases, husbands return from cities empty-handed and often with HIV infection. As our study shows, husbands' migrate because they find it easier to abandon their families rather than watch them die of starvation (it is considered very shameful for a man to be unable to feed his family). Women, on the other hand, feel more responsible for their children's well-being and even when there is of lack of food mothers never abandon children (Author, 2007). In Dodoma, it is quite obvious that women play a very significant role in maintaining and managing household food security undergoing difficult situations until their husbands return. The migration of population often has severe health consequences on the households as the farm labor is reduced and the health of farmers, who contract diseases (e.g., HIV), declines.

Movement In

Government employees and businessmen are the main groups that move into the villages. Government employees are usually assigned permanent jobs in the village and they start a new life in the community (Madaha, 2007). These include teachers, health workers, agricultural extension officers, and Village Executive Officers (VEOs). Some agricultural extension officers move in and out throughout the year. They are assigned a number of villages, usually to conduct training, survey, and meetings aimed at boosting agriculture. These groups do not pose significant health risks, though HIV cases are reported among them as well. On the other hand, those who do business (the so-called "Middleman") move into the villages seasonally usually during the months of crop harvest from May to July. They usually buy products at very low prices from village farmers, for instance groundnuts, sesame, and grapes and sell them in urban areas. The business people from urban areas often get infected with HIV that is spreading to rural communities when they indulge in casual relations with women in villages.

The local communities perceive those who move into the villages (such as teachers and other government employees) as the "incomers" that have higher life standards and higher social status than those moving out to migrate to cities.

In recent years, there had been an increase of drought in Tanzania affecting the agriculture and migration pattern as the majority of rural people move to urban areas in search of employment and some move out seasonally for petty businesses. Not many succeed in finding jobs and hence return to home, often secretly, in the last days of their lives after being infected with HIV. This adds a heavy burden to family members in the villages. During massive migration, movement of people is a negative phenomenon as many of the strong young men migrate to urban areas and the village loses main labor power required for agricultural production. More distressingly, returning back with diseases further impoverishes the families in villages who use the little income they have to treat the infected and use their time to care of the sick instead of working on the fields.

Consequently, time and money which would have been used for investment in developmental projects of individual households are used for the care of the poor health of returnees.

CONCLUSION AND RECOMMENDATIONS

Conclusion

In Dodoma, generally the rate of out-migration is higher than in-migration because life in a village is quite difficult. The climatic conditions are not suitable for agricultural production, which consists mainly of cereal production and requires a lot of rainfall. According to our respondents, to counter these processes a significant number of drought-resistant crop varieties that thrive in the area could be planted. Harsh climatic conditions, as claimed by respondents, make majority of the people move out of the villages to urban areas to seek employment or move out temporarily for small businesses. However, those who migrate to urban areas usually fail to find secure employment and return to their villages within a short time. Many of them are infected with diseases, in most cases with HIV.

The trend of population dynamics (moving out) poses serious health threats because many of the strong young men categorized as "youths" and "husbands" migrate to urban areas contributing to the loss of family labor. It is not easy to find a permanent job in urban areas that do not offer opportunities for unqualified labor, so many people who migrate to cities return to their respective villages, many sick with HIV/AIDS. Data from many countries show that the concentration of poverty is shifting from rural to urban areas. Although many rural people move to the cities seeking to improve their well-being, they often remain mired in poverty and squalor. Rampant violence, flimsy housing, and filthy living conditions, along with hunger and malnutrition, are becoming a reality for many people as cities grow (IFPRI, 2008; Infoforhealth, 2008). It would be much better if villagers use local opportunities available in their villages instead of migrating to cities that worsens the life of their families (Kinver, 2008).

Potential Policy Recommendations

Peasants in the region are largely small-scale family farmers working in agriculture affected by inadequate rainfall, poor soil conditions, and low crop yield production. Road accessibility is poor especially in some villages of Mvumi division. The communication and market system is under-developed and often fragile. The focus of farmers to promote their entrepreneurship, a process of diversification, and marketing innovation, in the area should coherently support the local initiatives and the innovative-ness of farmers, especially when migration fails to successfully execute development interventions. If migration is to be reduced the following are recommended:

1. It is believed that growth of cities, the development of new resources, and territories depends upon settlement, temporary and permanent, of individuals in diverse locations away from their place of birth and upbringing (Jackson, 1969). However, urban areas of Tanzania are already saturated with people because nearly half of active people in urban areas are unemployed. Unemployment in rural areas of Tanzania is much less and it is mainly due to underutilization (URT, 2007). In rural areas, there are a lot of unused resources that provide economic opportunity to majority of Tanzanians. It is recommended that the government and other development partners should improve the infrastructure in rural areas to allow full utilization of human and nonhuman resources.

2. In Dodoma, women temporarily migrate to known destinations to sell their agricultural products. Consequently, they come back home with an income that is equally shared among all members of the household, and children, especially, benefit from the earned income. Government and development agents should devote particular attention to helping women, if they want to improve the living standard in the area.

3. Majority of the returnees are HIV positive. Family members and other relatives are the ones responsible for the provision of homecare for the victims. Accordingly, HIV education is critically needed to protect family members from HIV infection as married women and men migrate seasonally to urban areas that have high rates of HIV infections and not knowing about protective sex may end up contracting HIV. Similarly, businessmen and other groups migrating to the region, seasonally or permanently, pose a risk to the local population. Also, education on care for people with HIV/AIDS is needed for families who care for the sick with HIV/AIDS.

4. Tanzanian government claims that fertility and mortality are the most important population components as compared to migration component (National Bureau of Statistics, 2006). Also, government policy on HIV/AIDS ignores migration problems which are, according to our study, the

main cause of HIV/AIDS infections. Undoubtedly, migration will be a major problem of the 21st century and will therefore pose certain social, economic, and political challenges for policy makers who will need to control migration if life in African societies have to be improved (African Union, 2008). Thus, governments in African countries should devote greater attention to migration issues. It would be wise for the country to establish a National Migration policy.

5. Community Cereal Banks are an important social asset in Central Tanzania. However, there is inefficient operation of Community Cereal Banks as far as management of the funds in circulation and food loans are concerned. This is mainly a result of negative community perception with regard to developmental organizations run by Europeans. It is therefore recommended that leadership of the banks, NGOs, and Local Government Authorities (LGAs) in collaboration with other developmental partners in the area should launch campaigns aimed at changing the attitude or mind-set of both bank members and other community members. This can be done through village meetings across all villages as well as the use of folk media across the villages carrying the message of encouraging support of bank operations. Understanding the community perception and past interventions may ensure successful implementation of any development projects.

6. Considering that the region faces frequent drought, particularly in Central Tanzania, it is recommended that farmers should engage in production of drought-tolerant crops such as sorghum, sunflower, groundnuts, simsim, and millet. Moreover, the irrigation system should be improved to stabilize agricultural production in Tanzania. Stable production would improve food security, increase farmers' productivity and incomes, and produce higher valued crops such as vegetables or flowers. Increased production would directly slow the migration process.

7. In Central Tanzania, farmers lack reliable information on markets and have no entrepreneurial skills. Consequently, a middleman exploits the farmers paying unfair prices for their agricultural products. Creation of farmers' organizations could support rural families and therefore reduce negative effects of migration. Farmers' organizations have a potential to empower the rural populations to increase their productive capabilities and as a result to reduce poverty.

8. Since youth (school dropouts and seventh-grade leavers) constitutes a significant proportion of those migrating to urban areas, not finding jobs in the cities add to impoverishment of their families. Tanzanian youth constitutes nearly 65 percent of Tanzanians. It is a potential labor force,

population of activists, and agents of change in their communities and countries. While much effort has been made on the eradication of poverty, little attention has been directed toward youth unemployment that is a fundamental cause of poverty. Paying little attention to youth constitutes poor governance (Shaidi, 2008). The situation affects the growth of the Tanzanian economy and increases poverty. Tanzania needs to create an environment suitable for youth employment. Government and other development partners should launch programs aimed at equipping youth with the skills necessary for opportunities available in the rural areas. This will in turn reduce the negative outcomes of migration and boost government efforts to reduce poverty and stimulate economic growth.

NOTES

1. The strategy can be downloaded at www.tanzania.go.tz/pdf/nsgrptext.pdf
2. According to the World Health Organization (WHO), health is as a state of complete physical, mental, and social well-being and not merely the absence of disease or infirmity.

REFERENCES

Aderanti, A. (1991). South-North migration: The African experience. *International Migration' Washington: International Organization for Migration Quarterly Review, 29*(2), 205–222.

African Union (2008). *The migration policy framework for Africa*. Addis Ababa: AU. Retrieved from http://www.africa-union.org/root/au/Conferences/Past/2006/November/SA/EU/EXCL276(IX)_Strategic_Framework_for_Policy_Migration.doc

Author, R. (2007). *The role of food security groups networks in poverty reduction: A case study of Chilonwa division in Chamwino district, Dodoma region, Tanzania*. Dissertation, Sokoine University of Agriculture. Unpublished manuscript.

Bah, M., Cissé, S., Diyamett, B., Diallo, G., Lerise, F., Okali, D., ... Tacoli, C. (2003). Changing rural-urban linkages in Mali, Nigeria and Tanzania. *Journal of Environment and Urbanization, 15*(2), 13–24.

Berg, B. L. (1998). *Qualitative research methods for the social sciences* (3rd ed). Boston, MA: Allyn & Bacon.

Black, R., Hilker, L.M., & Pooley, C. (2004). *Migration and pro-poor policy in East Africa*. Working Paper No. C7. Development Research Centre on Migration, Globalisation and Poverty, University of Sussex.

CBASSE (2008). *Demographic change in sub-saharan Africa*. Retrieved from http://www.nap.edu/openbook.php?record_id=2207&page=250. Accessed on September 12, 2010.

CIA (Ed.), (2004). *CIA World Fact book – Tanzania*. Retrieved from http://www.cia.gov/cia/
    publications/factbook/geos/tz. Accessed on July 1, 2008.
Dalen, H. P., Groenewold, G., & Schoorl, J. J. (2003). *Out of Africa: What drives the pressure
    to emigrate?* Discussion Paper TI 2003-059/3. Tinbergen Institute, Amsterdam, Rotterdam.
Disaster Control Priorities Project (2007). *Natural disasters: Coping with the health impact.*
    Retrieved from http://www.dcp2.org/file/121/
IFPRI. (2008). *Living in the city: Sustainable options for ending hunger and poverty. Challenges
    and options for the urban poor.* Retrieved from http://www.ifpri.cgiar.org/pubs/ib/
    ib9.pdf. Accessed on January 10, 2008.
Info for health (2008). *Meeting the urban challenge.* Retrieved from http://www.infoforhealth.
    org/pr/m16edsum.shtml. Accessed on March 12, 2008.
Insch, G. S., Moore, J. E., & Murphy, L. D. (1997). Content analysis in leadership research:
    Examples, procedures, and suggestions for future use. *Leadership Quarterly, 8,* 1–25.
IOM (2008). *World migration 2003, Chapter 17.* Retrieved from www.iom.int/publications/
    documents/en. Accessed on May 5, 2010.
IOM (2008). *Tanzania facts and figures.* Retrieved from http://www.iom.int/jahia/Jahia/pid/384.
    Accessed on May 5, 2011.
IUSSP (1998). *African population conference.* Dakar: IUSSP.
Jackson, J. A. (1969). *Migration.* London: Cambridge University Press.
Kinver, M., (2008). *The challenges facing an urban world.* Retrieved from http://news.bbc.co.uk/
    2/hi/science/nature/5054052.stm. Accessed on January 15, 2010.
Krippendorff, K. (2004). *Content analysis: An introduction to its methodology* (2nd ed).
    Thousand Oaks, CA: Sage Publications.
Lerise, F. (2001). *The case of himo and its region.* Briefing Paper series no. 1, Rural-Urban
    Interactions and Livelihood Strategies, International Institute for Environment and
    Development, Northern Tanzania.
Lerise, F. (2001). *The case of lindi and its region.* Briefing Paper Series no. 2. Rural-Urban
    Interactions and Livelihood Strategies, International Institute for Environment and
    Development, Southern Tanzania.
LVIA (2005). *Evaluation report of food security program.* Kongwa: LVIA.
Madaha, R. (2006). *Territory diagnosis and market opportunity identification in Chilonwa and
    Mvumi divisions in Dodoma Region Tanzania and Mkuyuni Division in Morogoro Region
    Tanzania.* Consultancy report for NGO: LVIA, Dodoma, Tanzania. Archives of the
    NGO: LVIA, Dodoma, Tanzania.
Madaha, R. (2007). *The role of food security groups networks in poverty reduction: A case study
    of Chilonwa division in Chamwino district, Dodoma region, Tanzania.* Unpublished MA
    dissertation, Sokoine University of Agriculture, Tanzania.
National Bureau of Statistics. (2006). *Tanzania main statistical tables: Selected from national,
    regional and district profiles, 2002 population and housing census.* Dar es Salaam: Ministry
    of Planning, Economy and Empowerment.
Neuman, W. L. (1994). *Social research methods* (2nd ed). Boston, MA: Allyn & Bacon.
NIDI (2008). *Push and pull factors of international migration.* Retrieved from http://
    www.nidi.knaw.nl/en/projects/330106. Accessed on September 17, 2008.
Nkwilima, E. M. S. (1999). Constraints and prospects of the HADO project. In: I. S. Kikula,
    C. Christiansson & C. G. Mung'ong'o (Eds.), *Proceedings of an international workshop
    on man-land interrelations in semi-arid environments of Tanzania* (pp. 51–54). Dar es
    Salaam: Dar es Salaam University Press.

Research and Analysis Working Group. (2009). *Poverty and human development report 2009.* MKUKUTA Monitoring System Ministry of Finance and Economic Affairs, United Republic of Tanzania. Retrieved from www.povertymonitoring.go.tz/.../PHDR%20 2009%20text.pdf. Accessed on August 10, 2011.

Portes, A., & Böröcz, J. (1989). Contemporary immigration: Theoretical perspectives on its determinants and modes of incorporation. *International Migration Review, 23*(3), 606–630.

Shaidi, J. (2008). *Youth development in Tanzania: Ari Mpya Nguvu Mpya Kasi Mpya.* Retrieved from http://www.oit.org/public/english/employment/recon/eiip/download/workshop/ youthtan.pdf. Accessed on September 12, 2010.

Silverman, D. (1993). *Interpreting qualitative data: Methods for analyzing talk, text and interaction.* Thousand Oaks, CA: Sage Publications.

UNESCO (2008). *Selected Studies on dynamics patterns and Consequences of Migration.* Retrieved from http://unesdoc.unesco.org/images/0005/000528/052897eo.pdf. Accessed on September 17, 2008.

URT (2007). *Tanzania poverty and human development Report 2007.* Dar es Salaam: Government Printers.

URT (2008a). *National population policy 2006.* Dar es Salaam: Government printers. Retrieved from www.tanzania.go.tz/pdf/Idadi%20Eng.pdf.

URT (2008b). *Dodom region socio-economic profile.* Government Printers. Retrieved from http://www.tanzania.go.tz. Accessed on April 11, 2008.

URT (2008c). Statement by Hon. Juma Ngasongwa, minister for planning, economy and empowerment of the United Republic of Tanzania during the General Debate of the High Level Dialogue on International Migration and Development' Queen's University. Retrieved from http://www.queensu.ca/samp/migrationresources/HLDstatements/ tanzania-e.pdf. Accessed on September 19, 2008.

Vice-President's Office. (2005, June). *The national strategy for growth and reduction of poverty.* United Republic of Tanzania. Retrieved from http://www.povertymonitoring.go.tz/ Mkukuta/MKUKUTA_MAIN_ENGLISH.pdf. Accessed on August 11, 2011.

Wallerstein, I. (1999). *The end of the world as we know it.* Minneapolis, MN: University of Minnesota Press.

Wallerstein, I. (2001, March 16). Democracy, capitalism, and transformation. Paper presented at the Demokratie als Unvollendeter Prozess, Vienna.

WHO. (2010). *The world health report. Health systems financing: The path to universal coverage.* Geneva: WHO. Retrieved from http://www.who.int/whr/2010/. Accessed on August 10, 2011.

Woodrum, J. (1984). 'Mainstreaming' content analysis in social science: Methodology, advantages, obstacles and solutions. *Social Science Research, 13*, 1–19.

Yin, R. K. (2009). *Case study research: Design and methods* (5th ed). Thousand Oaks, CA: Sage Publications.

HEALTH, GENDER, AND DEMOCRACY IN NEPAL

Shiba S. Banskota

ABSTRACT

Nepal has made progress in raising the living standards of its people over the last 50 years, and yet the country's human development, especially the development of women remains among the lowest in the world. Development outcomes have varied inequitably manifesting themselves in gender, caste, ethnic, and geographic disparities. Women cut across all these categories and within any one group remain the most marginalized sections of the society. Women find themselves in a vicious circle that drives the discrimination against their gender. With low status, they lack the decision-making power to control access to health care and other resources, which perpetuates the low status, with no obvious place to break into the circle.

NEPAL: AN INTRODUCTION

Nepal is at a historical crossroad. Modern Nepal was established in the 18th century and the governing principles have been based on the practices of Hinduism (Whelpton, 2005). There were few rights of the people, and the rulers had every liberty to do as they pleased. Caste system was widely practiced and patriarchy was deeply entrenched. In 1854 the first National

Democracies: Challenges to Societal Health
Research in Political Sociology, Volume 19, 161–172
Copyright © 2011 by Emerald Group Publishing Limited
All rights of reproduction in any form reserved
ISSN: 0895-9935/doi:10.1108/S0895-9935(2011)0000019014

Civil Code was made public and this codified most of the customary laws, establishing a relationship between castes.

Nepal's first constitution was introduced in 1948, but very little of it ever got implemented. This was followed by new Constitutions in 1951, 1962, and 1990. Each new constitution followed a major political event. At the moment there is a new Interim Constitution implemented in 2007, basically designed for a Constituent Assembly that would draft a new constitution for the Federal Republic of Nepal.

In 1948 the constitution came in as a response to the growing opposition to the Rana[1] rule in Nepal. The Ranas had usurped power from the Shah kings who were still around as de jure sovereigns. With increasing political opposition to the British in India, political disturbances also started to increase in Nepal. Coming close on the heels of the independence of India, the 1948 Constitution was an effort to politically appease the people of Nepal. But it was a gesture that was too little and came too late.

In 1951 the Ranas were overthrown and a de facto kingship restored in Nepal. An Interim Constitution was drafted with the objective of organizing a Constituent Assembly, but growing political instability did not facilitate this process, and after eight years of frequently changing governments each lasting less than a year, it was decided to introduce a new constitution for parliamentary democracy similar to India. (Whelpton, 2005) After this was drafted elections were held in 1959 for electing for the first time, a democratically elected government. The Nepali Congress Party won two-thirds of the seats and after just 18 months in office, the king imposed emergency rule and dissolved Parliament. In 1962 a new partyless Panchayat[2] Constitution was implemented that gave unlimited powers to the king.

In the late 1980s political disturbances started once again in Nepal. The democrats and the communists joined hands to restore multiparty democracy in Nepal. After struggling for a few years, the new constitution restoring multiparty democracy was announced in 1990. Political instability continued on account of a struggle for power among the political parties, a relatively active monarch, and the inception of the Maoist movement and eventually the "people's war" in 1996. A tragic incident occurred at the Royal Palace where a large number of the Royal family members were murdered in 2000. Instability continued to increase and the new king imposed emergency rule in 2005, and ruled until he was forced to hand over power to the people after all the political parties joined hands to restore peace and work together for a new Nepal. The dissolved parliament was reinstated with new provisions for the Maoists to participate in Parliament.

In January 2007 the new parliament with the Maoists introduced the Interim Constitution followed by declaring Nepal a republic and ending over 200 years of monarchy in Nepal. From the point of view of gender, the Interim Constitution was very significant because it ruled that at least 33 percent of the candidates in parliamentary elections must be women.

Many political changes have occurred rapidly and with each change, there are important gender questions about rights, freedom, and discrimination. At a time when the country is preparing for a new constitution, what are the prospects for democracy and women's health in Nepal?

Even when marginal provisions were made to reserve seats for women by earlier constitutions, most political parties grossly neglected to comply with these provisions. The 1990 Constitution introduced multiparty democracy, but it failed to reduce the powers of the king and neglected many aspects of gender equity. After 1990, in less than 15 years, there were other major political crises, which focused on a new Interim Constitution and the establishment of a Constituent Assembly for preparing a new constitution for a Federal Republic of Nepal. Women from all groups and areas played a major role in bringing about these recent political changes in the country, but will the country be able to reciprocate and provide equal justice to its women citizens, including protection of health and equal access to health care?

Nepal has made progress in raising the living standards of its people over the last 50 years, and yet the country's human development indicators especially for women remain among the lowest in the world. Development outcomes have varied inequitably manifesting themselves in gender, caste, ethnic, and geographic disparities (See Table 1 for details by caste and ethnicity).

Women cut across all these categories and within any one group remain the most marginalized sections of the society. Women find themselves in a vicious circle that drives the discrimination against their gender. With low status, they lack the decision-making power to control access to health care and other resources, which perpetuates the low status, with no obvious place to break into the circle.

The low status of women has deep roots in the social, cultural, religious, political, and geographical conditions of the country. Following the recent political changes since 1990, women have made significant achievements in winning over equal treatment, but every step has been a difficult process. Women have joined hands not only with the democratic political parties, but many also joined the armed struggle of the Maoist movement in protest against the continuing discrimination along caste, ethnic, gender, and geographic lines in the country by the upper caste Hindu groups. Women's voice, which is barely heard even in households today, is beginning to resonate at all levels across the country for a better future as well as a more equal future.

There are many lessons that have been learned from the past, and yet some practices tend to die hard. Ethnic diversity, social oppression, and

Table 1.   Human Development by Caste/Ethnicity.

Human Development Indicators Group	Nepal	Brahmin	Chhetri	Newar	Hill Ethnic	Madhesi	Dalit
Life expectancy	55.0	60.8	56.3	62.2	53.0	58.4	50.3
Adult literacy (%)	36.72	58.00	42.00	54.80	35.20	27.50	23.80
Mean years of schooling, 1996	2.254	4.647	2.786	4.370	2.021	1.700	1.228
Per capita income (NRs), 1996	7,673	9,921	7,744	11,953	6,607	6,911	4,940
Per capita PPP (US$), 1996	1,186	1,533	1,197	1,848	1,021	1,068	764
Life expectancy index	0.500	0.597	0.522	0.620	0.467	0.557	0.422
Educational attainment index	0.295	0.490	0.342	0.462	0.280	0.221	0.186
Income index	0.179	0.237	0.181	0.289	0.152	0.160	0.110
HDI	0.325	0.441	0.348	0.457	0.299	0.313	0.239
Ratio to national HDI	100.00	135.87	107.31	140.73	92.21	96.28	73.62

Source: Adapted from NESAC, Nepal Human Development Report (Nepal South Asian Centre (NESAC), Kathmandu 1998) and J. Gurung, Promotion of Sociocultural, Economic and Political Participation of Dalits and Other Disadvantaged Groups: A Strategic Approach (Draft) (Submitted to the Enabling State Program (ESP), Kathmandu, 2002).
Note: Hill ethic groups include Sherpa, Gurung, Magar, Rai, and Limbu; The Madhise category includes Rajbanshi, Yadhv, Ahir and Tharu (an ethnic group); the Dalit category includes Dalits from the hills and tarai.
Table derived from Pradhan and Shrestha (2005).

gender equality may prove to be very difficult issues to be addressed by the present Constituent Assembly in a satisfactory manner because in such cases progress is either in quantum leaps or very gradual over the years. Nonetheless, there are hopes for a quantum leap in support of gender equality and women's health because for the first time in the history of Nepal, there is a 33 percent representation of women in the Constituent Assembly. This strength of women representatives can be used to promote favorable provisions regarding health and women's health in Nepal. The critical question is will the woman representatives work as a caucus to focus on women's health issues, or will they be divided along more conventional basis of party, ethnicity, language, and class lines as in the past? A majority of the delegates belong to the Maoist Party that has a fairly strong class orientation in its approach to most issues. This brief chapter is an effort to review the challenges in health, especially women's health, and democracy as supported by women's participation in democracy in Nepal.

HEALTH SITUATION IN NEPAL

There are many aspects of health that have some role in determining the political participation of women as pointed out by Wejnert (2008).

According to UNICEF (2006, p. 155), one woman dies every two hours in Nepal due to pregnancy- and childbirth-related complications. Only 19.8 percent of all the births are under the supervision of skilled attendants (Nepal millennium development goals [NMDGs] progress report, 2005, p. 44). While there are many problems in the health sector, reducing infant and maternal mortality are among the biggest challenges for Nepal. Waterborne diseases, respiratory infections, and nutrition-related problems are the bigger killers of children. "Girls are nearly 1.5 times more likely to die between their first and fifth birthday than boys ... reflecting gender discriminations in child rearing and health care seeking practices, since biologically boys are more likely than girls to die in this age group" (ibid., p. 38). Compared to the average infant mortality rate (IMR) of 67.3 per 1,000 live births in males and 68.4 in females in higher castes, the IMR was 70.4 in males and 69.8 in females among ethnic groups. Dalits were in a much worse situation with an IMR of 88.3 in males and 84.5 in females. Immunization against measles and other major diseases has improved, but there are wide disparities in accessibility in terms of boys and girls, rural–urban residence, ecological zone, and development region (MOHP, New ERA, & Macro International Inc., 2007 in NMDGs progress report, 2010, p. 42).

The recent data also shows that Mid and Far Western Regions still have a way higher infant mortality rates than the rest of the country (see Table 2).

While availability of health services at affordable prices is a major problem in the country, lack of infrastructure and the prevailing

Table 2. IMR (Infant Mortality Rate) and U5MR (Under 5 Mortality Rate) by Development Regions.

Development Regions	IMR	U5MR
Eastern	45	60
Central	52	60
Western	56	73
Mid-Western	97	122
Far Western	74	100

Source: MOPH (2007) in NMDGs progress report (2010, p. 42).

sociocultural conditions and practices have also impacted very negatively on all aspects of the health of women and children in Nepal. There is no respite for women when pregnant especially in rural areas and reflects the poor status of women across all the groups in Nepal. Early marriage of the girl child as well as frequent pregnancy is another major problem that cannot be addressed only by law. There are legal provisions for marriage but it is difficult to enforce for lack of reporting. Thus, awareness raising of both female and male is critical for positive changes.

"Thus far, democratization's costs to women have been largely overlooked, not only in terms of economic opportunities but also in terms of their impact on women's health. These costs, however, that limit women's empowerment and endanger national health cannot be ignored" (Wejnert, 2008).

Democracy brings with it mostly positive societal changes, which have been discussed. However, Wejnert (2008) has argued that in addition to benefits there are also costs associated with democratization, and to women the costs of democratization are much more substantial than to men. Some of these costs may be random or situational, but most of them are deeply rooted in social structures that reproduce and perpetuate systematic inequities and discrimination against women. It is important to analyze how democracy impacts different women based on their specific locations in the society.

Democracy opens the door to market economy and subsequent growth of a capitalistic global market and changes in countries' political and economic systems. Nepal also saw transformations in social structures – including in the class system, in minority–majority relations, and in the labor market.

The democratic government offered a variety of opportunities that were previously unspeakable. Nepal's new Constitution (1990) established a more inclusive state and declared Nepal as "multi-ethnic, multi-lingual and democratic" and that all citizens are "equal irrespective of religion, race, gender, caste, tribe or ideology." People started speaking about their needs, making demands on the government, and started monitoring political activities. Prior to democratization in Nepal, women's issues were framed in the rhetoric of development and welfare and not rights. It has now opened legal provisions to protect and advance the interests of women. *"Democracy must widen and deepen if politics and political institutions are to promote human development and safeguard the freedom and dignity of all individuals"* (Nepal human development report [NHDR], 2009).

Six factors were listed by (NHDR, 2009) and identified as contributing to women/girls' subordinate position in Nepal that were: *disparities in education; limitations on the rights of women to own and inherit property* until the recent past; *poor health*, especially in the realm of *reproductive health; low access to labor markets, employment and productive assets/resources; gender-based violence;* and *lack of fair representation in decision-making.* Socio-economic mobility has been restricted due to patterns of ownership of economic resources, distribution of income and wealth, and access to employment opportunities with no social security safety nets.

ACCESS TO HEALTH FACILITIES

Girls continue to have a higher mortality rate than boys (NHDR, 2009, p. 68). Access to health care and nutritional status of children is worse among the excluded groups, resulting in their low human development as shown earlier. Many interrelated factors affect women to access health facilities including cultural, religious, social, as well as economic challenges.

Access to health services is also limited due to geographical difficulties, poor infrastructure, and lack of qualified health workforce as well as language barriers among excluded groups. According to the survey carried out by the UNFPA/World Health Organization and the Institute of Medicine Tribhuvan University in 2006, more than 600,000 women were suffering from uterine prolapse and 200,000 were in immediate need of surgery. Uterine prolapse is related to poverty, gender discrimination, denial of their human and reproductive rights, and has been recognized as a consequence of gender-based violence and lower level of maternity care.[3]

The democratization process in Nepal with its theoretical and practical opportunities has led to social transition to new ways of making livelihood to fulfill basic needs of food, shelter, education, and health care. In the period of Maoist conflict (1996–2006), the existing health system was jeopardized, which made access more difficult for the people. During that period migration increased, and many people, including women, migrated from rural to urban areas and to neighboring countries and to different parts of the world. For those women who were left behind, sexual favor from women in return for loan, employment, and other opportunities became common. Among women who migrated to other countries, the majority were from economically and socially deprived families.

Women migrant reported excessive workload, 29 percent mild and 28 percent severe. Other problems and violations of rights included denial of food (15 percent mild and 6 percent severe), denial of shelter (14 percent mild and 4 percent severe), denial of health and medical care (17 percent mild and 12 percent severe), denial of holidays (22 percent mild and 18 percent severe), denial of contacts with family (18 percent mild and 11 percent severe), denial of payment as contracted (17 percent mild and 4 percent severe), verbal abuse (31 percent mild and 6 percent severe), humiliation (29 percent mild and 9 percent severe), physical abuse (10 percent mild and 4 percent severe), and sexual abuse (1 percent mild and 5 percent severe) (Bhadra, 2007). They also reported that they were victimized by unscrupulous manpower agents and middlemen promising high paying jobs (Anbeshi, 2010).

Migration has threatened to spread HIV and women and children are the particularly vulnerable groups (NMDGs progress report, 2010). Nepal's 2010 United Nations General Assembly Special Session (UNGASS) report highlighted that labor migrants accounted for almost 40 percent of the total estimated HIV infections in the country, which is followed by the wives and partners of men infected with HIV (26 percent). Women in rural areas were at risk due to their inferior status in society, and difficulties negotiating condom use with partners who returned from work outside the country. Women accounted for 29 percent of the total HIV infections. Many women and girls trafficked to brothels in India returned to Nepal with HIV (UNGASS, 2010).

VIOLENCE AGAINST WOMEN

Violence against Women (VAW) encompasses an array of abuses targeted at women and girls throughout their life, which includes physical, sexual, and psychological abuses. Although VAW has long been on the international agenda, it has only recently become important in the Nepali gender policy context, resulting in the passing of the Domestic Violence and Punishment Act, 2065, accompanied by the declaration of BS 2067 (2010 AD) as Anti-VAW year (Anbeshi, 2010).

Various NGOs advocating on women's health have pointed out that regardless of the government policies on women's sexual and reproductive health, and international human rights instruments such as the Convention on Elimination of All Forms of Discrimination Against Women (CEDAW) and the International Covenant on Economic, Social and Cultural Rights (ICESCR), violation of women rights is on the rise. Widespread women's health problems and violence against women are yet to be addressed partly because of limited access to services as well as the trend in ignoring the problems as part of the physiology that every woman goes through. In cases where it is identified as a problem, social taboos prevent women from seeking help. When VAW is reported there is no follow-up for prosecution due to the fear of ridicule or retribution and also due to an inefficient criminal justice system.

REPRODUCTIVE HEALTH

Nepal's MDG progress report, 2010, highlights that the Maternal Mortality Ratio (MMR) was 281 deaths per 100,000 live births, which is a significant decrease compared to 415 of 2000. Pregnancy-related complications account for the majority of deaths (FHD, 2009). These figures are also varied by caste and ethnicity.

Adolescent pregnancy and motherhood have also been a major health issues in Nepal. In 2006, 19 percent of women aged 15–19 were pregnant or had given birth to their first child (MOHP et al., 2007).

In case of child mortality, the IMR and the Under Five Mortality Rate (U5MR) have shown significant progress. In 2006, the IMR decreased to 48 deaths per 1,000 live births, and the U5MR to 61 deaths per 1,000 live births. The report highlights that it is a 39-percent decrease in the IMR and 48 percent in the U5MR from the 1995–2005 figures (NMDGs progress report, 2010).

In Nepal the contribution of unsafe abortions to maternal deaths and morbidity was acknowledged with the passing of a new law on abortion in 2002. Feminist groups have used international instruments like the CEDAW, the ICESCR, and the ICPD to push for liberalizing restrictive abortion laws in Nepal. Greater emphasis on women's reproductive health is a positive sign, however, it should not undermine women's other health risks. The effort to reorient policy and health services is still ad hoc and immature.

DISCRIMINATORY SOCIOECONOMIC AND CULTURAL PRACTICES RELATED TO HEALTH

Practices like Chhaupadi have negatively impacted the health of women and girls from the Far Western regions of Nepal. During menstruation and childbirth women and girls are considered impure and are forbidden to lead their normal life. They are restricted and kept in animal sheds where incidences of rape and animal attacks are common. Women are not allowed to enter their house and often engage in difficult manual labor outdoors. The negative physical and mental consequences of the practice are hard to imagine. They are deprived of nutritious food and exposed to unhygienic conditions. Women are led to believe that violating such practices would bring bad luck upon their family and community. This practice is still prevalent and widespread in the Far Western part of the country. The Supreme Court of the Government of Nepal has declared the practice of Chhaupadi unlawful but law enforcement is still a challenge (Sen & Östlin, 2007).

Child marriage and polygymy are also prevalent that have increased the frequency of exposure to sexual activity contributing to a greater level of exposure to the risk of pregnancy among young women. The practice of polygyny has decreased in the last decade from 6 percent in 1996 to 4 percent in 2006 (Pradhan & Pant, 2007, p.27).

Women's economic dependence also contributes to health vulnerabilities and risks. Thus, unless structural violence and rights are not instated, addressing women's health problem remains a challenge. The trend in the policy and planning sector of national and the international government bodies has been to focus on women and their health because they recognize that poor health of women can have a long-term impact on the economy and human development (NMDGs progress report, 2010, p. 23). It cannot be denied that this is true from the perspective of national development; however, from a feminist perspective it should be underlined that this way of thinking eventually places more emphasis on national development and de-prioritizes women's concerns.

NHDR (2009) has stated that political democracy in Nepal has repeatedly collapsed because it was not accompanied by social and economic transformation, pointing to the fact that the state needs to invest in ways to close the gaps between those who are excluded and those who are not.

CLOSING COMMENTS

Gender issues may have been universalized, but there is diversity of interest due to economic, caste, ethnic, and religious differences. Women across social groups tend to differ in their opinion on many of these complex health- and gender-related issues, making it very difficult for them to work cooperatively on national health concerns. It has been easier for them to go either under an ethnic, religious, or caste umbrella. The need for some new thinking in practice – in approaching gender health issues is at hand.

The presence of elections and quotas are preconditions but not sufficient to address women's health problems. A true democratic political environment necessitates the inclusion of a wider cross section of diverse social groups in leadership and decision-making. Strengthening democracy is not just about increasing the numbers of women in government but also about making gender equality part of the political agenda. To bring about transformative changes, reforming discriminatory laws and policies against women through constitution and legislative reform is a positive step. Although, the law guarantees the health rights of women, there is a further need to understand how these rights are practiced in reality, if they are not to end up worsening the position of women.

Health issues of women are personal to some extent, but after a point they become deeply embedded in the social and political system. Democracy may have changed some of the laws in Nepal, but it has not significantly altered the reality on the ground where women's health has continued to be suppressed, neglected, and in some instances even worsened under the present democratic confusion in Nepal.

NOTES

1. Rana rule (1846–1951) in Nepal, the period in which control of the government was in the hands of the Rana family.
2. The political regime in Nepal (1961–1990) with partyless system and absence of popular participation and consisting of centrality of the King.
3. http://nepal.unfpa.org/en/programmes/reproductive.php

REFERENCES

Bhadra, C. (September 2007). *International labor migration of Nepalese women: The impact of their remittances on poverty reduction.* Working paper series no. 44. Asia-Pacific Research and Training Network on Trade (Revised on January 2008).

FHD. (2009). *Nepal maternal mortality and morbidity study 2008/09. Summary of preliminary findings.* Kathmandu: Family Health Division.

MOHP, New ERA, & Macro International Inc. (2007). *Nepal demographic and health survey 2006.* Kathmandu: Ministry of Health and Population, New ERA, and Macro International Inc.

Nepal millennium development goals [NMDGs] progress report. (2005). Government of Nepal, National Planning Commission, United Nations Country Team of Nepal, United Nations House, Kathmandu.

Nepal millennium development goals [NMDGs] progress report. (2010). Government of Nepal, National Planning Commission, United Nations Country Team of Nepal, United Nations House, Kathmandu.

NHDR. (2009). *State transformation and human development.* Nepal human development report. Government of Nepal, United Nations Country Team of Nepal, Kathmandu.

Pradhan, A., & Pant, P. D. (2007). *Trends in demographic and reproductive health indicators in Nepal: Further analysis of the 1996, 2001, and 2006.* Demographic and Health Surveys Data.

Pradhan, R., & Shrestha, A. (2005). *Ethnic and caste diversity: Implications for development.* Working paper series no. 4. Asian Development Bank, Kathmandu.

Sen, G., & Östlin, P. (2007). *Unequal, unfair, ineffective and inefficient gender inequity in health: Why it exists and how we can change it.* Final report to the WHO commission on social determinants of health.

United Nations Children's Fund [UNICEF]. (2006). Situation of children and women in Nepal. UNICEF, Nepal.

United Nations General Assembly special session [UNGASS] country progress report. (2010). Nepal. Retrieved from http://www.unaids.org/en/dataanalysis/monitoringcountryprogress/2010progressreportssubmittedbycountries/nepal_2010_country_progress_report_en.pdf.

United Nations Population Fund [UNFPA]. Retrieved from http://nepal.unfpa.org/en/programmes/reproductive.php

Wejnert, B. (2008). Effects of global democracy on women's health 1970–2005 cross world analysis. *Marriage & Family Review, 44*(2/3), 154–172.

Whelpton, J. (2005). *A history of Nepal.* Cambridge University Press.

Women's Rehabilitation Centre [WOREC]. (2010). Anbeshi – A year book on violence against women in Nepal, Kathmandu: WOREC, Nepal.

GLOBAL DEVELOPMENT, POPULATIONS' HEALTH, AND DEMOCRACY: POLICY RECOMMENDATIONS

Barbara Wejnert

ABSTRACT

Three important lessons can be drawn from the health situation in the developing and democratizing world. The first lesson is that the societal health does not occur in the vacuum of societal life or social structures, but it simultaneously inspires development of all major spheres of political, economic, and cultural life of society. Second, health policy transpires simultaneously in all major social institutions, including economy, political institutions, and culture. Furthermore, because all social institutions are interconnected, the initiation of health reforms causes enormous, multilevel changes in all social strata and affects the performance of all essential institutions. Third, according to the World Health Organization, health is considered an integral part of human security, human rights, and peace. Consequently, societal health is determined and depends on the fullest cooperation of governments, world-scale communities, and local health-care providers.

Democracies: Challenges to Societal Health
Research in Political Sociology, Volume 19, 173–184
Copyright © 2011 by Emerald Group Publishing Limited
All rights of reproduction in any form reserved
ISSN: 0895-9935/doi:10.1108/S0895-9935(2011)0000019015

Based on the material covered in this volume, three important lessons can be drawn from the health situation in developing and democratizing world.

LEARNED IMPORTANT LESSONS

The *first* lesson is that the societal health does not occur in the vacuum of societal life or social structures, as it is often presented (Lederer, 1992), but it simultaneously inspires development of all major spheres of political, economic, and cultural life of society. This includes family life, individual achievement, education, and life choices of each individual society member. Therefore, starting with movement Health for All (HFA) initiated in 1977 by the World Health Organization, societal health is also recognized as complementing part of human and societal development. Almost 35 years ago, the World Health Assembly announced that the primary goal of future development is attainment of societal health that permits people in all societies of the world to lead socially and economically productive lives by the 21st century. Changes need to be made in the allocation of resources so that funding is linked to states performance in implementing the new approach, as well as to population size and populations' needs.

Second, health policy does not exist alone, as it used to be often presented (Lederer, 1992), but it transpires simultaneously in all major social institutions, including economy, political institutions, and culture. Furthermore, because all social institutions are interconnected, the initiation of health reforms causes enormous, multilevel changes in all social strata and affects the performance of all essential institutions, from governments and political institutions to the banking and trade systems, industry, and arts.

Third, according to the World Health Organization, health is considered an integral part of human security, human rights, and peace. The existing need to protect these rights and ensure adherence to the responsibilities they mention is reflected in the concepts of "health security" that considers health equity and "health accountability" that concerns the quality of health care. Health security is founded on the principle that all human beings may live free from the risk of preventable illness and injury. All individuals should also have equal access to quality health care that is both affordable and relevant. Since health conditions are dependent on nutrition and food security, health security includes the right to food in sufficient quantity and quality, information needed for self-reliance, and a working and living environment where known health risks are controlled.

Therefore, the fundamental right of every individual regardless of race, ethnicity, religion, and nationality is equal access to the health-care facilities and medical help available in the world. Consequently, societal health is determined and depends on the fullest cooperation of governments, world-scale communities, and local health-care providers.

As this volume shows and asserts, specific steps by national government of each country are needed to improve the quality of societal health and health-care services. These include integrating state economy, family's income, long-term planning of health care, organization of networks of health services, prioritizing needs at the rural level, training medical staff and professionals, including professional nursing, doctors, auxiliary nurses and nurse-midwives, and traditional birth attendants; accelerating prevention and control efforts of a spread of HIV and other communicative diseases; developing and spreading education about diseases and hygienic practices especially among vulnerable population of migrant workers and secluded rural populations; and increasing the availability of medical treatment among rural population. It also should include state policies protecting female children who are at risk of child marriage, policies protesting child marriage and addressing the need to combat marital violence. The state policies should include implementation of such broadly understood health policies, including policies protecting societies from family violence.

As this volume shows, factors influencing people's status and health care include culture and tradition, governmental policies or the lack of such policies, education, technology, and availability of resources. Several chapters demonstrate that particular economic or political structures of capitalism and democracy are not automatically able to deliver high-quality health care. Likewise, the assumption that wealthy countries do a better job in health-care provision than poorer countries must be reconsidered. Not only have chapters in this volume noted a considerable initial drop in the quality of health care when countries adopted a capitalistic democracy, these chapters also noticed countries that provide very good health care with considerably fewer resources.

The protection of societal health and individual rights to healthy life also means empowering people to make the right choices in health and building their capacity to keep themselves and their families healthy. This calls for various forms of social and economic support and better knowledge and awareness. It also calls for intersectional collaboration of various social systems as an essential element in health development and health-care planning. Health accountability begins with the obligations of the states and the responsibilities of health professionals to provide health services to all. It also includes the state's acceptance of responsibility for the impact on health of development and other state policies.

In other words, the material presented about societal health, democracy, and democratic transitions drawn from the *political-*, *economy-centered-*, *policy-*, and *culture-centered* analyses, could be utilized in future studies on health and health prevention as well as in practical attempts at adoption of a new health-care system and health-care reforms. I now briefly turn to the contents of each type of analysis.

THE POLITICAL-CENTERED ANALYSIS

During the years prior to democratic transition, many totalitarian countries (especially communist states) began a journey toward societal development on what seemed to be an even road. On this road, if governments of nondemocratic states met occasionally with twists and turns, this was only part of the process of exploring the different paths that authoritarian governments and ruling elites might devise for public regulation to buffer its citizens against health rights and health prevention wants. In an era when many industrialized nations were developing competitive market economies and democratic rights for their citizens, these regimes sought to help nonworking people, but small ruling elites secretly covered this political strategy with ideological propaganda.

However, the change toward democracy of many nondemocratic countries imposes a supportive and caring attitude of governments toward health of their citizens. Three chapters by Sawa-Czajka, Wejnert, Prakash and Rodriguez with Austria and Landau on democracy, democratic transitions, and the transition of state health policies in democratizing Poland, India, as well as the well-established democracy of the United States are prime examples of discussion on an impact of political situation in democratic countries on societal health. Although the chapters cover countries from three different continents – Asia, Europe, and North America – that significantly vary by the level of socioeconomic development and societal structure, the conceptual issues remain similar. Authors unanimously and loudly convey a single message to secure future social, political, and economic development of a country, health of citizens is one of the most viable factors that needs significant attention and care of democratic governments. The care ought to be expressed in the form of protection of health of children, especially children of social minorities; or health of women who due to their generally lower social status are more vulnerable to limited health services regardless of the need of a greater medical attention in terms of reproductive health care and pregnancy-related medical problems; or health of under privileged rural communities frequently deprived of access to medical care facilities and medical staff.

It is possible to draw two conclusions from these politically centered discussions. *First*, transition to democracy or existence of democratic political system does not guarantee equal societal access to available health-care facilities and medical services in any country. Governments need to make a special effort to provide secure health care to all citizens. *Second*, health care and the condition of societal health are functions of the socioeconomic position of citizens of countries. General division of people based on political privilege, which means those who are connected to political leadership or to political resources and simultaneously to economic resources versus people outside of political connections within a particular political system, coincides with division based on those who are more versus less exposed to the best health care and the best available medical services.

THE ECONOMY-CENTERED ANALYSIS

In continuation of the road metaphor, the less economically developed but democratic states are lagging on the otherwise universally traveled road toward modernity, high quality of living standards, and a competitive market economy. Thus, they lag in the creation of suitable economic living standards that could provide possibly the healthiest living conditions comparable to those in Western democracies. These states are far off from the fast-developing Western world and its medical technological innovations or innovative medical treatments, or if such medical innovations are available they are limited only to the wealthiest members of developing societies. Prime examples on such inequality of access to medical facilities are discussed in chapters by Prakash, Wejnert, Sawa-Czajka, Alagan and Aladuwaka. It is true that exposure to global corporatism is not always the most beneficial to local national economies in the developing world because it often produces large economic disparities and social inequalities (Bornschier, Chase-Dunn, & Rubinson, 1978); however in most cases it provides higher living standards and a better quality and greater quantity of available medical help and medical services. Because of a greater access to economic resources and innovative medical services most developing countries strive to be incorporated into Western markets. As a result, in most societies of the developing countries, demands to improve living conditions incorporate requests for privatization and market competition. Mirroring the economic opportunities of Western democracies, market competition was assumed to constitute the ultimate key to the overall improvement of health, societal living conditions, and quality of life.

However, as several chapters of this volume address, the market reorientation of states has resulted in the emergence of a large income gap, social inequality, need for state health-care reforms, and complex employment problems due to the overproduction of highly educated young generation in comparison to jobs availability. Subsequent difficulties typically experienced by societies of transitional economies that are approaching market economy system and hence are in the process of formation of new capital are broadly discussed by Madaha and Wejnert, as well as Banskota, Alagan and Aladuwaka. The chapters discuss unemployment and broad rural–urban migration as they lead to societal health problems such as spread of HIV/AIDS, violence against women and female children, and malnutrition. Harsh economic conditions that cause deprivation of societal health are indirectly connected to the transition to democracy as the modern democracy is highly associated with global market economy. The complicated problems of economic reconstruction and prevailing social inequality in new democracies frequently lead to societal disappointment and dissatisfaction, causing in some instances return to semi-totalitarian societies (e.g., in Nepal).

By presenting the interconnectedness of new political institutions with new economic developments, this volume allows readers to see the sustainability and success of democratization as highly dependent on many preexisting domestic economic conditions of the states. In any future analysis on the impact on health of democratic transitions and the economic restructuring associated with democracy, the consideration of such preexisting economic conditions might be an essential component of dialectic, analytic scholarly debates regarding the potential success of newly implemented health policies in the transitional economies of democratizing nations. The value of discussion of these complex issues connecting health with economic situation is particularly high since the chapters are written both by academics, former members of research institutes and practitioners – activists of the non-governmental organizations (NGOs).

THE POLICY-CENTERED ANALYSIS

It is easy to understand why democratic states developed distinct social policies during transitional times, but only if the politics of such policymaking are situated within a broader, organizationally grounded analysis of democratic political development. In the same vein, to understand policies of well-established democracies, such as the United States, one needs to consider a broad spectrum of conditions within the political and economic environment during the years of the democratic transition and established democracy. Theda Skocpol correctly explains that:

> Social policies in the United States (and elsewhere) have not developed simply in tandem with capitalistic industrialization or urbanization; they have not been straightforward responses to the demands that emerging social classes place upon governments. Governmental institutions, electoral rules, political parties, and prior public policies – all of these, and their transformations over time, create many of the limits and opportunities within which social policies are devised and changed by politically involved actors over the course of a nation's history. (1992, p. 527)

Hence, until recently in many countries democratized governments did not respond to many societal demands concerning citizens' well-being and emerging social problems. The policy-oriented chapters by Madaha and Wejnert, Prakash, Banskota, Khakimova, and Rodriguez with Austria and Landau examine some problems relevant to policy. The list of such problems is long and diverse, and includes issues such as poverty, emergence of the underclass, unemployment, prostitution and drug use, rapidly increasing gaps in income and living conditions, and disparities in the economic development of rural and urban communities. Madaha and Wejnert's chapter concentrates on problems of health policy, with specific emphasis on an impact of unemployment, prostitution, drug addictions, and spread of HIV/AIDS on health especially health of rural workers migrating to cities. Prakash and Wejnert address issues related to the welfare and health policies and recurring changes of these policies across regions of Southeast Asia and East Central Europe. Khakimova's chapter focuses on the problem of rural poverty and unemployment that leads to an increasing number of abandoned rural mothers with children because husbands migrate from rural communities to cities and usually establish new families, stopping support for their families in villages. The malnutrition and well-being of the abounded rural mothers and children are further discussed.

The central message of all these analyses is that new democratic governments need to respond to many quickly evolving social problems. Hence, in the near future, a concentration on domestic policy and the domestic problems of social security and societal quality of life inevitably ought to be on the political agenda of the democratic governments and need the immediate attention of policymakers if democratization processes are to continue.

THE CULTURE-CENTERED ANALYSIS

The emphasis on changes in culture assisting democratic political transformations represents examples of a new conceptual trend to refocus theoretical analysis on the interconnectedness of health with the three basic elements of societal life: politics, economics, and culture. Parrot's discussion about practice of child marriage in Afghanistan, where child daughters below 10 years of age are married, or practice of polygamy, or complete subordination of females to male family members is presented as a cause of lack of provision of health care to women including maternal health care, as well as frequent occurrence of broadly spread family violence. This chapter unveils many social ills that continue to exist regardless of formally accepted policy by this country that forbids such practices. In a similar situation to women in Afghanistan are women in Nepal, who are also deprived of rights including rights to provision of medical care and medical services and human rights caused by female subordination as analyzed by Banskota. Two more chapters analyzing the impact of culture on health conditions, especially women's health, discuss problems of culture-induced deprivation of the social position of women and degradation of women's health in Sri Lanka. Authors Alagan and Aladuwaka analyzing the aftermath of the Tsunami disaster argue that regrettably, many disaster relief and recoveries projects ignore the population's health issues especially the health of women and women's needs. The relief projects also ignored gender discrepancies. In societies that are early democracies or low developed economies, the limited help and protection of health of vulnerable population multiplies the price paid by women and children during natural disasters like the Tsunami. Thus, as it is argued, different cultures and governments do not have the knowledge and skills to focus on women's needs adequately in a disaster situation.

At the same time, the spread of family violence induce by heavy alcohol consumption among workers of tea plantations in Sri Lanka also causes significant decline of health especially among rural communities. Since family violence so commonly occurs, it became part of culture and an ingrained part of marital and family life. Women accept family violence as a natural course of life, and even believe that husbands expressed their love by physically abusing their wives. If abuse does not take place it is interpreted that husband does not love his wife.

POLICY RECOMMENDATI(
IMPROVE SOCIETAL HEA

There are several recommendations concerning impr
health that chapters in this volume focus on. These reco₁.   .. ᴠe
grouped under several headings.

Improvement of Accessibility to Information about Health Through Communication Education

Misinformation, myths, or folklore can prevent people from getting appropriate medical help and care. Parrot, Prakash, Khakimova, Aladu-waka and Alagan discuss several cultural beliefs such as stigma against HIV/AIDS patients, belief in inevitability of child marriage and polygamy, or family abuse that significantly affects health, especially health of mothers and children.

Provision of Mechanisms for Improving Available Resources

In general, the United States does not specifically deny health care or reproductive care, and as a group, people in general do not suffer from malnutrition. Compared to the health care in most developing nations, we are rich in resources, education, and access to all forms of technology including the Internet. And yet, the United States falls below a large number of developed nations and some developing nations on a variety of health measures such as prevention of spread of HIV/AIDS, maternal and child health-care measures such as maternal mortality, infant mortality, and infant immunization. This suggests that other factors must be operating and resource-rich nations like the United States as well as nations with fewer resources need to find a way to overcome these challenges to assure improvement of societal health.

In rural areas of a new democracy of Tanzania, there are a lot of unused resources which present economic opportunity to the majority of Tanzanians. It is recommended that the government and other developed nations should improve the infrastructure in rural areas to allow full utilization of human and nonhuman resources. Such an opportunity could prevent enlarged rural–urban migration that leads to many health problems that society needs to face, including the spread of AIDS as many returned migrant are HIV positive. Family members and other relatives have to provide homecare for the victims and cover their medical expenses which leads to further empowerment of rural families. Thus, Tanzanian and governments of other countries should devote greater attention to the migration issue and its connection to the population's health.

In India, on the other hand, efforts of established organizations developed under the umbrella of the Civil Society Organizations with Multi-Stakeholder Partnership are producing positive results and contributing to the improvement of societal health. This experience and knowledge could be replicated by other countries in combating obstacles to societal health.

Provision of Strategies for Change

(1) Empowerment of women through education and their increased access to financial services.
(2) Counseling of husbands against alcohol consumption and family violence.
(3) Awareness and advocacy campaigns for Prevention of Domestic Violence Act.
(4) Mobile courts should be introduced as an effective strategy for reaching out to victims of domestic violence and child marriage especially in the rural areas.
(5) Women's participation should be increased in decision-making bodies.
(6) There should be a separate wing of police dealing with women's issues, attached to police stations, health facilities, and medical services. Some countries, for example, Poland, have already initiated this practice; this should be replicated in other countries as well.
(7) NGOs working in different fields should be made proactive to the issues of health, domestic violence, and prevention of HIV/AIDS so that prompt assistance could be rendered to the victims.
(8) Information and communication technologies could give a major boost to the economic, political, and social empowerment of rural women population, and to improvement of societal health via political, economic, policy, and cultural measures. Information and communication technologies can help improving societal health in combating communicative diseases, gender-based violence, securing nutrition, and improving societal hygienic practices.
(9) The public sector should continue to play a key role in providing health services such as control of infectious diseases, maternity care,

preventive health care that promote equity and economic efficiency and confer widespread benefits. However, not all health services – even those that are publicly funded – need to be provided by the state. The challenge for the government is to help direct and improve privately provided services through appropriate regulatory arrangements and by encouraging an expansion of their scope to include promotion and prevention, in addition to curative care.

(10) The expansion and strengthening of existing services will reduce the disease burden and the associated costs, including productivity losses. To sustain these improvements and to contain the disadvantage of decreased health, especially health of social minorities, health systems must be more gender sensitive, and education and employment opportunities must be expanded. Both demand-and-supply-side considerations need to be taken into account, although efficient, high-quality services will generate their own demand in the long run.

(11) Action (or operational) research includes a variety of formal and informal research projects that can be used to introduce, test, or modify program strategies and activities and measure their impact and cost. Because many countries' central and state governments often lack the capacity to carry out such research, NGOs, academic institutions, and other private sector groups with the requisite expertise should be utilized to carry out action research. Action research on service delivery and information technology projects is suggested for the following: safe motherhood messages; anemia prophylaxis and treatment; increased contraceptive choice; reduction of unsafe abortion practices; referral of and transportation of patients for emergencies; nutritional supplementation for adolescent, children, pregnant and lactating women; quality of care; and public–private medical service collaboration.

Democratic governments can take several steps to meet societal health needs, in addition to strengthening services. Through legislation, legal enforcement of policies against harmful practices such as domestic violence and gender bias can be curbed. Working closely with civil society, particularly with NGOs and health oriented societal groups will make services more responsive to health emergences and problems, and improve utilization of medical services and their impact. Action research should be used to investigate and test alternative approaches to improving the delivery of services and showing greater responsiveness to the population's health needs. If demand is to be effectively created or enhanced, information, education, and communication strategies must be consonant with the perspectives and belief systems of communities. Therefore, careful qualitative research will be needed as a basis for designing messages to convey knowledge and modify behavior. Mass media and interpersonal communication should be used to improve knowledge and practices related to safe motherhood practices, nutrition, HIV/AIDS prevention, and gender relationships. Effective strategies include targeting specific households, providing information on the importance of health care and the availability of services, promoting dialogue with womens' groups, and encouraging men to involve themselves in family planning and women's health. Such strategies must be decentralized to respond to local sociocultural variations.

To protect societal health and to combat diseases, joint efforts of social groups, organizations, voluntary services, medical staff, and medical doctors should be undertaken in democratic and democratizing countries alike. Only the uniform, multilayer effort will lead to general improvement of future health of societies regardless of their economic status or political conviction.

REFERENCES

Bornschier, V., Chase-Dunn, C., & Rubinson, R. (1978). Cross national evidence of the effects of foreign investment and aid on economic growth and inequality. *American Journal of Sociology, 84,* 651–683

Lederer, I. J. (Ed.) (1992). *Western approaches to Eastern Europe.* New York, NY: Council on Foreign Relations Press.

Skocpol, T. (1992). *Protecting soldiers and mothers.* Cambridge, MA: Harvard University Press.